Y0-CDL-409

SEX and the UNIVERSITY

RUTGERS UNIVERSITY PRESS
NEW BRUNSWICK, NEW JERSEY, AND LONDON

Daniel Reimold

X SEX and the UNIVERSITY

Celebrity,

Controversy,

and a Student

Journalism

Revolution

Library of Congress Cataloging-in-Publication Data

Reimold, Daniel, 1981–
  Sex and the university : celebrity, controversy,
and a student journalism revolution / Daniel Reimold.
      p. cm.
  Includes bibliographical references and index.
  ISBN 978-0-8135-4805-0 (hardcover : alk. paper)
  — ISBN 978-0-8135-4806-7 (pbk. : alk. paper)
  1. College student newspapers and periodicals—
United States. 2. Journalism, College—United States.
3. Advice columns—United States. 4. College
students—Sexual behavior—United States.
5. Sex counseling—United States. I. Title.
  LB3621.65.R45 2010
  378.1'9897—dc22

                         2009048296

A British Cataloging-in-Publication record for this
book is available from the British Library.

Copyright © 2010 by Daniel Reimold
All rights reserved
No part of this book may be reproduced or utilized in
any form or by any means, electronic or mechanical,
or by any information storage and retrieval system,
without written permission from the publisher.
Please contact Rutgers University Press, 100 Joyce
Kilmer Avenue, Piscataway, NJ 08854–8099. The
only exception to this prohibition is "fair use" as
defined by U.S. copyright law.

Visit our Web site: http://rutgerspress.rutgers.edu

Manufactured in the United States of America
Typesetting: Jack Donner, BookType

For my parents

CONTENTS

PREFACE

I have been passionate about college journalism since high school. As a junior and senior, I treasured the visits I made with my father to campuses throughout Greater Philadelphia and beyond. There is simply something about a lively college campus that puts a smile on my face and a giddyup in my heartbeat. Some students on a college tour seek out the main academic buildings, the athletic facilities, the freshmen dorms. I searched for newsstands. I felt I learned more about the schools I visited through one issue of a quality student newspaper than from a full tour, admissions rep sit-down, and website visit, combined. When I selected a college, I immediately sent an e-mail to the student newspaper's faculty adviser requesting to be considered for the position of editor in chief. Okay, so I overshot a little. In my sophomore year, the dream came true. Cue the smile and the giddyup. Neither have let up since.

As a student, teacher, adviser, reporter, editor, blogger, and researcher, I have operated within the framework of the student journalism field and also explored the theories behind it and the issues that provide it with the power to transform lives, shape experiences, and offer meaning to the campus routine. Student media are absolutely integral to university life. Their audiences are impassioned. Innovation is occurring at an ever-faster clip. Free press fights rage on. The influence they exert within journalism and higher education has become boundless. And amid it all, they are oozing an electrifying, omnipresent sexuality that continually stirs the media and academia into a tizzy.

In an online comment following a story in *The Nation* last fall that identified me as a leading expert of the student press sexualization phenomenon, a snarky reader posted a question that I have been asked endlessly since embarking on this book project: "Wow. I wonder what it takes to become such an expert?" The question's sexual subtext always makes me laugh. To clarify, no, I did not seek to explore sex in the student press due to an overwhelming interest in sex or any deep-rooted sexual kinkiness or fetishisms. Instead, a few years ago I started noticing that more media coverage and free press fights were centering on student sex columns and sex magazines than on anything else within college journalism. It seemed that at schools across the United States and into Canada debates were happening about the pieces' and publications' eye-popping editorial content, earning them an array of conflicting labels: the Rx for sex, sexual bibles, literary moaning sessions, softcore porn bullshit, sexual soapboxes, sappy love babble, a state-of-the-romance address, and the latest journalistic frontier. I became curious. I went to Google, then LexisNexis, then individual student newspaper websites and library archives. I sent e-mails, made phone calls, and spoke with people face-to-face.

In general, I simply did what I wish more people would do with the student press: I cared enough to pay attention, close attention, and I did not stop until the complete story was told. My ultimate rationale for the book's existence is best summarized in the editorial note that opens the inaugural issue of *Boink*, the student sex magazine co-founded by a Boston University student: "Everyone knows sex sells. . . . And it sells because it's a basic and vital part of being human, like eating and sleeping . . . only more fun. Why shouldn't it be discussed as freely as what you had for dinner last night?"

The discussion laid out in these pages would not have been possible without the basic, vital support of my parents—accompanied by my brothers, grandparents, and an extended family so large and caring it takes two full days to celebrate Christmas. I am further indebted to two of my former teachers, Robert Dickinson and Jackie Koch. They inspired me to pursue writing as a passion and profession, especially Mrs. Koch. Whenever she looked at me, I loved the writer I saw reflected in her eyes. In many ways, I owe her everything.

My sincere gratitude extends to Patrick Washburn for his guidance and enthusiastic support of this project. An additional heartfelt thank-you to my editor, Leslie Mitchner, whose patient, insightful supervision helped shape this work into something I am proud to publish. This book stands on their shoulders. A final thanks to others who have been huge helps with this project or more general life inspirations: Albert Barbetta, Joseph Bernt, Rosemary Boccella, Marilyn Campbell, Lynne Edwards, Samuel Freedman, Wendy Greenberg, Carolyn Kitch, Mary Ellen Malloy, Andrew Mendelson, David Mould, Chester Pach, Daniel Riffe, Carol Robidoux, Jan Slater, John Strassburger, Den Sweeney, Nicholas Taylor, and Ed Trayes.

SEX and the UNIVERSITY

Sex, Sex, SEX!
The Explosion of Sexual Expression in the Student Press

1

Sex has "mesmerized, titillated, and amused" Glory Fink since she was a little girl, even before she knew what the word meant. In second grade, she fell in love for the first time, setting her sights on a classmate. "He was sweet but shy," she recalled. "I wanted him to notice me, but he didn't. One lunch period in a fit of frustration, I said very loudly to him, 'Chad, if you don't pay attention to me, I'm going to sex you up!'"

Fink describes the subsequent lunchroom scene in cinematic terms—eerily silent, with "sandwiches hung in midair" and an angry teacher who summoned her forward with a "Finger of Doom." She feared a fate far worse than time-out, including being disowned by her parents. As she shared, "I would be homeless and have to live in a cardboard box with rats like on *Hill Street Blues*—all this because of one little word." While ultimately not forced to fester with rats, the experience did influence Fink to avoid discussing sex except at sleepovers until she reached eighteen, when she enrolled at the University of Southern Mississippi. In her words, "By that time, I felt sure I could avoid the devil as well as the penalty of death that surely came to children who ventured too far off the path and into the valley of forbidden words."[1]

Yet it was during her college years that the word, its titillation, and similarly furious Fingers of Doom unfurled in Fink's direction. She may have avoided the devil while at USM, but she was deemed one by many. Fink's devilish plaything: a student newspaper sex column. As a writer for "Pillow Talk," a sex column in the *Student Printz*, Fink tackled topics such as foreplay, safe sex, body waxing, bondage and sadomasochism, and modern romance, all with extreme tolerance and the same fervor she first used to pick up Chad. "All over the world people hook-up, go steady, make out, experiment with heavy petting, have affairs/flings, move in together, and, once in a while, get married," she wrote near the start of one "Pillow" piece. "I am not your mama, your spiritual advisor or your Great Aunt Sally so there will be no judgments here from me. You don't like it? . . . Put the paper down and go somewhere else. Have the finger waggers left?"[2]

In fact, their numbers were growing across the state. They centered their objections on Fink, her column, and the word screaming in capital letters as the headline to her opening article, the word that first got her in trouble more than a decade before: "S-E-X." As one report noted, Fink's writing "immediately stirred controversy. And more controversy. And even more controversy. And yet even more controversy." Throughout her columnist stint, angry e-mails and phone calls poured into the *Printz* newsroom, with one critic asking the paper's editor in chief, "Who the hell do you think you are? . . . What is this smut you got going in the newspaper now?" The university president also denounced the column, proclaiming in an open letter of disgust that Fink's work was "offensive to the quality and respectability of our student body and institution." Steve Crampton, the chief counsel of Mississippi's Center for Law and Policy, even called for the government to intervene. "We need to take our concerns to the State Legislature," Crampton announced soon after the column's debut. "The long and short of it is, it's not good for the university, however much they [*Student Printz* staffers] may enjoy being the little rebels of the moment."[3]

Since the late 1990s, Fink and her fellow college newspaper sex columnists have become the most prominent catalysts behind an unparalleled sexual rebellion in the student press. Student sex columns and full-blown campus sex magazines have appeared with increasing regularity at or near campuses in the United States, Canada, Britain, and parts of Asia, including Hong Kong and India. The pieces and publications mesmerize, titillate, and amuse on their own, but make no mistake: It is their student creators who are the real stars. Students earn an array of positive and fiery nicknames for their work: rebels of the moment, sexperts, sex scribes, smut spreaders, pornography peddlers, dictionaries of sin, dating gurus, sexual Sherpas, sluts with a pen, collegiate Carrie Bradshaws, heirs to Ann Landers, shock-and-awe writers, well-read little nymphos, and the Loch Sex Monsters.

They are thrust into what one columnist called "a kind of baby fame" in which their own selves wash away, replaced by a persona that their student fans praise, the media parse, and critical readers attempt to pick apart.

The story of the student press over the past decade has been this praising, parsing, and nitpicking, and the sex at the center of it all. As the *Minneapolis Star Tribune* asked readers, "What's the buzz on campus these days? Sex. Not who's having it, but who's writing about it." Or as Fink once noted about the drama in her own life, "All this because of one little word."[4]

In this book, I explore the celebrity status student sex columnists and sex magazine editors receive, the controversies they cause, the sexual generation they are helping define, and the student journalism revolution they represent. I also dive into the content of the columns and magazines, uncovering for the first time what they are saying about students' sex and social lives. Sex is the book's driving engine. At its heart, though, is a much larger aim—to begin filling the Grand Canyon–sized gap that exists within the body of scholarly work on journalism in respect to research focused on the campus press. Research into student media at the college level is sparse, and in book form is basically nonexistent—an especially troubling fact given the significance of the collegiate press within journalism and at the colleges and universities where most student media outlets are based.

Student media are the beating hearts of higher education, pulsing at the center of nearly every first-rate university worldwide. While they have been essential components of campus life in the United States since the early twentieth century and matured into respected news sources in the 1960s, they are currently enjoying an unprecedented editorial and technological renaissance—existing as more professional, interactive, eager, and able to compete for eyeballs and Googling fingertips than ever before.

Amid endless economic, administrative, and Internet bombshells, the campus newspaper remains the student press gold standard. Instead of the big men, they have been dubbed the "big media on campus," popularly serving news and entertainment to an influential student demographic while others around them fail. "It's not breaking news that the newspaper industry is losing the attention of young readers," a *Wall Street Journal* report confirmed. "But one sector of the industry is defying the trend: college papers. Hip, local, relevant and generated by students themselves, college newspapers have held steady readership in recent years while newspapers in general have seen theirs shrink." More than eighteen hundred campus newspapers are currently published across the United States. They collectively reach more than eleven million students, many of whom view grabbing a copy of a paper on campus as "almost automatic," according to the *Baltimore Sun*. They have become the main source, and at times only source, to which students turn for news. Nestled within this high readership rate and hip relevancy, student sex columns are the newspapers' hottest commodities, prevailing as "talk of the town" features on a level that editors joke even goes beyond the campus police blotter, major sporting event recaps, and crossword and Sudoku puzzles.[5]

The columns register the most online views, sport the most related comments, and are often the most e-mailed features on the newspapers' websites. And they are frequently the best-read features in print, proved in part by circulation numbers indicating that more copies of the newspapers are picked up on the day a sex column is run than at any other point in the week. According to *USA Today*, "Print copies [of student newspapers] . . . practically fly off the newsstands on the day 'sexperts' appear." In certain cases, the columns single-handedly, and dramatically, increase newspapers' circulation numbers and web traffic. For example, a column written by Yale University student Natalie Krinsky in the *Yale Daily News* during the 2001-2002 academic year received between two hundred thousand and five hundred thousand hits each week, more than ten times the normal traffic for all other *Daily News* content. The columns' other noticeable positive effect has been the large amount of discussion they create. "We got more feedback about the [sex] columns throughout the year than we got about the pending war in Iraq," said former *Post* editor Phil Elliott, who oversaw a pair of sex columns in 2002-2003 at Ohio University and currently serves in the White House press corps. "Forget the fighting. Students wanted to talk about sex."[6]

Tom Ashbrook, host of National Public Radio's *On Point*, said during a show on the student press sex craze, "The dance around sex finds a new beat, a new expression in every generation." College newspaper sex columns—and their close cousins, campus sex magazines—are the acknowledged leaders of the sexual dance for the current generation of students. They are intimately discussing and dissecting student social interaction, courtship, and sex at a time when sexual activity, sexual dangers, and sexual ignorance are prevalent and sex has become "the very wallpaper" of students' lives. Their content has jump-started a sexual conversation that is otherwise absent or severely lacking within the news media, schools, the political and religious arenas, and the homes of many students. They have even received *Playboy*'s blessing, with a feature in the magazine noting, "Right now, nobody knows more about the sexual goings-on in the collegiate trenches." One report labels them as nothing less than the "Campus Kama Sutra."[7]

The pieces and publications are also modern students' most significant reflections on sex and socialization free of adult interference or outside interpretation. They provide the most personal, verifiable retellings of students' own sexual stories, in their own words. They literally coin terms and define acts, issues, and trends that previously had no name or no scrutiny outside campus bars, house parties, and darkened dorm rooms. The student writers and editors are neither health experts dispensing advice in clinical language, nor adults opining about sex with moral or parental authority. Instead, they present themselves as ordinary students, offering observations about what a columnist called "sex, pleasure, and the taboo" in a recognizable, peer voice. In this sense, the sudden appearance and dramatic surge in columns and magazines are enabling students to redefine the sexual messages that in the past were aimed *at* them instead of created *by* them. "My generation, this is what we need to be talking about, and it's a discussion that needs to happen on our own terms," said Gillian Maffeo, a former sex columnist for the *Crestiad* student newspaper at Cedar Crest College. "We're not Baby Boomers or part of Generation X. We're Generation Sex." A writer for the campus sex magazine *Boink* similarly said, "This is kind of our protest to say that we're in charge of our sexuality, we can do what we want to do."[8]

This protest is journalistic as well as sexual. Over the past decade, the columns and magazines have sparked the most contentious, far-reaching legal, religious, and intergenerational debates about sex, the student press, and the place of both within higher education. They are the most prominent modern student press combatants in the fight for free speech, and have blurred once-solid journalistic boundaries separating information deemed public and private, art and pornography, and gossip and news. To this end, the pieces and publications represent a shifting of gears with respect to journalism, reframing sexual issues, euphemisms, and images previously considered unpalatable and unpublishable as newsworthy and part of everyday student discussion. "It seems sex is the topic of conversation on campuses across the nation," *Outloud* newsmagazine announced. "We used to flip through our college newspaper with plain old questions in advice columns. Today, we've gone further to answer more intimate and darker questions."[9]

Coupled with this intimacy is a fame and infamy for student sex columnists and magazine editors that is unmatched by anything else student journalists have experienced. Student sex scribes are both celebrities and causes célèbres on their home campuses. Former sex columnist August Brown at Stetson University, echoing the sentiments of many, said he became an overnight "rock star golden child of journalism." The student writers and editors are stopped for autographs, cold-called by literary agents and *Playboy*, hit on, honked at, gawked at, and stalked. They are solicited for sexual advice while in classes, at bars, and, for one columnist, while she was in her college's student center donating blood. Their names are etched as graffiti onto campus building walls. They regularly pass groups of students reading their pieces aloud and stumble across hard copy cutouts or web printouts of columns taped to the walls of dorm rooms, fraternity houses, and local restaurants. They receive hate mail, love letters, marriage proposals, and Facebook friend requests from complete strangers, wealthy alumni, international readers, and even inmates at maximum-security prisons. "Honestly, I didn't think writing a sex column would be such a big deal," columnist Rachael Parker wrote in the *Penn* at Indiana University of Pennsylvania. "I've been recognized at parties and heard shouts of 'I loved your article!' across the Oak Grove. Someone even hugged me at the homecoming parade."[10]

Along with being popularized, the sex writing position is often impression-forming, cementing itself foremost in people's minds when developing opinions about the columnists. "Whenever I'd be introduced to other students, they never came in with a neutral opinion," said former *Tufts Daily* sex columnist Amber Madison, now a respected author and speaker on sexual issues. "So either people would come in thinking I was awesome and the coolest girl they'd ever met or they'd hate me before they even met me. . . . I'd have a lot of friends and a lot of enemies, and none of them knew me at all." In this respect, along with their popularity in print and pseudo-celebrity on campus, the toughest part of students' column-writing experience is their inability to separate themselves from their columnist personae in the eyes of friends, fellow students, sexual partners, and strangers on the street. As Jessie Gardner, a former sex columnist for the *Orion* at California State University, Chico, put it, "So one night in September 2003, I fell asleep an average college student and woke up a 'sexpert.'"[11]

It is an awakening more than a hundred years in the making. College newspaper sex columns and student sex magazines are the latest in a long line of media outlets and individuals confronting, and at times revolutionizing, society's sexual standards. The mainstream, dissident, alternative, and underground media have been the primary catalysts for redefinitions in America's sex and relationship spheres since the sexual reform press stirred debates about "free love" and women's sexual rights beginning in the 1870s. According to historian Rodger Streitmatter, the media serve as "foot soldier[s] in the Sexual Revolution that has transformed this nation." While researchers such as Streitmatter, Beth Bailey, David Gudelunas, and John Semonche have documented the professional media's influence on sex and courtship, this book breaks new ground as the first exploration of sexual expression within the student press.[12]

In the first half of the twentieth century, campus humor magazines satirized sex. During the 1960s and 1970s, underground student newspapers politicized and celebrated it. Beginning in the 1980s, the college news media periodically covered it. The current phenomenon, however, stands apart for its pervasiveness, its mainstream acceptance, and the passionate tenor of the responses it has provoked. Student sex columns spread rapidly through campus newspapers in the United States and Canada in the late 1990s and early 2000s. They now appear in newspapers at institutions of every type and size—from the community college level to the Ivy League. Campus sex magazines are also starting to grow in number, more than ten years after a publication titled *Squirm* debuted at Vassar College.

To better understand the origins, popularization, and meanings of columns' and magazines' sex talk, I spoke in person, by phone, and occasionally via e-mail with more than one hundred fifty current and former sex columnists writing for student newspapers across the United States and

Canada; related editors (specifically those who supervise the columnists and deal with public reaction); columnists' family members, relationship partners, and close friends (chosen in part to better understand the personal implications of students' columnist stints); editors, photographers, and writers at campus sex magazines (including the founders of nearly every major magazine); and professional sex and health experts and advocates, including the CEO of the National Campaign to Prevent Teen and Unplanned Pregnancy.

Between interviews, I reviewed the astonishing amount of relevant popular press coverage, numerous related Student Press Law Center reports, and stacks of primary documents, including private e-mails columnists have received from impassioned and angry readers. I also delved into student press sex talk of past generations, in part by digging through archival collections of campus humor magazines, underground and alternative newspapers, and industry journals, including *College Press Review* (later renamed *College Media Review*) and *Trends in College Media*.

Finally, I leaped into sex in print, evaluating the magazine content and also completing the first thematic analysis of the influential messages sex columns are sharing. To conduct the analysis, I read and reread (at times for fun) more than two thousand columns written by one hundred twenty student sex scribes. I selected both popular and lesser-known columns; those written by male and female students; and those published within student newspapers at schools of all types and sizes in the United States and Canada. Many of the selected columns were written by columnists chosen for interviews, in part to determine if a synchronicity existed between their stated writing goals and the content they produced. My analysis focused on columnists' reflections related to the topics of most pieces: student socialization and sex.

For most columnists, these reflections are personal. "In order to make it readable and make it compelling, it had to tell a story," said former *Cornell Daily Sun* sex columnist Heather Grantham. "And what stories do I know better than my own?" Columnists note, however, that they tell their stories in a voice at least somewhat unlike their own. Most adopt a persona of sorts, typically a more confident, sarcastic, sexually aggressive version of themselves. The aim is not to fool readers, according to columnists, but to hold their interest. "I'm just a normal person like anyone else," said former

Carolinian columnist Brook Taylor at the University of North Carolina, Greensboro. "I don't have a constant flow of boys and girls through my door all the time. I have my dry spells like everybody else. The only difference is, they can get away with it. I kind of have to pretend . . . and keep up that facade that I'm getting laid when I'm not. I've never lied in my columns, but you do have to keep up the image." Former *Michigan Daily* sex columnist Erin Kaplan compared the columns' authenticity to the airing of a reality television show, in which some events are staged or irrelevant parts deleted for larger dramatic effect. "If you show all the boring parts in between, you're just wasting time," she said. "It is highlights, definitely highlights—always something students want to read."

On one level, the columns do exist as a glorified highlight reel, delivering exactly what undergrads looking for a laugh or an eyebrow raise expect to see when the word "sex" appears in the lead sentence or headline slot. They tell stories of crazy, once-in-a-college-career moments and spread the sex-and-relationship campus legends we all hear about but never actually witness or experience firsthand. Student readers at a university in Philadelphia described the columns to me as "drive-by lust" and "pure sexual fantasies" on par with Internet pornography.

Not so fast, say a growing number of experts and investigative reports. In recent years, the campus social scene has come under increasing scrutiny in research studies; fictional works based on ethnographic reporting, such as Tom Wolfe's *I Am Charlotte Simmons*; and even political attacks like young conservative Ben Shapiro's *Porn Generation*. The competing voices differ in their interpretations of deeper meaning but they all agree on one central truth: The social and sexual culture described in the columns is not a drive-by fantasy. The columns are accurate. Even while compressing the culture into eight hundred words a week and amping up the sarcasm, the columns are realistically describing the highlights and lowlights of modern undergraduate love and lust.

And their descriptions are startling. The columns document a dramatic social and sexual shift on modern campuses. They describe dating (in the old-fashioned dinner-and-a-movie sense) as dead, and monogamy and romance as dying. Instead, students interact like "an orgy of rabid monkeys." They engage in an abundance of drunken encounters and fleeting relationships solely to achieve what one columnist emphatically summarized as "sex, sex, SEX!" Columns define this casual-sex-centric or "hookup" culture as "a fast-paced fly-by-the-seat-of-your-pants free-for-all" where "fucking is in constant fluctuation" and social anarchy reigns supreme. As *Heights* sex columnist Anna Schleelein wrote about her arrival at Boston College, "I had plunged head first into an entirely new world of sexile, ridiculous alcohol consumption, no parents, pre-gaming, post-gaming, during-the-game gaming, and doing more work on less sleep than I had ever before in my life. It's a unique world that can only be found here, where . . . it's possible, if not probable, to not know if you're dating someone, or conversely to spend every night with someone monogamously when neither one of you 'wants a boyfriend/girlfriend.' I don't pretend to understand it; it's sex and the university."[13]

Sexual, Revolutionary
The Pioneering College Newspaper Sex Column

2

> It was really mostly about getting over ourselves, and our other-
> wise super serious objectives. It was about doing something fun,
> something beyond just straight journalism.
>
> ERIN ALLDAY
> *former managing editor,* Daily Californian

The most well-known sex column in a college newspaper was conceived amid a political uproar that had nothing to do with sex or the column at all. On November 3, 1996, after engaging in "a very heated discussion," the eleven-member editorial board of the *Daily Californian*, the independent student newspaper at the University of California, Berkeley, voted six to five in favor of running a staff editorial endorsing Proposition 209. The state initiative called, in part, for the elimination of race, ethnicity, and gender preferences in public university admission decisions. The conservative stance of the editorial, which was published the next day on the newspaper's front page, above the fold, enraged liberal-leaning students at Berkeley—a university known for its pro-affirmative-action policies and liberal politics since the free speech movement of the 1960s.

More than four thousand copies of the newspaper carrying the editorial were stolen soon after they were distributed. Michael Coleman, the paper's editor in chief, and his staff decided to reprint the editorial on the front page of the following issue, published on Election Day, November 5, when the proposition was scheduled to be voted on. Just after dawn that day, as soon as the delivery trucks had distributed the papers to the two hundred sixty drop-off points across campus and in the city of Berkeley, thieves made off with the newspaper's entire press run of twenty-three thousand copies. It was an organized pilfering that the Student Press Law Center confirmed as the largest newspaper theft in college journalism history. Three suspects later questioned were determined to hold ties with the student-run Coalition to Defend Affirmative Action by Any Means Necessary.

On November 7, a group of student protesters rushed angrily up the stairs of Eshleman Hall to the sixth-floor *Daily Californian* newsroom, ripping thousands of copies of the newspaper to shreds and tossing them off a fifth-floor balcony. Coleman also received an anonymous death threat on his voice mail. The message connected the thefts and the protest with the editorial, and warned him to watch his back and to carefully "consider what stances you take." The next morning, the exterior walls of the house he roomed in were vandalized, including a chalked message: "Fuck the *Daily Cal.*"[1]

More than a week later, still operating under the swirl of controversy that the editorial, political protest, and thefts had provoked, features editor Matthew Belloni and opinion editor David Katz, both seniors, were relaxing in the newsroom. The large windows behind them framed the south side of campus, and a borrowed boom box blasted music from the local alternative rock radio station. With their editorial work for that evening's deadline complete, their discussion of Proposition 209 turned to talk about "Ask Isadora," a syndicated sex and relationship advice column that ran for seventeen years in the *San Francisco Bay Guardian*, an alternative weekly popular among students. According to Katz, while they "marveled at the shamelessness of the column," Belloni suggested running a student version, "less raunchy, gossipy, and snarky and more clinical . . . something to increase reader interest but also actually provide good advice."

The key to the success of such an enterprise, the pair agreed, would be its focus on a topic that was the polar opposite of politics in terms of the depth and intensity of related student attitudes. According to Belloni, who graduated from UC Berkeley in 1997 with a political science degree and now serves as an editor and columnist for the *Hollywood Reporter*:

The proposed sex column was very different. We knew those people who were storming our halls wouldn't be up in arms about sex. Berkeley's a weird place. It's more politically explosive than anything else. Sex is just accepted, in all forms. . . . There are certain issues people would be enraged about, and sex just wasn't one of them. So, for all the risk, we knew we needed something at the time that would simply be accepted and not at the center of a larger student controversy or media storm like we were still experiencing with the editorial fallout. We really didn't think it would be a big deal at all.

Currently, more than a decade after the column's debut, Belloni's prediction is fascinating for the irony of its immense modesty. Far from uncontroversial, college newspaper sex columns have instead greatly overshadowed the political brouhaha from which the first major one sprang, becoming the most publicized and pervasive phenomenon in student journalism. Press reports have dubbed the sex columns "the best new trend in college newspapers" and, conversely, "a plague . . . [that has] hit the college newspaper world like a hurricane." In 2006, *The Student Newspaper Survival Guide* called the columns "a staple of 21st century college newspapers."[2]

The definitive spark behind these staples: the *Daily Californian*'s "Sex on Tuesday." The column, also known in Berkeley by its acronym, SOT, is the longest-running and most prominent student sex column appearing in a U.S. campus newspaper. According to separate reports, it is "something of an institution," one that has "titillated, disgusted, and intrigued readers of the *Daily Californian* every week" and served as a model for the many student newspaper sex columns that followed.[3]

Let's Talk About Sex

While the brainstorming session that led Katz and Belloni to devise the sex column lasted only minutes, the real groundwork for its emergence in print stretches back nearly one hundred years and involves all manner of college media. "Sex on Tuesday" and its subsequent student sex column companions are not generational hiccups. For close to a century, in humor magazines, yearbooks, independent and underground publications, and official school newspapers, the U.S. campus press has pushed boundaries and stirred trouble related to sex, sexuality, social interaction, and the human form.

Campus humor magazines were the earliest sexual provocateurs. Beginning in the late 1800s and continuing through the 1930s, sex was the punch line or setup to countless jokes, satirical stories, and risqué illustrations in student humor magazines nationwide. Along with poking fun at other topics timelessly ripe for sarcasm in a college setting (including politics of the day, football, studying, clueless freshmen, the Greeks, and life after graduation), the magazines possessed what one researcher called "a preoccupation with sex." The publications joked about sexual activity, social rites of passage such as proms and house parties, and all stages of courtship—from blind dates and on-the-street flirtations to marriage. In the magazine portrayals, on-campus promiscuousness was as common as a frat pin. Students were described as happily trapped within a social whirl filled with endless dates and sexualized pursuits such as spooning, necking, petting, fencing, toddling, vamping, and engaging in the university press (dancing with bodies closely pressed together) and the personal house party (an intimate make-out session). In illustrations, women were begged for kisses, with the promise, "What you don't *no* won't hurt you." And coeducation (rather than education) was regarded as the ultimate area worthy of study. As a fictional conversation between a student and dean was recounted in the *Yale Record*:

> Student: "Sir, I want permission to be away three days after the end of vacation."
> Dean: "Ah, you want three more days of grace?"
> Student: "No, sir. Three more days of Gertrude."[4]

The most common joke appearing within the magazines during their "heyheyday" in the 1920s centered on a student's dating slate being so full that the identity of a significant other was often forgotten or confused. As an aside in the *Harvard Lampoon* noted:

> He: "You know I love you—will you marry me?"
> She: "But, my dear boy, I refused you only a week ago."
> He: "Oh! Was that you?"

The *Washington Dirge* at Washington University in St. Louis put it even more simply: "He—Is that you darling? / She—Yes, who is this?" In the magazines, run mostly by men with (at least outwardly) heterosexual desires, female sexuality oozed off the pages. In illustrations, women appeared in short, skin-tight, and strapless dresses. Their heels were high. Their dress necklines were plunging. And men's smiles were wide. As the University of Washington *Sun Dodger* shared, in a back-and-forth between fictional students:

> Male: "I understand they're going to do away with sorority pins."
> Female: "How's that?"
> Male: "There's nothing left to pin 'em to anymore."[5]

This sexual forwardness and waywardness among women, at least in male editors' fantasies, was often linked overtly with popularity. In the *Princeton Tiger*, for example, a young man was described as asking his date, "What makes you always so popular? . . . And she said with a grin, [a]s she powdered her chin: 'I keep all the boys in the dark.'" Or as a gag in a 1928 issue of the *Punch Bowl* at the University of Pennsylvania, titled "Wake Up, Little Girl," rhymed, "There was a co-ed named Nanette / Whose mama forbade her to pet / So she laid off the stuff / 'Cause ma said it was rough / Is she wearing a frat pin? Not yet." Overall, a mix of asides appearing in separate publications during the 1920s starting with the phrase "I kissed her" best reveals the main sexual emphases present in humor magazines of the time—from the commonness of women's cosmetics and the importance of one's sexual reputation to the rush of the goodnight kiss and the impediments to sexual bliss:

> I kissed her in the garden. / And my brain was rather gladdish; / My coat lapel was powder white / My lips and cheek were reddish. (*California Pelican*)

> I kissed her in the parlor, / I felt myself grow faint; / I breathed a lot of cheap perfume—/ I tasted too much paint. (*Colgate Banter*)

> I kissed her in the vestibule, / I yearned for more and more; / I went to kiss her once again—/ But kissed the closing door. (*Notre Dame Juggler*)

I kissed her in the lamplight, / And wondered if she knew my past; / She said, "I've heard a lot about you"—/ Then I knew it couldn't last. (*Grinnell Malteaser*)

I kissed her in the ante-room; / The last kiss, I declare, / For tho we didn't know it then, / Her demon aunt was there. (*Brown Jug*)

I kissed her in the moonlight, / My head was in a whirl; / My mouth and eyes were full of hair—/ My arms were full of girl. (*Princeton Tiger*)[6]

While on the whole the magazines' aim may have been laughter, the content proved much more serious and significant as the first prolonged stretch of coverage and commentary related to sex appearing in the campus press. Their "sex as dirty joke" style also occasionally caused conflicts similar to those stirred by sex columns and magazines today. The most dramatic: debate about the November 1939 "Sex Issue" of the *Buccaneer* humor magazine at the University of North Carolina that left the publication's entire press run in ashes.[7]

The controversial issue, which joked about an array of student sexual urges and events, had a jocular feel. As an invented conversation, presumably between two male undergraduates, noted: "She is a nicely reared girl, isn't she?" / "Yea. She doesn't look so bad from the front either." Vaguely provocative illustrations showed women in various states of undress and fully nude. A separate full-page cartoon depicted a mustachioed photographer remarking that a topless woman posing before him had "the most beautiful pair I've ever seen." In the cartoon's final frame, it was revealed that the pair causing his excitement was not the woman's breasts, but her hands, featured in a soap advertisement for which he had taken the picture. Separately, students' responses to a campus survey were included, pertaining to the question, "Is Sex Here to Stay?" A few of the roughly three dozen replies: "Yes. And the longer the better"; "I hope so. It would be an awful world without it"; "Adam and Eve started it, and we've had it since then"; and "Sex is here but it's not to be *talked* about."[8]

The *Buccaneer*'s sex talk, through the survey, stories, visuals, and short asides, prompted swift, angry reactions both inside and outside the university. As the dean of students noted after its publication, "Criticisms have come from high school students, from high school teachers and principals. They have come from members of the State Legislature and from parents of students of the University. . . . Carolina students have said that they would not dare have a copy of the *Buccaneer* found in their homes. . . . High school boys tell me that their parents will not let them go to Carolina because the University permits the *Buccaneer* to be published." A quickly convened campus forum run by the student government president discussed the issue's inappropriateness, with one participant even questioning the upbringing of the student editor who oversaw its completion. All copies of the issue were eventually confiscated and burned in the Chapel Hill city incinerator. More than four hundred dollars was then appropriated for the printing of a new November issue, free of sexual explicitness or innuendo.[9]

In the period following World War II, college media overall similarly steered clear of sexual topics. While some student newspapers delved into divisive subjects, including the rise in campus communist groups and ROTC programs, the student press at the time was known mostly for the narrowness of its coverage. As *College Press Review* reported, "The 1950s was the decade of the quiet, clean, and informative college newspaper, the decade where newspaper features promoted adoration for faculty members, and the student government." Or as scholastic press researcher Sherri Taylor noted, "If the '50s was truly the period of the calm before the storm in relation [to] the '60s, the college press was representative of what was to come."[10]

Sex's coming out in the student press happened with astounding regularity and frankness during the 1960s and 1970s. During a two-decade-long stretch in which sexual issues of all kinds appeared more unabashedly within public debate, street protests, and professional media, college journalism also entered into the throes of an unprecedented "lingering sex and pornography phase." Student press outlets began conducting and publishing their own surveys of students' sexual activity, modeled on the earlier Kinsey reports. They provided how-to manuals for performing abortions (even while still illegal) and reported on students' decisions to undergo the procedure. And they fought for the greater availability of contraceptives on campus, and against the parental mentality pervading many campus health centers suppressing them.

At the end of the 1960s, the ultimate demonstration of student journalism's emergence as a central sexual forum came in the form of correspondence. In 1969, the *Exponent* at the University of Alabama in Huntsville published a brief letter to the editor written by an undergraduate who called herself "Virginia (Virgin for short but not for long!)." In the letter, "Virginia" invited students to attend the first meeting of an on-campus Free Love Club. "I think it's time the students got a little more loving, and I want to give as much of myself as I can, and I am 41–28–36, long blonde hair, and very friendly," she declared. "I want to lead this club because I think I'm uninhibited enough to make other students uninhibited too." As an *Exponent* editorial noted, two days later, at the appointed spot and time, "an unprecedented mob" of several hundred students and faculty showed up for a fifteen-minute "lust-in" waiting for "Virginia" to appear. While she was a no-show, the throng chanted "We Want Virginia" and catcalled any woman who accidentally strolled nearby. With students still abuzz about the event days later, the *Exponent* reported, "The newspaper had at last found, through a letter, the common denominator of many of the UAH students—sex."[11]

Along with inciting lust-ins, the rise in sexualized content and explicitness among student media of the time led to administrative threats of censorship and legislative action; the suspension, confiscation, and banning of many publications; and, in a few cases, even the pressing of criminal charges. It also led to a movement underground. While a smattering of underground newspapers in the 1960s and 1970s were funded and officially recognized by universities, most were independent but possessed strong campus ties and particularly targeted student readers. Content in the publications ran the gamut, including exposés and editorials related to student-initiated political movements, the Vietnam War, the draft, rising recreational drug use, youth gambling, racism, civil rights, Third World plights, environmental fights, and sex. Or as a popular saying at the time summarized the content mix more concisely: "Peace, Pussy, and Pot."[12]

In respect to the second part of that slogan, sex saturated the pages as the focus or subtext of many publications' opinion and news pieces. Erotic advertisements also were among the most popular parts of many papers, including business ads for sex toys and classified ads selling stag movie collections and soliciting sex and relationship partners of all orientations and inclinations. Sexualized assertiveness and titillation also appeared in human form, through photographs and drawings of nude men and women engaged in sexual activity. In sum, the underground press celebrated sex exuberantly and promoted it as a pursuit to be shared by many and carried out in abundance, in public, at all times, and for the sake of pleasure and protest as much as intimacy.[13]

The mainstream student press finally became serious about sex in the 1980s and 1990s, increasingly covering newsworthy issues such as the identifying of alleged student rapists, the military's implementation of "don't ask, don't tell," the mainstreaming of gay and lesbian lifestyles, and the spread of HIV/AIDS. In 1985, Phil Angelo, the faculty adviser for the *Lantern* student newspaper at Ohio State University, counseled students to begin covering the topic. "Sex is news," Angelo wrote in *College Media Review*. "Witness the large amount of coverage given to herpes and AIDS. Changes in sexual habits and mores are news."[14]

Interestingly, however, for all its many and varied student press predecessors, "Sex on Tuesday" stands most directly on the shoulders of the *Daily Californian*'s own financial woes. The newspaper had struggled to turn a profit since the early 1990s, a prospect made tougher by its independent status, leaving it with no student fees or university support to help prop up the budget. "A few years before I came on board, the paper was struggling horribly, to the point that in my sophomore year [1994–1995] it was published only twice a week, not even daily, which makes it much easier for students to pass by those stacks and just forget it's there," said Michael Coleman, who is now vice president of digital media at the *Arizona Republic*. "The staff at the time had apparently even considered bankruptcy. The situation was just bad."

To reverse the financial slump, top staff constantly focused on ways to increase reader interest and, subsequently, draw in greater advertising revenue. "Mike [Coleman] was really into trying new things," said former managing editor Erin Allday, now a staff writer at the *San Francisco Chronicle*. "He was kind of ahead of his time in a way. You know, nowadays, newspapers are trying new things and doing anything they can to get readers into the paper. And he was already thinking that way back then. He was always throwing out ideas, always pushing the envelope, and putting in quirky, eye-catching stuff." Specifically, during Coleman's tenure, sports coverage was ramped up; more attention was paid to presentation choices; and a greater amount of campus news was featured. This last effort related to the staff's desire to break away from the publication's reputation as the all-inclusive broadsheet of Berkeley, and instead establish itself as a more student-specific newspaper of record. "There was always a notion that we weren't just the paper on campus, but also serving the area beyond the school," Coleman said. "It's great and fine, but the needs of a Berkeley resident living a mile from campus and who has lived there thirty years and the needs of a student are incredibly different."

Top editors viewed a column about sex as the most blatant way to promote a student-first mentality. "Everyone talks about sex, especially college kids, when they're at the bar or sitting around campus," said Katz, who is now an editor at *Esquire*. "But most mainstream media outlets were afraid to touch it as a topic. We knew, though, with the college demographic, and their interest level in it, it would be something we could take on and be provocative, which would obviously attract more people to the paper."

By the mid-1990s, sex had cemented itself into the U.S. cultural fabric— from Madonna and Jerry Springer to teen magazines and MTV's spring break specials and *The Real World*. At the time of the column's start, the Clinton-Lewinsky scandal, a singular act that brought sex into the news ad nauseam, had not yet broken. The Internet, and its accompanying point-and-click sexuality, had also not yet arrived within the mainstream. But sex still reigned supreme among existing commercial media and had begun skewing ever younger, epitomized by explicit "booty rap" and a Hollywood "teen fever" that produced sexualized films and shows aimed at youths, such as *Clueless*, *Dawson's Creek, American Pie*, and *Beverly Hills, 90210*.[15]

To modern young adults, early 1900s Victorian chasteness was completely alien. The "no sex, please, we're American" philosophy of the 1950s was similarly anachronistic. The free love protests and sexual counterculture of the 1960s and 1970s had faded and normalized. The 1980s "Just Say No" label had morphed into the much more open slogan "Let's Talk About Sex," the title of a popular early-1990s hip-hop song. College students embraced this mantra, through talk, thoughts, fantasies, and especially actions.[16]

The college sex culture of the mid-1990s was "adventurous" and "self-confident." Those were the two most common words students used to describe their sex lives, as reported in a massive 1996 sex study that surveyed close to two thousand collegians nationwide. In the study, backed by *Details* magazine and published in the book *Sex on Campus*, researchers found that roughly 80 percent of student respondents were sexually active, with more than half having sex once a week or more. A majority of students also reported masturbating regularly, experimenting with anal stimulation, and having sex outside, in a car, and while under the influence of alcohol or drugs such as marijuana, LSD, ecstasy, and cocaine. A large percentage had one-night stands, talked dirty to their sexual partners, and fantasized about or actually enjoyed threesomes or sex with a close friend. The most compelling finding: During an average week, a majority of students said they thought about sex and love more than schoolwork.[17]

In return, a greater amount of educational content at colleges and universities had begun to focus on sex, sexuality, and sexual health, including accredited courses. Outside of class, naked parties, coed dormitory rooms, condom machines in residence hall restrooms, and sexual education workshops were becoming commonplace on campuses nationwide. Student groups centered on issues of sexuality and sexual health awareness were also founded in much greater frequency. In between courses and extracurricular activities, students were choosing to stay single longer and expressing a greater willingness to experiment with sex and even their sexuality. Simply put, the time for a student sex column had come.[18]

Ultimately, however, for the *Daily Californian* the most fortunate circumstance of the column's start was not the timing, but the paper's independent status. "If I had to stress one thing, it's that I honestly don't think the column would've happened if we'd been a university-controlled paper," said Belloni. "We may have been broke because of it, but the independence was a huge factor. It was only us deciding this. I couldn't imagine going to an editorial review board and pitching the idea. We were totally independent, with our own standards. . . . And I'm sure our advertisers weren't too excited about it at first, until they saw the revenues coming in."

Hey, Have Sex on Tuesday

According to the individuals who conceived it, the main resistance to the newly proposed column centered on the fact that such an explicit topic had a mostly alternative news pedigree. Once word spread about the planned feature, a few former *Daily Californian* editors still in the loop called Allday and Coleman to complain that they were squandering the paper's tradition of serious editorial work for a "sellout 'Savage,'" a reference to Dan Savage's syndicated "Savage Love" column that is published worldwide mainly in alternative publications. Allday also dealt with grievances lodged by a vocal minority of the eleven-member editorial board, a group with which she initially sided for a number of reasons. In her words:

> It's important to understand that we took ourselves very seriously back then and this column was definitely not viewed as serious jour-nalism behavior. We had just come off a period of major financial problems. . . . For awhile, we had not been the newspaper we wanted to be. We wanted to take ourselves seriously since we hadn't been able to for so long. . . . And so, okay, yes, a sex column's cute and funny, but we're stealing it from a weekly, which has a different vibe from a daily and college newspaper. And while it's fun, I definitely asked myself at first, "What purpose does it serve?"

Coleman was persistent that the column's purpose was to be interesting and to better acquaint the publication with the true passions and thought processes of modern students. "So much stuff that's published in a college paper is super dull," he said. "You know, the story of what goes into a city council meeting or how the water polo team did last night. So I liked the idea that a sex column would be a little provocative on purpose, to really get at the heart of what students actually talked about and cared about." In addition, part of the alternative appeal was that editors were not aware of any other college newspapers publishing a similar feature. Belloni said he remembered, even when discussions turned sour on sex, the sense shared by the staff that they might truly be breaking ground for what at the time was "something not just sexual, but revolutionary, you know, in the rather conservative, print newspaper sense."

The editorial board formally approved the column proposal in late November 1996. The board decided it should run weekly in the opinion section, in part to fill the newspaper's most glaring gap in terms of interest and space. The columnist position has long been among the most esteemed, sought-after spots on the *Daily Californian* staff, with only five undergraduates granted the post each semester or academic year. Each student writes a weekly column that is run with a prominent head shot and is featured as the only editorial content on the otherwise-advertising-heavy page 4. The decision to place the sex advice feature in a preexisting column spot was made soon after the editorial board had dismissed a columnist, according to Coleman, "mostly just for being bad and boring." Editors agreed that a regular report on sex might rejuvenate what was normally one of the most well-read and debated parts of the newspaper. "We had these columnists and, you know, they were college kids, so it was really hit-and-miss," said Allday. "By whatever quirk of fate, a lot were really boring during the fall [of 1996]. Some just weren't very good at it. Well, we thought, 'Put the sex column in there. How could anyone possibly make that boring?'"

Editors selected Tuesday as the column's regular publication day to similarly drum up greater reader interest, specifically to boost circulation on the day each week when the least number of newspapers were picked up. Belloni said that Tuesday issues did not offer any other major enticement for students to grab the paper, such as the sports section that appeared on Mondays and Fridays or the arts pullout section published on Wednesdays. Moreover, editors feared the column would be overlooked or quickly forgotten if published near the weekend and, in Coleman's words, would be "too much for people getting back into the workweek to handle" if run on Mondays.

After the publication day was decided, staffers focused on selecting a name. "I actually remember the biggest debate being on the name," said Allday. "We didn't have any idea at first. We wanted it to be serious, but be a little bit light. We didn't want it to be dirty or scandalous. The joke was that there would be enough of that in the column itself." Staffers agree that Belloni coined the now nationally known designation "Sex on Tuesday." He said the name was partially meant to mock the publication day's otherwise-humdrum reputation. "Hey, you get a bunch of twenty-year-olds together and, of course, some of the names we came up with were sort of outrageous," said Belloni, who specifically recalled nominations such as "Give Me Sex," "Hot Sex," and "Sex in Class." "After awhile though, we realized that the title didn't have to be so out there. The subject matter was outrageous enough. We were basically calling out to the student body, 'Hey, have sex on Tuesday.'"

Editors soon thereafter decided that the chosen writer, while still an undergraduate like other columnists, should be a person outside the staff with experience in the health field. The board wanted the column to possess an authoritative presence, in part so that it would not hurt the paper's reputation as a serious purveyor of news. As Allday noted, "It would be fun and titillating no matter what, so we might as well have someone who was knowledgeable and not just talking dirty."

With the general qualifications set, an open call for columnists was conducted quietly in mid to late November, with a pair of quarter-page advertisements run on page 4 of the newspaper asking interested students to send in submissions. "It wasn't just picking a random person on campus and asking, 'Are you sexually promiscuous?'" Coleman said. "We needed someone who could put some thought into it. Not so much a scientific take but an informed one." Five students sent in sample columns by the start of December. After reading the submissions, the staff did not feel strongly enough about any of the applicants to fill the position. Subsequently, they carried out a more informal, proactive search. In early December, Katz traveled to the campus's Tang Center, home to University Health Services, to inquire if any student volunteers involved with the sexual education or women's groups might be interested in undertaking a journalistic extension of their work.

It was there that he came across Laura Lambert. At the time, Lambert, a senior studying to be a sex therapist, was balancing a full course load with work as an instructor for a female sexuality course. It was one of the more popular classes run through the Democratic Education sequence, a nearly three-decade-old program enabling Berkeley undergraduates to invent, design, and facilitate original courses on nearly any topic, including origami, *The Simpsons*, bioethics, and Israeli folk dancing.

Upon meeting Katz and hearing his pitch, Lambert expressed an immediate interest in the columnist position and days later came for an interview in the newsroom, where the staff learned about her additional work as a student coordinator for the Tang Center's Health and Sexuality Peer Education Program. Through her involvement with the program, she counseled students and organized campus outreach events, including a safe sex demonstration she conducted at fraternity houses. Coleman also knew her socially, and at an off-campus party a few nights after her interview he officially extended an invitation for Lambert to become the first "Sex on Tuesday" columnist. "She wasn't a writer at the time, but she definitely knew a lot about the subject and came across as ballsy about it, in a good way, an engaging way," Katz said. "She spoke very frankly and casually about sex stuff. She brought that kind of comfort and directness to her column."

A Variety of Sexual Positions

In mid-January 1997, Lambert began her career in journalism with raw oysters and writer's block. For her first column, written in question-and-answer style, Lambert chose to address a query she received from a student wondering whether raw oysters served as a sexual aphrodisiac. The problem: She had no idea how to begin. More than any other part of the sixteen pieces she wrote for the *Daily Californian* during the semester she served as "Sex on Tuesday" columnist, she spent the most time writing and revising the first sentence of her first column. "There was an introduction I really just went back and forth with," said Lambert, who later worked as a writer and editor for Planned Parenthood Federation of America. "It was sort of self-mocking, and I wasn't sure that's the way I wanted to be, like making fun of myself. I ended up including it, though, and that was my lesson: I have to be entertaining and informative. I have to make sure it's something people want to read."

The slightly wry opening, which included a double entendre, ran as part of a two-paragraph preface in which she outlined her sexual-health experience. "Over the past several years, I've held a variety of sexual positions," she wrote in the column, published on January 21, 1997, under the headline "Out for Sushi." "That is, I've held several positions that demanded that I deal explicitly with a variety of sexual issues."[19]

Throughout her columns, Lambert similarly swayed between educational and entertaining. "I admit, I never totally cleared out an identity for myself, any type of persona," she said. "I was doing this awkward split between [being] straightforward and informative and maybe trying to be at least a little airy and hip and sexy. Well, in a sexy librarian sort of way." This indecisiveness is evident from a language perspective, with Lambert switching repeatedly in columns from complex, clinical terminology to more colloquial phrasing, which included wisecracks, bad puns, and explicit slang. For example, she periodically used phrases such as "jerking off" and "getting off," and referred to great sex in one column as "can't-walk-the-next-day fucking." She similarly strove for playful simplicity in her descriptions of various sexual resources, including calling lubricants "tubes of fun" and referring to the protective accessory worn by males during sex by the jokingly formal title "Mr. Condom." For Lambert, the occasional irreverence enabled her to dig deeper into hot-button sexual issues by at least somewhat masking their controversial nature. The casual style also mirrored the randomness and peculiarity of some topics, such as a sarcastic question she posited in a column on the potential downsides of phone sex. "The only true drawback I can foresee to engaging in phone sex . . . is call-waiting," she wrote. "How annoying would it be to have some poor telemarketing sap call up right before you're about to come? Unless, of course, you're into that."[20]

More often, however, she stuck with technical terms and descriptors. For example, she described a woman's clitoris somewhat heavy-handedly as "a whole network of nerves and nerve endings (called legs) that extend from . . . the nerve-packed pea-sized nub at the top of the vulva . . . down each side of the labia toward the anus." A week later, in a column titled "Exploring a Man's Sensitive Areas," she referred to the portion of the male body known as "the G-spot" as "an internal organ of the male anatomy that produces ejaculatory fluid." Lambert said the detached, at times antiseptic, writing style stemmed largely from her approach to the column as an extension of her health center work and sexuality class teaching. "I thought of it as a health advocacy thing, especially at first, more than me being a health journalist or columnist," she said. "It was really organic, in that I felt I wrote like I taught. That made it a bit awkward at the start, because I wasn't attempting to become the Bay Area's next celebrity sex columnist."[21]

Lambert and the editors agreed on a question-and-answer format so that interested students or Berkeley residents could submit queries directly to her, heightening the column's reader-service aspect. By semester's end, however, only about a half dozen readers wrote to her via the exclusive e-mail address set up, leaving her to concoct most of the thirty-one questions that appeared in the columns. Her ideas for questions came from friends and housemates, curious students in her female sexuality class, and the dozens of health and sexuality booklets resting scattershot around her Tang Center office.

Apart from her brief personal greeting in the opening column and a similar good-bye in her final piece, a majority of the columns started right away, sans introduction, with a question. Lambert submitted question topics for Katz's approval via e-mail in the middle of the week prior to each column, with both of them constructing the exact question wording and attempting to have them appear as informal and genuine as possible. The goal, Katz said, was not to trick students into believing real readers were writing in, but to have topics asked about in a manner that a regular student could grasp, leaving out technical or medical jargon. While generally not standing out, the pair admitted their question creation became apparent at certain points, such as the faux questioner who used overly polite terms to describe how a question idea popped up while in a campus lavatory. "Recently," the questioner began, "while attending to some business in a Wheeler Hall restroom, I began perusing some of the colorful anecdotes etched into the stalls . . ."[22]

Besides the questions, headlines were the toughest aspects of the columns to create, although they offered editors the best opportunity to be entertaining and stir things up. A majority of the editorial board collaborated to brainstorm "Sex on Tuesday" headlines, often arriving at a final heading only hours before the pieces were published. "It was tough, but definitely the most fun we had all week," Belloni said. "It was a one-deck [one-line] headline, run over two columns, meaning that we were trying to be creative in a very tiny amount of space. We wanted to give it the right treatment for a sex column, but also avoid getting tons of angry letters."

After the staff eliminated more extreme choices, the chosen headlines mainly resorted to tacky puns—what Coleman called "the groaners or eye-rollers"—that were in some way related to the first question or main topic Lambert addressed. A majority played off outdated literary or pop culture phenomena, such as the Shakespeare-inspired "An O by Any Name" about creative ways to achieve orgasms; or the Broadway-musical-motivated header "Ragtime" for a piece about the female menstrual cycle. A number of headlines also turned to double entendres and sexually oriented wordplay, including the tame "Don't Give Me No Lip," atop a column about the transmission of cold sores through kissing; and the more risqué "Knuckle Sandwich," over a piece on fisting, which in Lambert's words involves "one partner inserting his or her entire hand into the other partner's vagina."[23]

Similar to the range of headlines, the topics in the sixteen columns published each Tuesday during spring semester 1997 ranged from ordinary to more extreme. Most skewed traditional, including advice and observations about oral sex, hand jobs, lubrication, masturbation, the use of personal advertisements for dating, and the difference between male and female sex drives. More serious sexual topics addressed in the columns included the dangers of unprotected sex, engaging in sex during menstruation, STIs (sexually transmitted infections), HIV testing, and unknown vaginal discharges. These exposés were interspersed with parts of columns looking at the lighter side of modern sex and relationships, including advice on riding a bicycle to increase one's sex drive, shopping for the perfect vibrator, and dealing with a roommate's noisy sexual activity. A smattering of columns also addressed less mainstream behavior, such as bestiality and sadomasochism, the frequenting of sex clubs and bathhouses, and rimming (the act of running one's tongue in and around a partner's anus).

When such cultural taboos were broached, the columns invariably advocated open-mindedness, such as Lambert's contention that students should stop being "weirded out" at the thought of having sex during a woman's menstrual period. She similarly scoffed at the stereotype that being diagnosed with an STI "is the day your sex life ends," noting that there were many options available to enable partners to continue enjoying a safe, active sexual relationship. Likewise, she eschewed the "silence . . . surrounding self-pleasure" (masturbation), imploring readers to embrace the act as a natural part of everyday life. In a separate column, she dispelled the notion that S and M and sex clubs were nothing more than dens of unsafe sexual pursuits, pointing out at length that such establishments offered more safe sex accessories and information than regular clubs.[24]

The columns' most central theme: Sexual communication and self-reflection are needed to make sexual experiences more pleasurable, productive, and protected. "It's not often that we give ourselves permission to think only about our own sexuality, free from our relation to any other person," Lambert wrote in a column about the need for a better understanding of one's own daily sex drive. She similarly stressed that "with everything sexual, communication is key," notably to ensure safe and consensual role playing. "You need to sit down with your partner, talk about what's going to happen and agree on some rules," she advised students interested in sadomasochism. "There needs to be a 'safe word' that really means stop. . . . The lines of communication, even in your S/M fantasy world, need to function loud and clear."[25]

Overall, Belloni said Lambert's open, nonjudgmental approach made students feel comfortable turning to her for answers about topics that otherwise might have made them whisper, walk away, or blush. He equated the column to receiving anonymous sex advice from a friend, without the embarrassment of actually asking a friend. "Her style was great because it wasn't based around the question, 'Can you believe people are doing this?'" Belloni said. "It was more, 'This is what it is and how to do it for people who want to be into it' . . . explained in a tolerant way meant to break down stereotypes and offer some new perspectives."

A Little Furor Every Tuesday

In the weeks following its debut, "Sex on Tuesday" created a buzz and, in Lambert's words, "a little furor every Tuesday" on campus and in Greater Berkeley. While the overwhelming response was positive, pockets of criticism came mostly in the form of what Allday described as "outraged grandma letters." Angry Berkeley residents also occasionally phoned the newsroom to complain—their calls almost always transferred to Katz when the staff realized how frustrated he grew while speaking to them and how entertaining the ensuing conversations became. "We were very happy overall about the fact that we quickly realized there was a buzz out there and that it was pushing new people to pick up the paper," said Coleman. He recalled running into a professor on campus while on his way to class who said to him "something along the lines of, 'Hey, see you've got an interesting new way to drive readership, wink-wink, nudge-nudge.'"

Lambert said it was initially tough to deal with criticism, especially when it hit close to home. Early in her column writing, her mother, a nurse, called to tell Lambert that the only people who needed to know information about sex were medical professionals and prostitutes, and that she did not see the point in the column since it did not address either of those parties. Her parents subsequently refused to read the column and never talked about it with her again. Lambert also needed friends and newspaper staffers to console her in the wake of a letter from a UC Berkeley student published more than a month after the column premiered. "I think we've had enough," it stated. "The *Daily Californian* should be a source for good journalism, not the gory details of other people's sex lives. The 'Sex on Tuesday' column . . . is nothing more than smut, and is entirely inappropriate in a reputable newspaper."[26]

Lambert said the condemnation and "smut peddler" reputation she earned in certain circles was offset, in part, by the positive feedback she received from students, including a casual comment from the newspaper's webmaster that his grandmother loved the column. "I also even got a bunch of job offers . . . from obscure little papers and newsletters for me to continue my column right after I graduated," she said, "which made me curious about just how many random people outside the intended audience were actually reading this thing." The personal recognition at times challenged her idealism about what she wanted the column to accomplish, exemplified by a student who interrupted a female sexuality class she was teaching in March 1997 to ask her to autograph a copy of the *Daily Californian* carrying her most recent column. "I remember being mad about it, and I kicked him out of the class and didn't sign it," she said, laughing at the memory nearly nine years later. "At twenty years old, I took myself really seriously, but I truly thought of it as writing for health advocacy and I didn't want to give myself a big head that would overshadow the content, and so I tried to avoid all the recognition that came with it."

Meanwhile, the recognition bestowed on the column prompted the editorial board to unanimously renew it for the following semester. In mid–April 1997, at the behest of editors, Lambert spread the word among students associated with the health center that the newspaper was seeking a new sex columnist. Interested students submitted two sample columns to Belloni and Katz and then interviewed with members of the editorial board. In May, at the close of her final column, a brief editor's note announced: "Laura Lambert is graduating, but sex will stay in school. Watch for our new sex columnist next fall."[27]

The column has continued to run every Tuesday that the newspaper has been published, including the summer months, featuring more than two dozen student writers. Coleman said he was confident from the beginning that the column would continue because editors had conceived and marketed it as a brand name, well-known on its own, and not just connected to the first writer who penned it. "We didn't want it to just be 'Sex on Tuesday by Laura Lambert,'" Coleman said. "We wanted it to live on and be an institutional or icon-like thing."

Serina Johnson, the second "Sex on Tuesday" columnist, faced the first semblance of the iconic status that future columnists achieved nationwide. Writing near the start of the Internet boom, she was shocked to learn how many readers living outside Berkeley were accessing the columns solely online. "I mean, I did not even get my first e-mail address until just before I started writing and then I find out soon after that people were subscribing to the newspaper's online edition just to get 'Sex on Tuesday' sent to them by e-mail," said Johnson, now Serina Culleton. "I remember talking to one of the tech guys, one of the newspaper's early webmasters, who said that the column had more than five hundred regular readers, just online, people who wanted it sent to them every week. Nowadays that's probably normal, but at the time the tech guy said it was phenomenal, you know, unreal."

She also received regular personal e-mails and was identified in public by her columnist persona. As she recalled:

When I went into Henry's, our bar on campus, my friends would introduce me by saying, "This is 'Sex on Tuesday,'" as if that was my name. I also totally started getting moved to the front of any lines, you know, to get into bars or different places when I was out. . . . I was told by a friend of the football coach that there were no newspapers around the rest of the week, but on Tuesdays the players would all have them and they'd be everywhere in the locker room. Just on Tuesdays, not on any other day. I always got a kick out of that. I never expected that type of following or attention.

In this sense, staffers agree that the irony of the column's endurance and lasting influence rests in the low-key expectations surrounding its creation and continued publication, in part because it started amid a swirl of other seemingly more important happenings. "I mean, our staff was there covering things when they caught the Unabomber, who was one of our professors, along with a few other major protests, and of course the affirmative action fight," said Belloni. "With all that, it's funny now to be remembered for a sex column, which almost came about as an after-thought." By comparison, Katz said that staffers' chief legacy with the sex column was related to nothing more than their recognition of, and courage to act on, the obvious. "When you're in college, it's probably the most sexually charged time of your life," he said. "Mondays, Tuesdays, any day of the week, you can't go wrong talking about it. We were just the first ones to realize that fact. I mean, it's not rocket science. It's sex."

Carrie Bradshaw of the Ivy League
The Celebrity of Sex Columnist Natalie Krinsky

3

> I was never worried. I never realized what I was doing. I never thought to use a pseudonym, never thought that it would impact my own life in any way.
>
> NATALIE KRINSKY
> *former sex columnist,* Yale Daily News

Itzhak Krinsky, the managing director of a leading Manhattan investment banking firm, received an e-mail from a younger co-worker in December 2001. The message began with the words, "You should read this—it's hysterical." It included the text of a recently published college newspaper sex column detailing the finer points of fellatio (oral sex performed on a man). It was provocatively headlined "Spit or Swallow? It's All About the Sauce."[1]

In the column, the writer, a female student, recounted her experience practicing oral sex in her early teens using bananas and carrots, eventually coming to a sarcastic, Shakespearean-level crossroads: "Thus, as Hamlet does, I say, to spit or not to spit? That is the question. Whether 'tis nobler in the mind to suffer the sour tastes of a thousand sperm or to bring a cup and take arms against a sea of troubles." She wrote that she decided in college to become an "avid swallow supporter," in respect to the male's secretion upon orgasm, comparing it to taking cough syrup. "Sure it's a little painful at first," she noted, "but eventually the taste will go away, and it's pure lovin' from then on." She concluded wryly, and with the use of a double entendre, by summoning the spirit of the approaching holiday, stating, "Whether you choose to spit or swallow this holiday season, may your days be merry and bright, and may all your Christmases be—white." Krinsky no doubt read the article more closely after seeing that the writer's last name in the byline matched his own. The columnist: his nineteen-year-old daughter, Natalie.

His accidental discovery of Natalie's extracurricular writing endeavor came just as she was also discovered nationwide and placed at the center of a media onslaught, all for her role as a college newspaper sex columnist. She was not the first to pen such a column, nor the most talented, but Natalie Krinsky is by far the most well-known student writer whose newspaper beat was sex. "Sex and the (Elm) City," the explicit, at times shocking, column she wrote for the *Yale Daily News* while at Yale University, unequivocally changed her life—leading to national press attention, television appearances, calls from literary agents, and an eventual book deal with a major publisher.

She followed in the footsteps of dozens of high-profile social advice columnists who have dispensed wit and wisdom to the American public for more than a century. The position first formed with "Beatrice Fairfax" and "Dorothy Dix," the original prominent figures behind "lovelorn" columns, as they were called during the yellow journalism era at the turn of the twentieth century. "Fairfax" arrived first, premiering in July 1898 in the *New York Evening Journal*. The column, penned by reporter Marie Manning, promised to advise readers on "troubles of your heart." As an introductory note published at the start of the first column announced, "All young men and women have love affairs. At such times they need advice. Often it is impossible to obtain it from their families. . . . *The Evening Journal*, through Miss Beatrice Fairfax . . . will answer, to the best of her ability, all letters on subjects pertaining to the affections." From 1898 to 1905, when Manning married and ceased writing, she addressed issues involving courtship, engagement, marriage, social etiquette, "the intersection of love and class," and sex, although the latter was normally only discussed in what researcher David Gudelunas called "heavily coded language." Her column was progressive for its nonchalance in discussing sex outside marriage, but overall it pushed traditional values. The national media celebrated Manning, as "Fairfax," to levels similarly enjoyed by Krinsky generations later, including making her the impetus behind an Ira and George Gershwin song and the 1927 silent film *The Lovelorn.*[2]

But it was Manning's contemporary, "Dorothy Dix," embodied by *New Orleans Picayune* reporter Elizabeth Meriwether Gulliver, who achieved the most fame for her columnist work. "Dorothy Dix became a figure pointed out on the streets, whispered about as she passed through hotel lobbies, sought out in one or two cases by American presidents," *Quill* reported in 1953. "She was hailed by the curious who ranged from heads of medical and bar associations . . . to troops of Japanese girl scouts, waiting hours for her turn to approach during one of her world tours." Her social and sexual advice column ran for fifty-five years, appearing in more than one hundred newspapers at the height of its popularity and reaching more than ten million readers worldwide.[3]

Beginning in the 1940s, "lovelorn" columns expanded, as local newspapers attempted to build on the success of "Dix" and "Fairfax" by featuring their own homegrown social advisers. The most famous advice mavens of the era, a pair who quickly outgrew their locales, also happened to be twin sisters. Their real names: Esther "Eppie" Lederer and Pauline "Popo" Phillips. The names by which they are still known to millions globally: "Ann Landers" and "Abigail Van Buren." In 1943, "Landers" premiered in the *Chicago Sun*, originally written by Chicago nurse and journalist Ruth Crowley. It did not become a national institution until 1955, however, when Lederer won a contest to become its newest writer, a post she held for close to fifty years. Her "shoot from the hip" advice endeared her to the young and middle class, and she is credited with unabashedly bringing issues of sex and sexuality into Middle America unlike any other media figure or outlet before her. "She helped open up a healthy dialogue about sex and relationships by raising topics in her column that had never before appeared in 'family newspapers,'" *Playboy* founder Hugh Hefner said. "She, her voice, and her opinions were so accepted in more conservative areas of the country, where wives and mothers respected her. . . . Without question she helped shape for better the social and sexual landscape of this country."[4]

Phillips, Lederer's younger sister by seventeen minutes, began her own column three months after Lederer's "Landers" debut. "Dear Abby" first appeared in the *San Francisco Chronicle* in January 1956. Success and syndication followed only months later, with Abby's "uncommon common sense and youthful perspective" etching an enormously influential place in popular culture and leading to a sibling rivalry for readers and newspaper placement.[5]

Beginning in the late 1960s, the underground press also featured a number of regular advice columns on health and personal matters that at times dealt explicitly with sex. The most well-known: "Dr. HIPpocrates," a column that mainly discussed what researcher Robert Glessing termed "aberrant sexual behavior." It began in the *Berkeley Barb* and was quickly picked up officially by fifteen underground publications nationwide and unofficially by many more. Separate historians label it a "first-of-its-kind medical advice column" and a "sort of 'Dear Abby' for the hip set." As historian Rodger Streitmatter noted, "Berkeley physician Eugene Schoenfeld, who wrote the column, answered questions from readers not in arcane medical jargon but in street language—and often with his tongue firmly implanted in his cheek." The column achieved a must-read status, competing with sexually explicit classified ads as the most popular part of the publications in which it appeared. The types of questions "HIPpocrates" handled: "Should a bent penis be straightened?" "Is masturbation harmful to one's eyesight?" and "Is it harmful to fart in the presence of others?"[6]

"Miss Manners" Judith Martin and "The Problem Lady" Cynthia Heimel also earned acclaim and huge followings in the 1970s for reshaping the mainstream advice column, adding some sass and more explicit feminist perspectives. In the early 1980s, Dr. Ruth Westheimer became "the first famous American sex-advice celebrity" for her motherly counsel on the radio and television programs *Sexually Speaking.* The most direct forerunners to student sex columns are similar professional press columns often published in alternative news media. Among the most prominent is Dan Savage's syndicated, graphic "Savage Love," which began in 1991 in Seattle's *Stranger* alternative weekly and currently appears in more than seventy newspapers nationwide and in Canada, Europe, and parts of Asia. According to Gudelunas, "He has achieved a cult-like status among the regular alternative weekly-reading set." One other cult-worthy sex and relationship writer is Candace Bushnell, who told CNN in an interview that her column for the *New York Observer* during the mid-1990s "was so popular that they sold newspapers and advertising off it. People in New York were faxing it to their friends who worked in the movie business in

LA and almost immediately I was getting phone calls from movie producers who wanted to buy it and ABC and HBO wanted to buy it." The column's name: "Sex and the City."[7]

With her success, Krinsky joined this hallowed and hyped sex columnist pantheon, existing in the media spotlight as both the "prototypical sex scribe" and a leading influence on the student sex column boom that followed. IvyGate, a popular blog covering the Ivy League, noted, "Natalie Krinsky should be credited for starting a revolution. After the Yalie's column . . . the college sex column has taken off like a beer goggled frat boy the morning after bedding Bertha." Yet—similar to the conditions surrounding her father's discovery of her column—Krinsky's sudden thrust into prominence and infamy, the revolution she is credited with starting, and the windfalls and downfalls that came as a result were mostly related to forces entirely out of her control.[8]

Shock Value Is My Best Friend

Natalie Krinsky never set out to become a writer, and she certainly did not aspire to be the sexual Sherpa of the twentysomething set, a one-woman "Ivy League revolution," or "college's answer to Dr. Ruth." During her freshman year at Yale, beginning in fall 2001, the olive-skinned eighteen-year-old with curly red hair and an "irrepressible giggle" immersed herself in the study of history, eventually deciding to major in the subject. She also spoke about potentially pursuing a career in banking or consulting, following in the footsteps of her father.[9]

The Canadian-born Krinsky was raised by her parents, Itzhak and Roni, both Israel émigrés, in a bilingual household, learning French first and becoming conversant in English at age four. A further immersion into foreign languages and cultures came at fifteen, when her family moved to Manhattan's Upper East Side, where her father began work with a top corporate finance firm and Natalie enrolled in the United Nations International School (UNIS). At UNIS, in addition to participating in several theater productions, writing for the student newspaper, and interacting with the roughly fifteen hundred students and staff from one hundred fifteen countries, she began learning Hebrew and occasionally visited members of her extended family living in Tel Aviv.[10]

During the trips, she formed a distinct cultural opinion of Israelis and, while describing herself as "pretty secular," found she felt a connection with individuals sharing her Jewish heritage. "Israelis are loud and obnoxious and never stand in lines," Krinsky once told the *Jewish Week*, tongue in cheek. "They push at airports. They yell, but they believe they are speaking at normal volume. They tell you exactly what they think, even if you never asked for their opinion. Deep down inside they are generous, kind and funny, but I remind you, these qualities are very deep." Years later, Krinsky's contemporaries at Yale described her as similarly brash, as an undergraduate who seemed to know exactly where she was going. "I knew and admired . . . Natalie Krinsky from afar," wrote Maureen Miller in a *Yale Herald* feature. "In my memory, she remains forever nattily dressed in stilettos and jeans, workin' the curly red locks, and about to walk right into me . . . if I don't get out of the way."[11]

Former *Yale Daily News* editor Christopher Rovzar, a year ahead of Krinsky at Yale, said her larger-than-life persona was evident even prior to her university enrollment, exemplified by a visit she made to campus in her senior year of high school. "I definitely remember my first meeting with her," said Rovzar. "I mean, you could already tell she was going to be one of the cool kids. She wasn't clumped in a group of the younger kids like everyone else, you know, nervously looking around. She was running all over, talking to upperclassmen . . . literally speaking different languages and clowning around." Her personal drive, in part, stemmed from a lifelong restlessness and desire to always be one step ahead, both in school and in love, as she confessed irreverently at the start of a "Sex and the (Elm) City" column:

When I was in kindergarten, I was the only girl allowed in the no-girls-allowed boys club. But I couldn't wait for grade school, because all the boys were cuter there. Plus THEY didn't play with themselves in public. And when I was in fifth grade, I had a crush on an eighth-grader because he was far taller than any of the shrimpy boys in my class—i.e. he was my height. Then I got to middle school, and all I wanted to do was get to high school so I could sit outside on the lawn smoking and I could kiss "guys" and go on dates. But not necessarily in that order.[12]

Krinsky confessed to later losing her virginity in slightly theatrical fashion, while a New York Knicks basketball game and the famed Budweiser Frogs commercial aired on a nearby TV. She recalled that while at first the experience followed the "missionary all the way and . . . mediocre at best" cliché, after several moments the intercourse dramatically shifted when her boyfriend suddenly flipped her over and attempted anal sex with nary a word of warning. "Yes, that's right, he went for the anus," she wrote in April 2008. "Sure, it was only one thrust—but I—unaware that this was even something people did, skyrocketed off the bed like a shuttle leaving NASA. I landed on the floor with a thud. I was in major pain. I looked up at him— shocked—I felt like a land war in Asia, being penetrated from all sides. . . . I told him to go get a bag of frozen pees [sic] for me to sit on."[13]

This flair for the dramatic was further honed while at Yale, in part through Krinsky's participation in regular women-only Saturday morning dining hall discussions focused on the incidents and mishaps that had occurred the night before. As a reporter sitting down to interview her noted, "Krinsky seems warm, smart, the kind of woman everyone wants as her best friend. She is articulate, thoughtful and intelligent, but not above saying 'That's hot!' and laughing when a strand of her curly, dark red hair falls into her mouth." Her wittiness and carefree spirit enabled her to fit in with a wide assortment of Yale students. "The great thing about Natalie is that she was friends with everyone," Rovzar said. "She hung out with athletes, theater kids, the girls who go shopping in New York on the weekends. She had access to basically every level of the social scene. She was renowned for her sense of humor and her no-holds-barred approach to life. That's why, right away, when the sex column idea came up, she immediately came to mind."[14]

In fall 2001, at the start of his junior year, Rovzar took over as editor of the *Daily News* Scene section, a pullout published each Friday. His chief aim was to enliven the slightly stale, "self-important" content, consisting mainly of film, theater, music, book, and restaurant reviews. He first broached the idea of a sex column to *Daily News* editor in chief Christopher Michel after several weeks on the job, contending that such fare would more accurately reflect what students actually talked about, a perspective Krinsky shared. "We still talk about politics and war and all those kinds of things," she said on NBC's *Today* show, "but I think that sex is a definite issue that a lot of college kids on campuses are facing, and you know, the same way that politics are important in our lives, sex is important, in a very different way, but equally." As Rovzar similarly said, "We were in the business of covering student life, and for better or worse, sex is an integral part of student life."[15]

After Michel approved the idea, Krinsky was the only person Rovzar considered for the columnist position, even though she was not on the *Daily News* staff and had no college or professional journalism experience. "She was just the perfect choice," he said. "There was really no one else logically who could pull this off, mixing the social stuff with the humor. She was friends with everybody, outgoing, and popular. She was able to really operate in any circle. For that reason, we thought she would really be someone . . . people would really want to read every time she wrote." In addition, top *Daily News* editors knew Krinsky would not be afraid to stir up debate and raise issues that other student writers might shy away from, a fearlessness she quickly confirmed. As she wrote at the start of one column:

> There are some things we are just not supposed to talk about. Warts. Drug habits. Third nipples. Nose picking. Your parents' sex lives. These are things that are not meant to be discussed. My mother used to teach me not to say certain things. I always did of course, like the time I told Mr. Frankel that Mrs. Frankel boinked the neighbor in the shower while he was at work. I simply loved the reaction I got. This is not something I've outgrown with age. Instead, I crave talking about things I shouldn't be discussing. Shock value is my best friend.[16]

Rovzar approached Krinsky with his pitch casually, while drinking with mutual friends on a Friday night. As Krinsky recalled, "He said, 'I think you would be perfect for it.' I didn't know if it was a compliment or not." Rovzar framed his pitch around his disappointment in the current content being published in the section, leading her to accept the columnist position as "a favor to a friend" more than any desire to fulfill a personal ambition. "He [Rovzar] had never seen my writing, we never talked about writing," Krinsky said. "I figured I'd write a column or two until he found someone else." Rebecca Dana, a *Daily News* staffer who took over as Scene section editor after Rovzar and later worked for the *New York Observer*, confirmed, "It was Chris's idea. It was Chris's idea. It was Chris's idea. That is the one thing that needs to be put out there, more than anything else. Chris totally doesn't get enough credit for this. I mean, he came up with the idea. He edited the columns. He advised Natalie through the whole thing."[17]

Rovzar envisioned a column that would provide a glimpse of what it meant to be a Yale student "beyond the ivy-covered walls." He wanted it styled after the fictional work of Carrie Bradshaw, Krinsky's "personal sex guru" and an individual to whom she was repeatedly compared in the media. "We liked how in the end, in *Sex and the City*, Carrie doesn't really talk about sex all that much, at least in the parts of the columns she's heard in voice-over talking about," he said. "It's cheesier, sort of cutesy one-liners, and more about love and relationships. We wanted it to be also, well, about sex, the act, the intricacies, and the ins and outs. In the end, it was a compromise with what ended up running. I was always satisfied with it. The best surprise was that Natalie turned out to be a really strong writer."[18]

What Kind of Sex Fiend Is She?

From the moment her column debuted on October 26, 2001, Krinsky admitted taking on a persona that was a stretch from her real self. While based on her own experiences and perceptions, she mainly aimed to present herself as a younger version of the Bradshaw character on *Sex and the City*, which was illustrated most directly by the feature's similar name, "Sex and the (Elm) City." As she wrote at the start of her first column, "Sarah Jessica Parker embodies all which I value—a raging New York City singles romp carried out in a great pair of Manolo Blahniks. . . . There was no way I was about to turn down being Yale's one and only Carrie Bradshaw."[19]

Krinsky repeatedly said the "singles romp" persona she presented in her column was "more ballsy and sarcastic" than her actual social self. Specifically, while portraying herself in print as a "swinging single" who partied almost every night, scoped out guys at clubs for "dance floor erec- tions," and attempted to single-handedly bring the hand job back into fashion, in reality she was involved in a long-term monogamous relation- ship during most of the time her column was written. She was also more of a homebody than her columnist persona, often staying in alone or with friends, cuddling with the stuffed pig and red-haired doll she kept on her bed, and watching late-night talk shows.[20]

Yet, however far from the truth, editors and the media cited her audacious, no-holds-barred persona as one of the main stimuli behind the column's and columnist's rapid leap into the limelight. The public was innately curious about the woman behind the columns, even more than the topics she explored. For example, prior to an interview with Krinsky, a *Hartford Courant* writer shared that her questioning thoughts ran the gamut: "What is one to expect when meeting a bona fide sex columnist? Will she be a vixen? Will her breasts spill out of her shirt as she puffs a cigarette and her thong peeks out of her jeans?" Or as a *Yale Daily News* writer observed sarcastically during a separate sit-down, "I've been on a date with Natalie Krinsky for ten minutes, and she hasn't had sex with me once yet. I'm talking nothing. She didn't stick her tongue down my throat when we met outside the restaurant, she didn't spank me when I got up to go to the bathroom, she hasn't even LOOKED at my crotch. What kind of sex fiend is she?" Krinsky dealt with myriad silly and serious misperceptions from peers, the press, and strangers after her column's premiere, including that she was a nymphomaniac or a confirmed expert on all things sexual. "People may have a tough time separating who I am from what I write, but the 'Natalie' in this column is a persona," she said. "It's not who I really am."[21]

This disconnect between her true identity and fictional self surfaced most significantly during the run-up and initial reaction to her most famous column: the treatise on oral sex etiquette that rocketed her to fame and outed her as a column writer to her parents. The boldly straightforward piece—still the most well-known college newspaper sex column—mixed sexuality, humor, and, ironically, high-brow bookishness. As the *Chronicle of Higher Education* recounted, "In less than two thousand words, Ms. Krinsky recalled sexual experiments with produce, reported on the fat content of semen, tweaked Hamlet's most famous soliloquy to reframe the question posed in her title ["Spit or Swallow?"], and revealed her personal preference." The column generated more than three hundred fifty thousand web hits in the week following its publication and remains the most-visited article on the *Daily News* website. It was also circulated through e-mail lists, electronic bulletin boards, and newsgroups across the Internet. According to a *Yale Alumni Magazine* profile, all the attention caused Krinsky to become overnight "'The Natalie Show,' a bona fide Yale phenomenon."[22]

The online message board linked to the column received tens of thousands of reader responses, some supportive and others more critical and even personally condemnatory. Rovzar, who said the column was "more for shock value than being particularly funny or smart," contended that the intense fascination and uproar centered on the irony of such a personal topic being discussed in such a candid and carefree manner. A vocal group of readers applauded Krinsky for showing that women could talk about sex unguardedly. Critics claimed she had degraded the sanctity of such activity, discussing it, as a conservative *Daily News* columnist wrote, "as if she were talking about decorating your living room."[23]

Krinsky, who admitted the piece "was probably the most risqué column I wrote," said the topic was not her idea. It emanated from a weeklong push by *Daily News* editor in chief Chris Michel, who later served as a deputy speechwriter for President George W. Bush. "Chris actually pressured her into doing it," Rovzar similarly recalled. "It was just something we were talking about and wanted to do a piece on, but, of course, she was uncertain, because obviously that's pretty personal, and something a lot of people wouldn't want to share with other people. He just kept hammering home how much of a windfall reaction it would get, and she finally just wrote it up."[24]

That single write-up, and the biweekly columns that followed, attained ever greater popularity. For a brief time, the newspaper's website featuring her pieces averaged more than four hundred thousand unique visitors per week. For a few months in mid to late 2002, the site became the tenth-most Googled page on the Internet. Krinsky said no one predicted just how famous and controversial the column would become, noting, "It's interesting that such a small fluke led to all this." As Rovzar agreed, "There were a lot of forces at work. Everything media-related just seemed to blow up all at once. A lot of it was out of our control." A portion of the media coverage in the months after the "Spit or Swallow?" piece focused on the simple fact that her work was widely read beyond the campus the newspaper served, a rarity for most student press content. Its high level of popularity led the *Harvard Crimson* to proclaim that Krinsky's column "increasingly . . . serves the college masses as a sexual bible, (re)introducing wayward undergrads to the joys of doing it right and doing it often."[25]

Additionally, the public seemed fascinated by the column's publication in a newspaper at an Ivy League university, and the contrast between these bastions of American privilege and the taboo nature of sex. In this respect, the media and students frequently noted that Krinsky's column was a sexually charged symbol that Yale "was clearly no longer an old boys' network" or "a stodgy conservative place." As Krinsky said, "People do have stereotypes or perceptions about what happens beyond the ivy-covered walls of Harvard or Yale or Princeton, and when those perceptions are contradicted, I think that excites and fascinates them. I think a lot of these institutions also seem 'mysterious' or 'untouchable' and some of the sexy stuff we're writing about is at once scandalous and relatable." Krinsky also found herself in the spotlight due to a months-long period of inter-media influence during the summer and fall of 2002, as columns and columnists were suddenly featured in quick succession in national and then local print news outlets, television shows, and radio programs. Specifically, columnists dealt with a huge surge in interview requests in the months following "The New Sex Scribes," a June 2002 *Chronicle of Higher Education* story that touched on the popularity of Krinsky's work in its discussion of the "small but growing number" of college newspaper sex columns.[26]

Krinsky at first treated the attention like a game, enjoying the opportunity to meet actor Taye Diggs, a long-standing celebrity crush, during an appearance on *Today*. Krinsky later shared with friends a request she received from a high school senior in Arkansas to accompany him to his prom, which she politely declined. Along with the prom invitations and side perks, she was often criticized, including being called a slut and denounced by those who felt she did not write enough about safe sex issues. She broke down in tears at times after particularly nasty voice mails and e-mails, some of which included admonitions that she was setting the women's movement back hundreds of years and variations of the message, "You're going to hell, Jesus hates you." She almost decided to quit writing after her parents first confronted her about the column and threatened to force her to leave the newspaper, a stance from which they eventually backed down. "That was not the best day of my life," she said. "My parents weren't exactly thrilled.

It's a shock to find you're paying all that money for an education you didn't even know your daughter was getting."[27]

Overall, Krinsky felt the outside criticisms often focused on her columnist persona and came with no recognition of the young woman behind the popularity and press coverage. "When I wrote the column I created a character who was much more blasé, more confident than I was," she said. "When people criticized the column, saying things like 'How did you get into Yale?' they didn't always realize they were criticizing a nineteen-year-old girl with feelings." As time passed, however, through the tears, TV and radio appearances, print news profiles, and stares from peers, Krinsky adjusted to a collegiate existence in the spotlight, and even began to revel in it. "I'm a hot commodity," she told *Yale Alumni Magazine* in 2002. "I'm really popular. I've become an icon on campus and I love it."[28]

A Veritable Confucius of Fornication

Apart from the media mania focused on Krinsky herself, the frenzy surrounding her columns most often centered on the everywoman approach she took in writing them. Specifically, she gained a following that far surpassed student writers of similar fare through her decision to strip away the health talk, up the humor quotient, and focus on speaking to students as a peer, not a sexpert. Throughout her columns, she continually mocked the authoritative status that readers and the press bestowed on her as a "veritable Confucius of fornication" simply because she wrote a thousand words every other week on the subject. As she noted in her final piece, "Ever since I started writing this column, people assume that I am a seasoned expert in a variety of things that I know nothing about."[29]

Krinsky never assumed the role of an expert or deferred to one. She asked questions instead of providing definitive answers. She shared personal stories and pet peeves, communicated with students in their own language, and even used them as sources. She also almost always addressed readers directly as a collective *you*, enabling even the most abstract issues to hit home in a direct, personal way, and conversely allowing her personal adventures to be framed as incidents to which everyone could relate. As a news report noted, "Krinsky was not the first college student to write a sex column, but she was the first to take an 'average bear' approach to writing about sex and relationships." And in her own words, "I'm just normal. I wasn't, and I'm not, any more or less experienced than anyone else."[30]

She remained open in the columns about her information-gathering techniques. She read magazines. She listened to the radio. And she informally interviewed friends and acquaintances, including once while eating dinner during a raucous fraternity party and separately while working out on an elliptical machine at a campus gym. The closest she came to using an expert was for a column headlined "A Trip to the Toy Store: Good Vibrations, Sweet Sensations," when she asked her more experienced friend Veronica, "who oozes sex . . . like lava out of a volcano," to show her around the vibrator section of a pornography shop.[31]

She also readily admitted lacking solutions to the more complicated or abstract questions concerning sexual exploration and college life. As she asked at the close of one column, "Is it wrong to [sexually] experiment? After all, we ARE in college. I am sad to report that, after much discussion and deliberation, I have no answers." Similarly, in terms of style, her columns were often presented as unpolished conversations, employing a friendly, no-holds-barred banter comparable to what students might hear in their dormitories or campus coffee shops. They were filled with rambling, run-on sentences, fully capitalized words mid-sentence, a laissez-faire attitude toward grammar, colloquialisms, popular culture references, and a mix of witty and worn clichés. "It was basically like she got into the head of every red-blooded college student and poured out what we were thinking all the time and even how we were thinking it," Dana noted.[32]

For instance, Krinsky referred to a friend's desire to engage in sexual activity with the sporting allusion "take him to the hoop and slam-dunk him." She compared fake orgasms to wearing a cubic zirconium ring instead of a "good, hard, quality . . . rock." She wittily observed that "guys our age enjoy their clothing much like they enjoy their women: not too clingy, easy to take care of, easily replaceable, and, above all, easily removable." And in a column headlined "Heading Down There? Don't Waste Your Time," Krinsky likened the difficulties men face while performing oral sex on women with getting lost while driving. As she wrote:

The truth is that they are often lost, even terrified when it comes to what to do . . . though they insist the opposite is true. They . . . easily lose their way but refuse to give in. Meanwhile, we sigh, and . . . crave a turkey sandwich. After all, there is no vagina compass leading to the clitoris. No vagina road map, dictating when to get off the turnpike. There is no friendly vagina ranger that might pop out from behind a tree, with the reminder that "Only YOU can prevent forest fires. And, of course, the right way is only five minutes down the road." Men insist on driving around aggressively down there for hours on end, not realizing that THEY ARE GOING IN THE WRONG DIRECTION.[33]

Beyond the graspable comparisons, Krinsky sought to give names to the many ordinary sex, relationship, and social occurrences that had never been directly identified. During her column writing, she coined more than twenty expressions, mostly in the form of acronyms. She referred to male arousal while dancing close to a female as a "Dance Floor Erection" (DFE). She labeled one discreet form of sex play as the "OTPHJ" (Over-the-Pants Hand Job). She called women who create to-do lists in their heads while having sex "Overly Organized Orgasamers (OOOers, if you will)." And she described a last-minute phone call to convince a partner to have sex as the "Maybe-If-I-Call-Right-Now-You'll-Come-Over-and-Get-Naked-with-Me-Again call," or "MIICRNYCOAGNWMA," an acronym later adapted for the headline of a *Village Voice* story on the sex column phenomenon. Overall, her eccentric euphemisms and writing style aimed to mirror the quirkiness of the topics she discussed. "The body is beautiful, of course," she wrote at one point, "but the things we do with our bodies in the sack are plain weird."[34]

Along with embracing the absurdity, Krinsky connected with her audience through her columns' publicizing of her private side. She granted her fans an intimate, warts-and-all peek into her upbringing, family life, dating ups and downs, social and psychological idiosyncrasies, and personal obsessions. Readers in this sense were not detached spectators, but kindred spirits. They traveled with her to a pornography shop. They experienced an awful first date with her. They heard her "hurling a string of profanities" at her waxing woman. And they imagined her trying on a "red sequined thong the size of Rhode Island (read: small) with two sparkling white balls of faux fur on the front," a gift from her roommate's mother.[35]

Krinsky extended this reader-writer connection by leaving herself emotionally and, at times, physically exposed. As the *New York Times* noted, "Ms. Krinsky's persona in her column is part hip, jaded Carrie Bradshaw from *Sex and the City* and part insecure, romantic and eternally single Cathy, from the comic strip." She acknowledged in print that she was self-conscious about her weight and felt insecure every time she dug into "macaroni and cheese in the shape of Scooby Doo. And Ramen Noodles. And Yorkside [pizza]." She admitted sarcastically to having a "thin mirror" in her bedroom, being a "razor whore" in respect to shaving her legs (even though she hated the activity), and spending inordinate amounts of time ensuring the curls in her hair had "a flattering come-hither face-framing bounce." She additionally chided herself in numerous columns for being overly fashion-conscious. As she recounted at one point about a walk to class, "I'm doing this sort of awkward run-walk-skip-trip because I'm one of only five morons on this campus who wears heels when I'm clearly aware that I have four miles and three and a half minutes between classes."[36]

Krinsky's public stature also rose because of her determination to discuss sex from a female perspective. She continually promoted female empowerment through sexuality and openly discussed the realities of being a college female in a sexualized world. Even columns that appeared male-centric were framed around concerns for young women. For example, in her first column, Krinsky encouraged the reemergence of the hand job as a sexual activity, an espousal that initially seemed to be solely for the benefit of men. Yet, as she wrote, in her view the comeback of this form of sexual stimulation would provide a buffer between kissing and oral sex—allowing women to feel less pressure to engage in more intimate sexual acts so soon. In general, she repeatedly championed a female student's right to embrace her sexuality as a celebration of her womanhood, and not simply for the old-fashioned purpose of finding a mate. As she noted throughout her columns, even in a world in which women were held up unfairly as individuals who "do not pee, do not emit bodily fluids, do not perspire and are on the whole perfect creatures who roam the earth looking delightful," she did not feel it was giving in to put on sexy lingerie or dance at a club in a manner that screamed, "You are the WO-MAN."[37]

For Krinsky, who had no long-held personal writing ambition, it was recognition of her own iconic status as "the WO-MAN" documenting the student sex scene that first led her to seek literary success. She also had the help of a mentor-professor with publishing connections. At the start of her junior year, Krinsky was admitted to an upperclassmen magazine writing seminar based on the strength of several writing submissions, including two of her "Sex and the (Elm) City" columns. The seminar was taught by Steven Brill, a magazine publisher who founded *Brill's Content* and Court TV. "When I was reading her writing samples, I said to my wife, 'Can you believe this goes in the *Yale Daily News*?'" said Brill, who graduated from the university in 1972 and currently serves as a lecturer in the school's English department. "When I was there, the *Yale Daily News* was editorializing for the Vietnam War. It was run by a bunch of nerds."[38]

During the semester, Krinsky received an average of two cold calls or e-mails per week from literary agents who wished to represent her and help turn the columns into a book. After first laughing them off, the messages began to plant seeds of ambition, leading her to visit Brill during his office hours for advice on how she might proceed. "I decided to really pursue writing once the column gained popularity," she said. "So, in essence, the column decided my career path." Prior to their meeting, Brill told the *Hartford Courant* he had become impressed by Krinsky's work in the seminar, including a business proposal project in which she put together a detailed pitch for a complicated financial magazine. He decided to introduce her to Joni Evans, an influential literary agent based in New York City who previously worked for the William Morris Agency and represented best-selling authors Ann Coulter and Peggy Noonan, among others. Brill subsequently worked with Krinsky on her book proposal, which she completed during the school's winter break in 2002 and sold to Hyperion, a general trade-book publishing house in Manhattan.[39]

"I started writing the full novel in June [2003]," said Krinsky, who was twenty-two years old at the time. "I thought it would be a great summer job. I probably spent the first two months in absolute paralysis. I have a big problem being by myself all day long." She wrote roughly fifty pages over the summer. Her deadline for submission was February 1, 2004. Once back at school, she used the campus "social environment" as creative writing fuel, enabling her to complete the book on February 7, 2004, at 5:46 A.M. She told the *Daily News* she was initially apprehensive about overshooting the target date, until "her editors told her that they had never received a novel so close to the deadline." She then quickly shifted her focus to her senior history thesis on the feminist implications of the films of former blaxploitation star Pam Grier, turning in the sixty-page report only three weeks later.[40]

The novel, *Chloe Does Yale*, chronicles the adventures of a titular character bearing a more-than-suspicious resemblance to Krinsky, as a Yale undergraduate who writes a "notorious and much dished-over sex column for the campus newspaper." The book contains anecdotes from the personal life of Chloe, a witty New Yorker with Jewish parents, interspersed with the full text of Krinsky's actual *Daily News* columns (with Chloe's name in the byline). In interviews, Krinsky described the book as roughly 70 percent fiction, although she said she understood why many viewed it as autobiographical, and she admitted to changing the names of friends and tweaking anecdotes after worrying that certain characters and situations might hit too close to home.[41]

According to reviewers and friends, Krinsky's ultimate success with the novel rested more on its surrounding hype and the locale it described than from her own writing talent in bringing the story to life. In the press, *Chloe* was excoriated almost across the board. The *Houston Chronicle* called it "a tired tale of a neurotic co-ed sloshing through campus life." *Publishers Weekly* described the plot as "mostly a series of tired college party anecdotes, punctuated by Krinsky's real-life columns." The *Harvard Crimson* noted that Krinsky "tried to straddle the line between witty philosophical inquiry on the life of an Ivy co-ed and a scandalous tell-all, but ends up doing an awkward split." The book boasted strong initial sales, however, in part due to a heavy promotional blitz that focused on Krinsky more than *Chloe*. It included interviews and features in media outlets such as *USA Today*, *Entertainment Weekly*, and Match.com's *Happen* magazine.[42]

The book also generated a great deal of attention among inhabitants of its featured location, in part *because* of its less-than-stellar critical acclaim. "Everyone [at Yale] kind of went crazy when the book came out," said Dana. "A lot of people said, 'This is not representative of Yale.' It didn't exactly help that it was not considered a masterpiece of any kind. People really kind of recoiled at having a piece of chick lit, not at the highest end of the genre even, be so closely associated with Yale." Through this furor, however, the Yale University bookstore reported ample interest in *Chloe*, including one hundred sixty copies purchased in February 2005, just before Krinsky returned to the school for a public reading. Dana said there was a short period when seemingly everyone on campus could be seen reading or carrying a copy of the book, highly identifiable by its bright-pink cover. She attributed this buying spree to curiosity about whether Krinsky had been accurate about university life, a nod to one news story's assertion that, more than anything else, the novel's "setting is the star."[43]

After college, Krinsky resettled in Los Angeles, where she works as a screenwriter and occasionally contributes to TheFrisky.com, an online magazine for women. In 2006, she publicly discussed her work on a second novel, adapting *Chloe* into a screenplay, and plans for a separate screenplay about a Beverly Hills homemaker who becomes mistress of a university sorority. The projects have not yet made it to bookstores or theaters. "It's nice to be credited with starting a trend," Krinsky said about the legacy of her column writing. "I don't consider myself a role model. I'm more of a prototype than a role model."[44]

In the end, her trend setting and subsequent stardom can be traced most directly to a host of outside factors that purposefully or inadvertently catapulted her into the spotlight even more than her own talent and personal drive. As fellow Yale student and *Daily News* columnist Greg Yolen wrote near the start of Krinsky's junior year, after she had become a full-fledged, nationwide spectacle, "Natalie Krinsky does not seek out fame. Fame . . . follows her around. This girl didn't invent sex. She just writes a column about it. . . . Natalie Krinsky is no sex goddess. She's just a sweet Canuck looking for a good time who . . . lucked into getting her own spot in the paper." Or as the *Daily Telegraph* put it, "The last subject Natalie Krinsky expected to major in, when she achieved her dream of a place at Yale, was sex. But within a year, the Canadian-born teenager had become the Carrie Bradshaw of the Ivy League."[45]

4 Kate Has Become Sex
The Impact of Sex Columns on Students' Personal Lives

I've been stopped in the street, pointed at, whispered about, hit on and hollered at. . . . Gaining celebrity status in such a small town was quite an adventure. Within the first ten weeks, I managed to make a name for myself as "the sex girl."

JESSIE GARDNER
former sex columnist, Orion

In fall 2003, Kate Prengaman became "Sex." She earned the nickname on the Ultimate Frisbee field, where participants often receive names based on a defining interest or characteristic. Prengaman's teammates began calling her "Sex" during her freshman year at the College of William & Mary, not long after the debut of "Behind Closed Doors," her weekly sex column in the *Flat Hat* student newspaper. "Nicknames are big in Ultimate," said Prengaman in July 2006. "You never play with your real name. Everyone has some sort of bizarre nickname. So, my nickname is bluntly 'Sex.' It's just 'Sex.' . . . When you want somebody to cut to get open, you yell, like, 'I want Liz' or 'I want Jenny,' and they make that next cut to get open for the disc. And our captains just loved the idea of being able to scream, 'I want Sex!' in the middle of the Frisbee field."

Prengaman's nickname stuck and spread off the field as well. Friends and classmates regularly whispered "Hey, 'Sex'" to her while in the library or screamed "Hey 'Sex,' we're over here!" to get her attention while she walked to class. Her Frisbee teammates at times even identified her by nickname in more awkward situations, including while waiting in line for a ride at a Busch Gardens amusement park and during President George W. Bush's second inauguration festivities in 2005 in Washington, D.C. "I have to remind people when my parents are coming to visit to just call me Kate," she said. "They do it in front of their parents and they don't even realize it, and then I have to explain to them why I'm called 'Sex.' I have to say, 'It's not because I'm a big slut. It's because I write a sex column.'"

Like Prengaman, many students' sex columnist stints have a considerable impact on their social, academic, professional, and family lives. The most common consequence is fame. The columnist position has elevated many to a place of prominence on campus normally reserved for top athletes or student union presidents. "Definitely the most shocking thing was the B-list celebrity we achieved," said Boston College alumnus RJ Milligan, a former sex columnist for the *Heights*. "I mean, we're student journalists, not rock stars."

With the rock stardom comes an identity shift. The sexual nature of the columns, and the personae that many columnists adopt, invariably bleeds into the public perceptions of students' personal selves. The attention leaves many columnists questioning where the student part of their life ends and the columnist part begins—or if there is any real separation at all. As Prengaman said, "It's just become who I am. It's so funny. It's so awkward. It's just 'Sex.' Kate has become 'Sex.'"

More Than a Developmental Curiosity

In sixth grade, Yvonne Fulbright made a fallopian tube out of clay. The model was part of a full female reproductive system molded to scale, including ovaries and uterus. Fulbright created the system with her father as part of a class project asking students at her school in State College, Pennsylvania, to recreate different parts of the human anatomy. As she recalled, the rest of the class chose innocuous bits such as the heart and the digestive system. Her selection required special permission from the school principal. "I give a lot of kudos to my teacher," said Fulbright, now a certified sex educator recognized by the U.S. secretary of health. "Of course, I was the only person who did it and nobody took on the male system. It was a definite learning experience." The reproductive recreation served as Fulbright's initial recognition of an interest in sexual education that would evolve from a class project to a lifelong passion, including a stint as sex columnist for the *Washington Square News* at New York University.

In general, the childhood experiences and personal lives of student sex columnists often directly influence both their decisions to write a column and the personae they take on in print. While many columnists cite a love of writing, an interest in journalism, and exposure to sexualized media as tangential muses, the principal motivation for their collegiate sex scribing is a heavy curiosity about sex from a young age. For Meghan Bainum, a former *Daily Kansan* columnist, it all began with what she called "the dictionary of sex": *Playboy* magazine. At the start of grade school, she stumbled onto a few of her father's *Playboy* back issues, which aroused an interest in sex that she confirmed in eighth grade while viewing her first pornographic film during a sleepover at a friend's house. "Sex was always just fascinating to me," she said. "Of course, growing up in a small town, my sex ed. was taught by the wrestling coach with the basic film that featured paint brushes dipping into different colors, i.e., the vagina. . . . I just started wondering why it was such a big fucking deal. . . . A lot of people in small towns do it the way their parents do it and accept the values passed down without questioning them. I was the one who questioned them. I was the questioner. I didn't shut up. I still haven't."

Stephanie Oliveira, a former sex columnist at the University of South Florida, also became interested in sex with a peek at naked pictures, not in *Playboy*, but rather a psychology textbook showing bodily changes during puberty. A few years later, at the start of her own adolescence, she began questioning the changes and the blooming sexuality accompanying them, through therapy sessions, conversations with her mother, and books such as *Sexplorations* and *Sex for Dummies*. "As I got older," Oliveira said, "I realized that there was something more than a developmental curiosity in me."[1]

Merry Grasska, the mother of former *Daily Californian* "Sex on Tuesday" columnist Mindy Friedman, said her daughter's sexual curiosity also developed at a young age, in part due to Grasska's own background and professional work in public health. "Health issues including sexuality were commonly discussed in our home, family gatherings, and social gatherings," she noted. "I had an opportunity to develop curriculum for school-aged children in the area of sexuality, HIV, and AIDS. Mindy and her brother (a year older) would preview the materials and critique them. Mindy might have been eight or nine years old and she was helping me carve out public health messages for public school students."

While public health, gender studies, human sexuality, and sexual psychology are most mentioned by columnists as areas of academic interest from which their columns sprang, others refer to more universal life experiences as inspirations. For Kate Carlisle, a former sex columnist for the *Cavalier Daily* at the University of Virginia, the experience was pubescent in nature. "Sometime around sixth grade it hit me," she wrote in one column. "Yes, IT. Puberty. I was the first girl in my sixth-grade class to be tortured by this genital hurricane. . . . First I got my boobs and then I got my brains; boobs in the sixth grade and brains in the eighth. As an elder in middle school I started becoming intellectual and curious about sexuality. I lost interest in the wholesome *Sweet Valley High* sagas and started enjoying the subtle and devious writing of J. D. Salinger and Anne Rice."[2]

Meanwhile, years before Julia Baugher achieved fame and infamy as a sex scribe for the *Hoya* at Georgetown University, the foundation for her sexual exploration arrived in care package, not column, form. "When I was a senior in high school," she said, "one day completely randomly my boyfriend told me, outright and with no sense of irony, 'Oh, by the way, you're horrible at blow jobs.'" Baugher recalled being "embarrassed and devastated, of course," but also motivated. "My dorky side kicked in," she said. "I decided to study, read up, learn, and practice all I could. I was just not going to take being bad at anything, oral sex included."

Baugher borrowed relevant books from the library and also bought books from the collection available at the Urban Outfitters clothing and accessories store. She studied them and practiced various techniques on bananas. "My response to anything that I'm doing wrong is that I'm obsessed with self-improvement," said Baugher, who joked that her mother's first sex talk with her came at age two. "Well, lo and behold, he comes back from summer camp or whatever the hell he was doing and, oh my God, I'm miraculously good at blow jobs now." Interest from female friends related to her self-improvement led her to create care packages that included highlighted copies of chapters from the sex books she had read, condoms, lubricants, and other items. Years later, Baugher laughed at the memory. "I loved being able to give advice and disseminate information," she said. "So I got quickly, quickly known for knowing all these things, but it wasn't because of, you know, like, copious amounts of experience. It was because I studied. I did the same thing in college for the column. If there was a situation, like, how do you flirt, I would read every book I could on it and ask everyone I knew and then boil it down and have this base of knowledge."

The knowledge base for former *Tufts Daily* sex columnist Amber Madison began at home in North Carolina, where she grew up in what she described as "like a hippie community" and what press reports termed a "quasi commune." During her *Daily* columnist stint at Tufts University, she confirmed, "As I was growing up, everything was pretty much naked. On a nice day, I'd lay out on my back deck completely nude. If either of my parents happened to walk through the house without clothes on, it just wasn't a big deal. I swam naked with my neighbors in the creek behind my house, and I can't think of one close family friend who I haven't seen in the buff." In this enclave—comprising twenty-four houses with shared land, a playground, and a pond—nudity and sexualized humor were coupled with extremely open communication about sexual issues. The openness instilled in Madison an early sexual awareness and fed a growing perception that other women her age were not being similarly taught about their bodies and sexualities.

In a writing course during the summer after her freshman year, she wrote an essay about the lack of formal and informal sexual education that modern young adults receive. She adapted the essay into her first *Tufts Daily* "Between the Sheets" column, noting, "I was lucky. My parents were very open with me about sex. I have always known I had a clitoris, where it is, and the importance of this organ. If my boyfriends were less enlightened, I would stop mid hook-up, draw a labeled diagram of the vagina, and then return to action."[3]

By comparison, the sexual actions proving inspirational for former sex columnist Anna Tauzin at Texas State University were partially sadomasochistic. More specifically, Tauzin's column writing linked to her work as a professional dominatrix, a position she first researched in high school after a conversation with a family friend. As she recalled, "He mentioned something about a sexual slave, and I was like, 'My goodness, what is that?' I pleaded with him to tell me more about this BDSM [bondage and sadomasochism], this culture, subculture rather, what is involved, what it takes. . . . Long story short, I entered the scene as a submissive and switched around and then figured out I could make money doing something I enjoyed." While at Texas State, she set her own hours, selected her own clients, and, separately, wrote a column about sex, which in her words "is a topic I obviously have a unique perspective about."

For some sex scribes, the life experiences that inspire their columns come not as children or adolescents but as college students. For example, Erin Granat's sex column in the *Nevada Sagebrush* at the University of Nevada, Reno, stemmed directly from her time in the college dating pool after breaking up with a long-term boyfriend. "I had a semester where I was dating, like, for the first time ever . . . and I had all these ridiculous things happen to me," said Granat, a twenty-year-old junior at the time. "I was just having material come out of my ears without even trying. . . . Just being introduced to the whole scene for the first time really motivated me to write about it." Former *Michigan Daily* sex columnist Erin Kaplan actually started writing her column before she knew it would be published, regularly jotting down sarcastic, essay-style ramblings as a means of venting about a difficult relationship. "I was just kind of going through an annoying, confusing situation with a guy I was kind of dating," she said. "So I started writing down what was pissing me off, and whenever I write I read out loud because that's just how I correct myself. And my roommate came in halfway through my reading it one day and she was like, 'That is so funny. You should totally send that to the *Daily* and get a column.' And so it began."

The single most direct influence on students' sex writing is the country's favorite sex columnist, an individual who does not actually exist. Manhattan singleton Carrie Bradshaw, portrayed by actress Sarah Jessica Parker, spent six seasons writing a column on sex and relationships for the fictitious *New York Star* on the acclaimed, popular comedy-drama *Sex and the City*. The show is based on an eponymous book and all-the-rage *New York Observer* column penned in the mid-1990s by a New York writer sharing Bradshaw's initials, Candace Bushnell. It premiered on HBO in June 1998, soon thereafter cementing toxic bachelors, modelizers, Post-it-note breakups, funky-tasting spunk, Mr. Big, and the acronym SATC (Sex and the City) into the sexual and intellectual consciousness.[4]

Sex and the City is not a show. It is a brand name. It is a lifestyle. It is an unparalleled mainstream sociocultural phenomenon. As a *New York Times* reporter admitted, "I kept my distance until it became clear to me that every smart, lively woman I knew between twenty and forty watched *Sex and the City* avidly. Devoured it, debated it, analyzed how it gave form, or at least gave stylish credence, to their quandaries and desires." It is not universally adored, however, with objections sounded about the show's perversities, materialism, all-white regular cast, gay-friendly but lesbian-light sexual depictions, slim body ideals, and self-centeredness. Others describe it is as inconsequential "consumerist fluff full of naked women and devoid of content." But the complaints pale in comparison to the frequency and vivacity of praise heaped on it by the media and fans, especially for its high production values and its unflinchingly honest look at the dating scene from a female perspective.[5]

The "ladies first" mentality and "girl power" thrust are major parts of the show's influence on student columnists and its larger character-ization as groundbreaking. "Never in an American film or TV series has sophisticated girl talk been more explicit," one press report noted, "with every kink and sexual twitch of the urban mating game noted and wittily dissected." The show appeals to women for both its ultra-realism and its glamorous fantasy—a televised tightrope between women as they really are and who they desire to be. The interactions between the female characters and the sentiments they express about life and love are deemed realistic, while their consumption, fashion, and seemingly endless free time are appealingly illusionary. "With *Sex and the City*, we can live vivaciously vicariously," *Newsday* reported, "mentally strutting in Manolo Blahnik heels as our virtual exclamation points." The women who strut on screen are fully realized, empowered characters, while the men are generally one-note "revolving doors." It is a reverse of most media depictions—women as subjects, men as objects. The related objective most frequently featured and celebrated: explicit, accurate, razor-sharp girl talk. As television historian Louis Chunovic noted, "This may be the first show in which young women really talk just the way they do in real life . . . about relationships and sex, and about men, and their many shortcomings."[6]

The series has enjoyed a cultural relevance far beyond its initial airing. It has spawned frenzied fandom, mega-merchandising and fashion trends, and a media oligarchy that includes DVDs, two movies, and a spin-off best-selling book and hit film *He's Just Not That Into You*. It also continues to serve as a reference point for everyday sex and dating situations and even as a catalyst for academic study into various aspects of gender, relationships, sexuality, culture, and media. And it has spawned student sex columns—hundreds of them—attempting to capture the romantic idealism, sarcastic soul-searching, and social curiosity of the show's main character. "I think the show played a very big part in the [college sex column] boom," said Dave Franzese, a former sex columnist for the *Daily Nexus* at the University of California, Santa Barbara. "Very much the same way that 9/11 created a lot of firefighters and soldiers, or the way that Lance Armstrong created a lot of cycling classes at local gyms . . . Sarah Jessica Parker could be blamed directly for girls writing about their vulvas."

Carrie Bradshaw embodies a new strain of the journalist-as-superhero persona long ingrained in pop culture—from Superman and Spider-Man to the reporting wunderkinds of *All the President's Men*. Carrie is super-woman, a successful journalist by day and It-glamour girl by night, saving the city's singles one clichéd sentiment at a time. She is Bob Woodward with a Prada clutch, a better tan, and a more alluring bustline. Columnists adamantly express their desires to both write like her—exploring sex so frankly, funnily, and frequently—and to literally be her and exist in her world. Many student writers called *Sex and the City* their ultimate pop culture backdrop while growing up. They held weekly viewing parties. They stayed home on rainy days and quiet weekends to watch repeats in excess. They continue to reference the show in conversations with family and friends. And they write columns following SATC themes, styles, and spirit. "What was our biggest influence?" asked former *Daily Evergreen* sex columnist Erin Thomas. "Four words: *Sex and the City*. It was so revolutionary for women. . . . Every student journalist girl wanted to do the same revolutionary thing for her paper."[7]

Media reports have dubbed the columnists, at times admiringly and at others mockingly, "collegiate Carrie Bradshaws," "Carrie Bradshaw redux," "a would-be Carrie Bradshaw," "bubbly Carrie Bradshaws-in-waiting,"

"Carrie Bradshaw 101," and aspiring journalists caught up in the "Carrie Bradshaw columnist fad." Student writers are almost always upfront about their columns' connections to *Sex and the City*. For example, *Daily Trojan* sex columnist Elspeth Keller at the University of Southern California stated outright, "No one's pretending that this column isn't a take-off on *Sex and the City*." Former *Pitt News* sex columnist Rose Afriyie similarly said, "*Sex and the City*, just growing up in this time period it's difficult to say that it wasn't an influence. Everyone could hear Carrie Bradshaw's voice in the back of their head when they first read my columns."[8]

Certain columnists do resent being categorized as simply followers of the SATC trend. "I never had HBO," Meghan Bainum said. "I was a poor student. I didn't know about the Carrie Bradshaw thing. And that's one thing I always hated reading about in stories or blogs about me, like, 'Oh Meghan Bainum just wants to be Carrie Bradshaw, blah, blah, blah.' And I was always like, 'I don't even know that bitch. I don't know who you're talking about. I'm not just doing this to be like some HBO star.'" Much more common, however, is an explicit recognition of the show and its main character as sources of inspiration and admiration. "I really can't overemphasize the impact of *Sex and the City*," former *Daily Northwestern* columnist Margo Scott said. "Every college girl I know is obsessed with that show, like seriously obsessed, like certifiably obsessed."

The SATC inspiration even extends to the core of many columns' identities: their titles. Dozens of columns openly imitate or playfully adapt the "Sex and the City" moniker, with designations such as "Sex and the University," "Sex and the (Elm) City," "Sex in the Classic City," "Sex in CINcity," "Sex on the Beach," "Sex on the Avenue," "Sex on the Hilltop," "Sex in Atlanta," "Sex in the Suburbs," "Sex and the Swattie," "Sex and the Bing," "Sex and the Sun," "Sex and the 'SC," "Sex and the Cigar," and "Minus the City." As Lehigh University student Kelly Height wrote in her debut "Sex in the South Side" column for the *Brown and White*, "I'm no Sarah Jessica Parker. My legs aren't as long, my nose isn't quite as obvious, my hair isn't as straggly and my shape isn't so perfect. It doesn't matter, though, because I'm still a young woman just like her having to live my life with the opposite sex. Aspiring to be that 'talk of the town' sex columnist, Carrie Bradshaw from *Sex and the City*, I write this column."[9]

Rock Star Golden Child of Journalism

For Beth Van Dyke, the moment came while shopping in a Linens 'n Things housewares store in Santa Barbara, California, with her boyfriend. The former *Daily Nexus* sex columnist at the University of California, Santa Barbara, had spent several minutes downplaying the fame she had achieved for her column, while her boyfriend protested, "I don't know, people seem to know who you are." As Van Dyke recalled, "We go into the store right after having this conversation, and I go to pay for something and the girl takes my debit card and looks up at me and is like, 'Oh my God, you're Elizabeth Van Dyke. Did you write the sex column?' And my boyfriend just started laughing, like, hysterically. There was no denying it after that."

The truth at the heart of Van Dyke's boyfriend's laughter is the unique type of fame and infamy student sex columnists experience during the time they write their columns—and in some cases for years after their columnist stints are complete. Julia Baugher called it "a kind of baby fame." Former *Dartmouth* sex columnist Abi Medvin said friends identified her as nothing less than "a campus icon." And Phil Elliott, former editor of the *Post*, similarly described sex columnist Brynn Burton at Ohio University as "an event on campus . . . a celebrity of sorts. She was *that* girl who wrote *that* column."[10]

Many columnists' most standout memories center on the moment they realize they have become public figures or gained at least a sliver of renown. For former *Cornell Daily Sun* sex columnist Molly McDowell, who wrote under her middle name Kate, the moment came when she learned that a piece she wrote on anal sex, headlined "Going Down the Dirt Road," received so many online hits that it temporarily crashed the *Sun* website. For Kimberly Maier, a former sex columnist at Oregon's Clackamas Community College, it was when she was asked to sign autographs for her fellow students. For Lane Taylor, a former columnist for the *Grizzly* at Ursinus College, it was when she looked up while waiting in the school's student center to donate blood and realized everyone around her was reading her column. For former *McGill Daily* columnist Denise Brundson at McGill University in Montreal, it was when a friend telephoned to say she had received an e-mail containing an online version of

Brundson's column, sent from a student at Algoma University—more than six hundred miles and an entire province away.[11]

Meanwhile, for Jessica Beaton, a former sex columnist for the *Johns Hopkins News-Letter*, the moment arrived in fall 2005 in the form of prominent alumnus Christina Mattin, the primary financial contributor behind the university's arts-focused Mattin Center. As Beaton recalled:

> I got a call from the head of our alumni relations office. She was like, "Christina Mattin wants to meet you." . . . She apparently had the newspaper flown to London where she lived so she could read my column with her daughter. She wanted me to come to the class of '75 alumni dinner [during homecoming weekend 2005], to entertain her and a couple of other alumni. That was an experience. . . . They loved the column. Like, apparently there were class of '75 alumni fighting to sit next to me. I'm just not that interesting, but apparently they were under the impression that I was.

Columnists are regularly recognized on their home campus and in surrounding communities. At times, they are simply stared at or whispered about. "I think most of the time I walk around campus, I notice people noticing me but not saying anything," columnist Alexis McCabe said in 2006 while still at the University of South Florida. "They kind of do the double-take, sort of along the lines of, 'Wait, is that who I think it is?'" Kate Carlisle similarly said there were "constant stop-and-stare sessions when I was on campus, like I was Madonna or something." Students also randomly hug columnists, scream their names from across the street, buy them drinks at campus bars, and ask sex and relationship advice regardless of the locale, including during lecture classes, football halftime shows, and while selling back textbooks at campus bookstores. Former *Arizona Daily Wildcat* sex columnist Caitlin Hall said a friend of a friend once asked her how she could stop faking orgasms with her boyfriend while on a car ride to the grocery store.

For a majority of columnists, the attention is surreal and at times overwhelming. According to Meghan Bainum, who appeared topless in the February 2003 issue of *Playboy* due to her column work:

What stands out most in my memory is starting to get noticed on the streets around Lawrence or walking to class or I had teachers say stuff. I'm used to being nobody my whole life, just someone who blended in and someone who did their thing. Now, suddenly the most unpopular kid in all of Mission Valley High School is having total random strangers stopping her and asking, like, sort of breathlessly, "You're Meghan Bainum? Wow, you're so cool. Your writing is bold. Your nipples are great." It was just, like, a complete overload.

As Elizabeth Stierwalt, a former sex columnist for the *Crimson White* at the University of Alabama, similarly noted, "After the column took off, suddenly I became a public figure. It sucks when you're out in sweats buying groceries and tampons and all of a sudden—'Hey, I think I know you . . . are you the, uh, chick who writes those articles?'"[12]

Along with the grocery store, the classroom is no longer a safe haven from columnists' rock stardom. Students are frequently singled out by professors during class, normally from the first day's roll call, with asides such as "Oh, *you* are the Brynn Burton?" or "The *notorious* Lauren Morgan." Christina Liciaga, a former sex columnist at Muhlenberg College, said she was once introduced at a faculty meeting as "Christina Liciaga, you know, the girl who taught us all how to masturbate." Professors often allude to columns during lectures or discussions, and in more personal asides after class and during office hours. Former *Columbia Spectator* sex columnist Miriam Datskovsky said her advanced oral French professor enjoyed the column so much she compelled Datskovsky to regularly discuss it with her in French.[13]

Overall, students' academic efforts often take a backseat to their columnist stints in the eyes of school officials, who view them with either contempt or awed curiosity. As Kate Prengaman recalled, after turning in an assignment in a large organic chemistry class, "I started walking away and she [the professor] whispered or hissed at me, like, 'Hey, Kate, psst, come here.' And I wondered how she even knew my name and then realized I had just turned in the assignment with my name on it. So, I walk over and she was like, 'No come here,' and motions me closer, like, uncomfortably close, and goes, 'Actually, I don't have anything to say. I just wanted to be close to you because you're the sex columnist and you're in my class and that's just so cool.'"

Outside the classroom, columnists receive a regular stream of calls to their landline and cell phones and messages to their personal e-mail and social networking site accounts. Some contain marriage proposals, invitations to swingers' parties, and nude photographs. Others are even more bizarre and threatening, leading columnists to notify local and campus law enforcement. For example, Anna Schleelein requested an unlisted dormitory and telephone number during the time she wrote her sex column for the *Heights* at Boston College, partly because of fan mail she received from a prisoner at the Massachusetts Correctional Institution, Cedar Junction. A separate angry e-mail sent to *Temple News* "Straight Up Sex" columnist Nadia Stadnycki informed her that she was so uptight only dogs could smell her flatulence. It included a PS: "I hope you slip in a puddle of AIDS and cut yourself." Stadnycki's response: "I laughed."

Columnists also cannot help but laugh at the bundle of letters and e-mails they receive containing requests for sexual rendezvous. "I'd get e-mails all the time from creeps who read my articles and wanted to meet to talk more about sex with me," said former *Dartmouth Free Press* sex columnist Valerie Arvidson. "Pertaining to my BDSM article, one was like, 'I need some help learning some knot-tying techniques. Would you meet up with me sometime?'" Former *California Aggie* sex columnist Anna Ritner received an especially large number of messages after a piece she penned a week before Valentine's Day, headlined "The Campus Lust List," that named the top five locations to have sex at the University of California, Davis. As she recalled, "There was one guy in particular I got an e-mail from that said, 'You are so hot. I get a boner every time I read your column in class. This is not a joke. I want you to meet me tomorrow at [a well-known campus building] at 8 A.M.' He proceeded to basically tell me that we were going to have sex. He gave me directions. He even attached a picture of himself."[14]

Nearly four hundred miles south, on the UC Santa Barbara campus, Dave Franzese received more than fifty friend requests on Facebook, mostly from women, immediately after he took over writing duties for the *Daily Nexus* sex column, "The Wednesday Hump." In his words, "It was just all these girls who wanted to see if I was on Facebook. Then, they found me and I would get these messages like, 'I want to meet you in the library. I want to be in one of your columns.' It was, like, seriously wild shit. And I'm not anybody. I'm writing about sex, which I barely even have a grasp on. I was literally getting messages like, 'I want to be in your column. I want you to take my anal virginity and then write about it.'"

Erin Kaplan's most memorable set of personal messages arrived as a result of the tagline included at the end of her first column. It read, in part, "If you would like to date Erin, she can be reached at [Kaplan's school e-mail address]." It was her editors' idea of a joke, but it prompted a stack of serious e-mails to show up in her inbox only hours after the column was published. "By the time I got home from class that day, I had more than fifty e-mails from people of all ages asking me out on dates," she said, laughing at the memory.[15]

Along with potential dates, the professional press regularly come calling as columnists become ever larger campus stars. At first, the attention focused on the novelty. In this respect, the national media spotlight shined brightest on the early wave of sex columnists writing for student newspapers at major universities, including Natalie Krinsky at Yale, Yvonne Fulbright at NYU, Amber Madison at Tufts, Jessica Beaton at Johns Hopkins, Miriam Datskovsky at Columbia, Meghan Bainum at Kansas, Anna Schleelein at Boston College, and Julia Baugher at Georgetown.

Baugher remains one of the most high-profile columnists. During her column writing, she appeared in features run in the *New York Times*, the *Chicago Tribune*, and the *Washington Post*, and as part of segments aired on Fox News, National Public Radio, and the popular radio program *The Big Show*, among many others. "The funniest thing is that I truly wasn't seeking any attention when I first started," she said. "Everything just sort of happened, really fast. Everyone was calling me up. It was all just coming to me." August Brown, a former sex columnist at Stetson University, similarly recalled, "I was sitting in the student cafeteria one day, and a reporter for the *Orlando Sentinel* just walked over and said, 'Hey, I want to do a profile on you.' . . . After the *Sentinel* profile ran, I naturally got a massive ego boost as a nineteen-year-old kid, because, you know, this big paper says you're like this rock star golden child of journalism in the area. It was a real trip."

The Sex Girl

James Whitaker wrote that he awoke each afternoon during the 2003–2004 academic year between three and four in the afternoon in a drug-and-alcohol-induced haze. After getting his bearings, the *Mustang Daily* sex columnist, now an alumnus of California Polytechnic State University, always searched his apartment for what he termed "left over prostitutes." This search included a quick scan of his bachelor pad's shag carpeting, mirrored ceiling, corner sex swing, and leopard-print bed sheets. After sending any women of the night home, he noted, "I do six or seven lines of coke . . . [and] stop at the medicine cabinet where I take my daily cocktail of pills for my chronic infestations of herpes, syphilis, gonorrhea, warts, and crabs. Afterwards, just for fun, I beat my chest in front of the mirror." His evenings, meanwhile, consisted of what he called "skirt chasing, ass grabbing, and offensive ogling," normally ending with a "gang bang" until dawn with his ex-girlfriend and "her three virgin lesbian friends."[16]

Whitaker's rundown of his daily routine, recounted in a spring 2004 *Mustang Daily* column, was a ruse meant to amuse readers. But it also provided a counterpunch to the bevy of stereotypes, criticisms, and false impressions heaped on columnists solely because of their sex writing. "A common misconception the world has about sex columnists is that we all lead the lives of porn stars; lots and lots of sex with no moral hang ups or problems with any of it," *Carolinian* sex columnist Brook Taylor wrote while at the University North Carolina, Greensboro. "In truth . . . most of us lead relatively normal sexual lives. Just like anyone else." Or as Whitaker summed up his sexual lifestyle in his satiric column's conclusion, while still in character: "Is anyone really that surprised? After all, any man who talks or writes about sex must live as desperate a life as I do. Surely it would be impossible for a regular guy to write such a column."[17]

Readers appear to often assume the position of sex columnist is not just a writing gig but rather a full-fledged, far-from-regular lifestyle, one filled with fetishes, sex toys, bondage gear, and mounds of erotica. "To quelch popular belief . . . I don't have any crazy whips and chains stowed deep in my closet, nor do I line my shelves with *Kama Sutra* books and seventies porn," *Temple News* columnist Nadia Stadnycki wrote. She subsequently noted in parentheses, "You'd be surprised how often I'm asked that."[18]

Female columnists especially say that overnight they become known on campus as "the sex girl." Students playfully scream it at columnists as they walk along campus or upon their arrival at social gatherings. They whisper it in class, often accompanied by the most common question columnists face: "Hey, sex girl, what's your column about this week?" Former *Pitt News* sex columnist Melissa Meinzer said that strangers said it to her "in bars and coffee shops more times than she can count." Students repeatedly called Erin Granat "Anal Sex Girl," an allusion to one of her more risqué pieces. Meanwhile, *Phoenix* sex columnist Sarah Walsh confirmed she became known as "Vibrator Girl" at Swarthmore College after penning a column on masturbation.[19]

Many columnists' frustrations are not with the nicknames themselves, but the accompanying assumptions that their extracurricular activity is a full embodiment of who they are as people. Former *Muse* columnist Kaya Anderson Payne, an alumnus of Canada's Memorial University of Newfoundland, said that almost instantly after starting the column her work began taking the place of her last name. "I was suddenly being introduced, 'This is Kaya, she writes a sex column,'" she said. "No pause. Just all in one breath. And I wanted to be like, 'Well, this Kaya, who does a lot of stuff,' and that was stressful." Former *Daily Californian* columnist Sari Eitches said most of her good friends from college were those she met before writing "Sex on Tuesday," partly because a majority of people who met her after the column began could not see past that part of her. "Anyone I met after the column started running associated me immediately and often only with 'Sex on Tuesday,'" said Eitches. "Some people would even call me 'Sex on Tuesday.' Or they would call whoever I was with, like a study partner, 'Oh, is that Mr. "Sex on Tuesday"?' It was just kind of a thing people linked too strongly with me." During her time at the University of Wisconsin, Madison, *Badger Herald* columnist Jenny Kalaidis similarly said, "There's no chance to ever just be me for a few minutes, without all the sex-column-strings attached."

With public labels slapped onto them ranging from "smelly pirate whore" to "one who celebrates promiscuity," columnists' dating lives are also affected.[20] Columnists are constantly concerned about potential relationship partners' true intentions, mainly whether they are interested in the real person behind the column or the persona deemed promiscuous in print.

As one former columnist, who asked to remain anonymous in respect to this particular memory, recalled, "I've even had the experience occasionally where I've brought a guy home and then halfway through the evening he goes, 'Oh my God, I can't believe I'm making out with the sex columnist. Holy shit. Oh my God, oh my God, oh my God.' . . . It's like, are they making out with me or the myth associated with my columnist status and what that means on campus?"

Both male and female columnists say students frequently view them as conquests more than companions. Students hope to either earn bragging rights by "scoring" with the sex columnist or to display their sexual talents for someone who can then share it with an audience. To this end, columnists often receive romantic interest from individuals only after their column is brought into the conversation. "You would literally see their eyes light up," said Datskovsky. "I sort of operate on the rule of thumb that any guy who wants to date me because of my column is not a guy I want to date or even hook up with." Columnists are repeatedly asked questions such as, "If I have sex with you, do I get an exclusive article?" or "Hey, if I take you out tonight and show you a good time, will you put me in your column?" According to Brook Taylor, "There was a point when the people who want to date you just want to date you because you're the sex columnist. They want to be able to say that they've been with the sex columnist. They're just the ego-trippers."

Brundson recalled a specific ego trip with a man she briefly dated who lived on her block. "One time I just had the greatest time with this guy in bed, like, just a phenomenal experience," she said. "It lasted several hours and multiple orgasms and I was like, 'Well, that was fantastic.' And I said, 'I don't think I've ever had a third orgasm at one time.' And he turns to me and was like, 'Yes, I did it!' And I said, 'Oh my dear God, what?' And he said, 'Well, I just wanted to be memorable so you'll give me a shout-out in your column.'" Brundson acceded to his wishes, but with a twist. She mentioned him in a column in the context of men who are good in bed but screwed up in real life.

Even when finding someone genuine, columnists then face the same set of trust issues in reverse: relationship partners who express concern about whether they are simply fodder for future columns. One columnist referred to the phenomenon as "Mr. Big phobia," a nod to the oft-mentioned love interest in Carrie Bradshaw's "Sex and the City" column. To combat this fear, many columnists agree to eschew any mention of friends or relationship partners in their pieces, or to only write about them anonymously or through the use of pseudonyms. Sometimes these noms de plume are general. For example, George Washington University's Jessica Smith, who wrote under the pseudonym "Eve" for the *GW Hatchet*, referred to her boyfriend in columns as "Pink" and individual friends as "Boobs," "Love," "Babe," "Blonde," and "Brown." Kate Carlisle's in-joke, meanwhile, was that she used friends' real names in her columns but put quotation marks around them so that to readers they appeared like aliases.[21]

In general, the more intimate the relationship, the more likely the person is to remain anonymous or out of the columns entirely. Columnists tend to only break their promises to keep a relationship column-free if the relationship itself ends. In this respect, numerous individuals decline dates with columnists because they are afraid of receiving a negative review in the following week's newspaper or a damaging write-up post breakup. Others who follow through and become full-fledged relationship partners repeatedly ask if a specific fight or observation will be adapted for use in an upcoming piece. "I've been in a relationship for awhile and he [her boyfriend] was the topic of my very first column and we've been dating ever since and he's kind of embarrassed about it and we definitely have the agreement that anything that happens between us is not going to be fodder for the column," said Margo Scott in 2007. "He threw that out there, like, day two, 'This is not for your column. This is not some research experimental thing that you can go write about.' We made that agreement. Happily ever after? We'll see."

They Told Me Not to Tell Grandma

As Miriam Datskovsky lay in bed after having sex with a young man she labeled a "horny bastard," he taunted her playfully, "I didn't think it would move this fast with a Columbia girl." Datskovsky recounted the postcoital reaction near the close of her debut "Sexplorations" column in the *Columbia Spectator*. She admitted in later columns that a sex talk initiated by her mother when she was in third grade scared her and elicited a prolonged "ewww," and that at the moment she lost her virginity, her mother was checking her e-mail downstairs in the family home.[22]

The autobiographical snippets are provocative in their own right, but they hold special significance for Datskovsky for one main reason: She knew her mother would read them. "The day my first column ran she insisted on reading it, despite my protests," Datskovsky said. "She called me back after she read it—'It's very well written,' she began. Giant pause. 'But as a mother, it's kind of hard to deal with you being so open about your sexuality.' . . . The next time she called back a good twenty-four hours had passed; she didn't want to talk about my column, she wanted to talk about my sex life. Possibly the most awkward conversation we've ever had."[23]

While writing first for their peers, columnists are also extremely cognizant of the impact their writing has on their loved ones. In general, the columns have a significant effect on students' interactions with their families—leading to either strained relationships or a greater level of intimacy that only the columns' topics can foster.

Many parents of columnists read their sons' or daughters' pieces online every week and e-mail them to relatives and family friends. "My parents loved it," said Dave Franzese. "My mom made it really weird and e-mailed her mah jong friends. . . . And then I'd go home and I'm wearing my sweater and these women are reading about me giving girls head. It was just weird." In her final column, *Cornell Daily Sun* sex scribe Jessica Saunders even thanked her parents for "support[ing] the fact that I sometimes get ass." She noted in the column that they specifically e-mailed a piece she wrote about a same-sex encounter, "Kissing Jessica Saunders," to every member of her family.[24]

Merry Grasska, Mindy Friedman's mother, wrote similarly that Friedman's father collected all issues of the *Daily Californian* in which Friedman's "Sex on Tuesday" column appeared and told everyone on his side of the family about them. In her words, "I recall that even at a family funeral Mindy's column had been the topic of conversation." *Bottom Line* sex columnist Amanda Baldwin at Frostburg State said her mother not only read all her pieces but also occasionally logged onto the newspaper's website and left positive postings in the comments section under the columns, using the pseudonym "Super Mom." At the same time, however,

Baldwin noted, "My dad's whole side of the family is very Catholic, so it's like, 'Sssh, don't tell.'"

A number of columnists do remain mum about their writing to parents, grandparents, and family members with more conservative religious, political, and social leanings. As Datskovsky said in 2005, "The worst of it all is that my dad's family, who are orthodox Jews, have no idea I write this column. I feel like I'm getting to the point where they're going to find out or I'm going to have to tell them. . . . The problem won't be so much that I write a sex column but that writing a sex column means I must be having sex. And I don't have a boyfriend."[25]

Some only cryptically confess their work to family, calling them relationship or general life advice columns. "My parents are very prudish, because they're Asian," said Kaiko Shimura, a former sex columnist at Swarthmore. "While clothes shopping in Tokyo, I mentioned it once to my mom, calling it more of a dating column. She said, with her eyes wide, 'You're writing a what?' So, I paused for a second and said, 'Oh, look at that skirt over there.' We didn't talk about it again after that." Caley Meals even asked her parents to stop reading her *Badger Herald* sex column. "It was inhibiting what I wanted to write," she said. "I'd sit down to write and see my mom's face. If she reads me writing about it, she assumes I've done it." Alex Freeburg, a former sex columnist at Minnesota's Macalester College, similarly danced a two-step, first telling his parents about his columnist status and then purposefully not showing them specific pieces. "I thought it would weird them out," he said. "They told me not to tell Grandma."[26]

Certain family members in the know about the columns openly express their disappointment and concerns about the students' current or future reputations. "There have been times I've seriously considered quitting because of just how much it sucks," said Brook Taylor during her writing stint. "I told my parents when I got the job and they weren't happy with it. . . . Then my dad found out you could read them online and there was a huge big thing with that. He was like, 'This is going to come back to get you. People are going to think bad things about you.' It made me feel horrible, because I really respect my parents and what they think. It just broke my heart."

Parents at times even opt for fully silent forms of protest. August Brown said that the biggest clue to his parents' slight dissatisfaction with his column writing could be found in the family photo albums they regularly update. While they include cutouts of all other articles he has written for numerous publications, the sex columns are noticeably absent. "We basically don't talk about it," said Melissa Meinzer. "My mother says it is a good thing that my grandparents are dead because this would kill them." Erin Granat said her father's discovery of her column writing played out like a classic film scene:

> I was at home, not long after I'd started [the column]. . . . I'd gone home for the weekend and I was racking my brain about how to break this to him. . . . I was coming down the stairs for dinner and I remember looking down the stairs into the kitchen and seeing my paper open on the kitchen table and being like, "Holy shit, have you read it yet or not? Do I have time to get there and close it and hide it? Am I going to get yelled at?" . . . It was just a split-second of "Oh my God." And he'd read it. He had definitely read it. And it was one of those reactions where it's worse than when they yell. He was just silent, silent for such a long time. Finally, he said softly, without looking at me, with this frown-to-end-all-frowns on his face, "I didn't know you knew about such things." I truly in that moment didn't know what to say back.[27]

Columnists' immediate families at times face a special set of difficulties, experiencing negative reactions or public scrutiny of their own simply because they are related to columnists. "It was very, very hard for my parents, and that's the reason I stopped writing the column," said Caitlin Hall. "Not because they're religious, but because they both work for the university I was writing it at and were really harassed by a lot of their co-workers and just got so tired of having to deal with it that they got angry at me eventually for writing it. . . . They asked me before I started writing it not to write it and then they continued to do so while I was writing it and so after a couple of months, I just said, 'Okay.'" Elizabeth Stierwalt mentioned in print that her father once faced a co-worker's complaint that she was penning "pornographic stuff." As she noted in the piece, "I guess it's kind of crappy not having a common last name like Smith or Jones. . . . I want to give thanks to my dad, Mike, for not disowning me."[28]

Through the strain, however, the columns occasionally do act as tremendous sources of family bonding. "The part that was particularly distinct was that I had an opportunity to appreciate Mindy's perspective on various topics," Merry Grasska wrote. "We also discussed how her research and activities related to the column affected her friends and relationships and also the responses from her readers." Some parents, after warming to the columns, even serve as unofficial editors. "I would consider myself a fan of her work, and I definitely read the columns each week," wrote Deb Thomas, mother of former *Daily Evergreen* columnist Erin Thomas at Washington State University. "Sometimes I would just laugh and think to myself, 'Oh Erin, you think you are so clever,' but I love hearing her voice when she writes. . . . She would often ask my opinion and ask me to proof her columns, which I took as quite a compliment."

Julia Baugher's mother, Robin, drew on her extensive professional writing experience, including a stint as a speechwriter for President Richard Nixon, to help edit Julia's "Sex on the Hilltop" column. She said the editing tête-à-têtes doubled as mother-daughter bonding sessions that went far beyond discussing the sexual topics at the crux of the columns. Specifically, the sit-downs stood out as the first significant inroads Robin had made with Julia since a rebellious phase in high school that, in Robin's words, transformed Julia from a "buttoned-down, Miss Perfection, kind of straight A kid" into "a larger-than-life Julia" who cut classes, stopped completing assignments, and resisted all things parental and academic. As Robin recalled:

I mean, here's my buttoned-down student who, you know, makes up her mind that's she going to become "popular" and does everything in the book to try to do that short of drugs and a lot of alcohol, and I'm ripping my hair out. . . . And there were fights: big ones. So, when you ask whether her column helped bring us closer together, yeah, it was a very, very important way for us to be close and keep up with each other. I mean, it was one of the few things we actually agreed on and that I could be openly proud of her about. She was in a pretty deep hole in high school with me, but for some reason we just saw eye to eye on this. . . . You know, I got it, I understood it, I accepted it, and I liked it. And it was all genuine, and she knew that.

So, it was not only a way to stay connected, it was definitely a way for us to be closer as well.

Apart from constructive editorial help, family members occasionally affect columnists' work in one last capacity: as sources of inspiration for column ideas. For example, Baldwin wrote about a trip she made with her mother to a local sex store to buy her first vibrator. Haley Yarosh, a former *Emory Wheel* sex columnist, wrote about her mother's harried experience with a bikini waxer, in a column she said caused controversy on campus "because no one wanted to hear about my mom getting that done, which I guess I can understand . . . although my mom thought it was hilarious."[29]

Most memorably, *Daily Nexus* columnist Beth Van Dyke wrote about a college student who once stumbled on a fraternity brother in an open field having intercourse with a sheep. While detailing every aspect of the scene down to the "Baa . . . baaa!" sounds made by the animal, Van Dyke did not reveal in print that the student eyewitness to the bestial act was actually her father during his undergraduate days at UC Berkeley. "My father thought my column writing was the most hilarious thing, and anytime he could get his hands on material he would read it and then give me suggestions," she said, laughing. "It would always lead into stories about his college years at Berkeley and his encounters with girls or other frat boys and stuff like that. I mean, oh dear God, you know, you never want to hear about your own parents having sex." Van Dyke laughed again, before adding, "I guess the same could be said about parents not wanting to read sex stuff written by their children."[30]

A Has-Been at Twenty-two

Julia Baugher is a star, on air, online, and in print. As of late 2009, the Georgetown alumnus and former *Hoya* sex columnist wrote a weekly column for *Time Out New York*, which buttressed past columnist stints at *amNewYork* and *COED Magazine* and freelance writing for publications such as *Seventeen*, *Men's Health*, *Cosmopolitan*, *Teen Vogue*, and the British edition of *Marie Claire*. As a former *Star* magazine editor-at-large, she frequently appeared as an entertainment news commentator for programs on a host of networks, including CNN, NBC, CBS, MSNBC, E!, and Fox News. Her current and former websites—nonsociety.com, itsmejulia. com, and juliajuliajulia.com—are treasure troves of her personal and professional goings-on, visited by more than ten thousand web surfers daily. In October 2007, *New York* magazine named Baugher "the most famous young journalist in the city."[31]

She says unequivocally that the "Sex on the Hilltop" column she penned between September 2002 and December 2003 was her stepping-stone to stardom. The media attention it garnered stirred the interest of talent scouts, triggered a development deal, and paved the way for her *amNewYork* gig after graduation. Yet, even amid her success, Baugher has not only attempted to move away from her columnist persona, but literally changed its name. Specifically, after her graduation from Georgetown, she was no longer known as Julia Baugher to anyone but her family and close friends. Upon entering the media universe of Greater New York City, Baugher placed her middle name last, adopting Julia Allison as her professional moniker, the one that now appears on her websites, next to her image on TV, and in the byline of her columns and freelance articles. In her words:

> When I came to New York, I changed my name because I really wanted to move away from the sex columnist designation. You know, I didn't want to be associated with it. I was very against it. . . . I do see that it enabled me to get a column in *am*, which I wouldn't have been able to get otherwise. To have a column when you're twenty-four . . . it was the best thing that happened for my career. And for that, I only have the sex column in college to thank, because I would have never gotten it otherwise. However . . . I do not get taken seriously as a journalist at all because of it. . . . I had a boyfriend at Georgetown who now writes for the *New York Times* and I'll tell you, the way he has spoken about my career, it's not even slightly derogatory. He's like, "Well, when you want to do some real journalism let me know."

As she later confirmed, "I do really wish I had used a pen name at Georgetown. You know, I have no out now. My real name is forever attached to Google results beyond embarrassing. . . . It's hard because I know I owe a large part of where I am now to it, but it's not what I'm all about anymore. It's not who I am."

Baugher is part of a growing contingent of former columnists who discover upon graduation that their sex columnist personae are not easily escapable, for better and worse. Miriam Datskovsky, who plans to write a memoir centered on how the column changed her life, said that even with her unrelated aspirations to attend law school and work in the human rights field, she realizes the bond that will always be present with her column. "On the one hand the column's this solid, concrete thing in my life," she said, "because I created it and it's there and it can't leave me, and at the same time I've had very low points with it and it's a very complicated situation. I'm effectively in a relationship with my column."

Columnists say it is tough at times to adequately explain this relationship in the outside professional world. Some downplay the experience or generalize the position, listing it on their résumés as a dating, lifestyles, or opinion column. Former *Dartmouth Free Press* sex scribe Heather Strack said, "I write on my resume 'columnist' instead of 'sex columnist,' and when asked, I say I write about 'social issues.'" Similarly, on a résumé Brook Taylor submitted to a newspaper in her hometown, she said, "I put that I'd been writing the column, but I sweetened it a little bit, you know, 'I write the love and relationships column.' . . . It's not lying. It's just kind of molding it to your situation."

Online search engines have made such molding evermore difficult, however, with potential and current employers often stumbling on columns via a quick Google search. The subsequent trouble that columnists face is not in explaining that part of their past, but in convincing superiors and co-workers that it does not wholly define them in the present. For example, Caitlin Hall said she endured continued scrutiny from her colleagues and advisers at Yale Law School. "The fact that it [the sex column] continues to come up in my daily life is kind of surprising to me," she said in 2006. "It's on the Internet, so people Google and my name comes up. . . . It's legitimately made me an unwitting celebrity in certain ways, in that I'm in law school now and a lot of my classmates found my columns online and it's something that's discussed a lot in a very uncomfortable way to me." A prominent law school admissions online discussion board even featured a user-generated dialogue focused on Hall in late

2005. It contained particularly hurtful comments about her column work and its implications for her law school enrollment, including the question, "Who will Caitlin Hall (prestigious bitch) fuck first at Yale Law?"[32]

A majority of former columnists express a desire to leave their writing stints in the past, either forgotten or downgraded in importance. "It's over for me now," Beth Van Dyke said. "I don't want to be cornered into the sex-columnist-for-life camp." Molly McDowell agreed, noting, "I retired, put it behind me." Or as Anna Schleelein similarly said, "At this point, I consider that chapter of my life closed."

By contrast, Paul Shugar, a former sex columnist for the *Post* at Ohio University, said it is all about mind-set. Shugar chooses to embrace his column work during job interviews as a gauge of a potential employer's open-mindedness. "Some smart interviewer will always run a Google search of my name and my sex columns will pop up," he said. "They think that's going to be the big stumbling block, and to me, I'm waiting for that question. . . . It's my biggest test for the newspaper I'm going to work for because if they're very anti-that . . . then I'm probably not going to want to work for them, because they're out of touch with what the industry needs to stay relevant. I can't escape what I've done and I don't want to. It's part of why I'm especially employable."

Shugar is among a small group of former columnists who actively employ their columns as a central springboard to professional success. For example, Amber Madison said student feedback to her column led her to tackle a book project devoted to straight sex talk. *Hooking Up: A Girl's All-Out Guide to Sex and Sexuality* received national press attention when published in fall 2006. Actress Amber Tamblyn called it "revolutionary for the 21st century female" and *Publishers Weekly* declared, "This is the book you wish you'd had as a teenage girl." She has since written a follow-up, *Talking Sex with Your Kids*, makes regular television appearances, and gives talks at schools nationwide. She is fast becoming the most trusted authority on modern issues of sex and sexuality and a conduit through which parents and children can talk openly about s-e-x.[33]

Yvonne Fulbright, who once described her column as "just one step in trying to be the next Dr. Ruth," also made tremendous strides in the publishing world soon after her column's completion. She has authored or coauthored a steady stream of books, including *Touch Me There!: A Hands-*

On *Guide to Your Orgasmic Hot Spots* and *Sex with Your Ex: And 69 Other Tempting Things You Should Never Do Again (Plus a Few That You Should)*. In sum, she has become a veritable sexual health brand name. She fronts her own company, Sexuality Source Inc.; and serves as the resident sexpert for outlets such as FoxNews.com, *Women's Health*, and *Cosmopolitan*.[34]

Other columnists have found similarly plentiful writing opportunities. Jessica Beaton's column at Johns Hopkins led to her selection as the voice behind "Ask College Girl," a bimonthly advice feature in *CosmoGirl*. Anna Schleelein was hired by the National Institutes of Health to spice up the clinical sex advice offered on the website MyStudentBody.com. Dozens of columnists have also gained national exposure through their placement on a website sponsored by E. Jean Carroll, the longtime writer of the "Ask E. Jean" column in *Elle* magazine. Margo Scott even received an offer to write for the Porn News Network, and McDowell was once e-mailed by a director of pornographic films who told her she could earn "a couple of thousand dollars for a couple hours of work." As a *Maclean's* report quipped, "In a zipped-up world, it seems, a little literary unzipping can go a long way."[35]

Yet, in the end, for some, the long way around has led right back to where they started. It is a destination no one knows better than Meghan Bainum. The University of Kansas alumnus was spotlighted in a bevy of local and national press reports from September 2001 to December 2002 for the sex column she penned for the *Daily Kansan*. As a *Kansan* article reported, "Her advice column was featured every Thursday and rarely failed to drop jaws with such irreverent topics as genital piercing, masturbation and anal beads. . . . As the degree of Bainum's risqué and raunchy topics increased, circulation and student buzz were proportionate. She became a sex icon—willing or not." In June 2002, the *Daily Kansan*'s former general manager and news adviser called Bainum's column nothing less than "a real showstopper. . . . My phone rang off the hook."[36]

Who was calling? The Associated Press, for starters. The Kansas AP bureau focused a story on Bainum's column in spring 2002, and a *Chronicle of Higher Education* feature followed in June. "Th[at] report snowballed into a mainstream media frenzy," the *Kansan* noted, leaving Bainum at the center of a seemingly endless loop of print, online, and broadcast news reports, including in the *New York Times, Cosmopolitan, Esquire,* and *Inside Edition.* She also briefly wrote a sex column for the *Chicago Sun-Times.*[37]

The apotheosis of her fleeting fame: an all-expenses-paid trip to Chicago to pose for *Playboy* in late October 2002. "It was the first time I had ever been to Chicago in my life," she said. "I was picked up by a car at the airport and was just like, 'Holy shit.' And here I am with my one little backpack that's all ragged and wearing these raggedy jeans. . . . I spent the one night in Chicago alone in my room [in the W hotel] because I was afraid to leave because I didn't think I'd be able to find my way back." After posing for photographs, she was ushered into the office of a magazine editorial director for a lunch meeting. As Bainum recalled, "He suggested that I write a column and that they'll put it in *Playboy* and the whole time I was wearing a bathrobe and someone else's underwear and was thinking this is the most surreal job interview I've ever been on. And it's in this huge penthouse office on Lake Shore Drive [where the *Playboy* corporate office is located]. You know, the chair I was sitting in probably cost more than my apartment. I was just totally big-eyed."[38]

Amid what she dubbed "the surrealist period" of her life came academic trouble, especially during what was her planned final semester in spring 2002. "I just remember that basically I flunked out that semester because I was so busy with my career," said Bainum. In her words:

My big memory of that time was having to do endless interviews. You know, some station somewhere wanted an interview, and then I did another one, and I was really being thrown into something that as a twenty-one-year-old, I had no idea. I didn't have a manager or an agent or a publicist or anybody. I had someone at the *Kansan* giving me messages. It was really me making my own decisions about things. It was really unbelievable. It almost became too much. After I flunked out of school, I didn't have money for so much and I was writing [a column for the *Sun-Times*] and I lost my Internet connection and shit blew up and I was behind on rent and I had to get all these jobs and it was just like too much for me to sustain just by myself.

Bainum eventually reenrolled at the university, graduating in 2004. She encountered little interest in her writing from local journalism outlets. She briefly wrote a sex column for the website Lawrence.com, but stopped "after being relentlessly attacked in online forums," according to the *Kansan*. Early talks with a television production company in Los Angeles also fell through. In September 2006 she started work at the Replay Lounge and Jackpot Saloon bar and music venue and the Blue Collar Press screen printing service, both based in Lawrence, Kansas, also the location of the university where her columnist stint began.[39]

In an interview, Bainum did not sell her story as riches to rags. Instead, she spoke with a sense of frustration while sounding a quiet note of warning: Fame, like the part of her shown in *Playboy* scantily covered with a thong, has a backside. As she noted:

> I couldn't sell myself in the way I wanted to and I didn't know how to do it, and so it just, like, slipped out of my fingers. That would be my advice to columnists writing now. Don't expect to come out at the other end in a penthouse in Chicago with a multimillion-dollar book deal and ordering people around all day while you type on your platinum laptop words that are dropping like honey into the open mouths of the waiting populace gathered below, because that ain't reality. Especially in our culture, you're a big deal and then people move on. . . . I always joke around with people that I was a has-been at twenty-two and kind of like the whole overnight sensation thing and now it all just went away.

Or as she wrote near the start of her final *Daily Kansan* sex column in December 2002, "In a weird, twisted way, I feel as if I'm trying to write my own epitaph."[40]

Love, Lust, and Every Kink In Between

The Columns Tackle Modern Students' Social and Sexual Lives

5

> Sex. Such a simple, small word. S-E-X. Three letters that have inspired shock, moral outrage, scandal, art, literature, the Anglican Church, and let's not forget, good ol' Siggy Freud. So what's the big deal? Everybody thinks about it, everybody does it . . . so why not talk about it frankly?
>
> LIZ TOWNSEND
> *"Sexploration,"* University News, *January 27, 2003*

In spring 2004, Kaya Anderson Payne became a "new-age hippie," a "detriment to society," and, conversely, "a legend in the student press." She started as the "Sex Geek," a columnist for the *Muse*, the campus newspaper at Canada's Memorial University of Newfoundland. During her tenure, Payne wrote about sexual positions, birth control, and STI prevention. "I didn't really expect people to notice the columns," she admitted. "'It's only a campus paper,' I thought. 'No one really checks out the back pages of the Opinions section.' But I was wrong."[1]

In her second semester as sex columnist, Payne became embroiled in what one report called "the campus scandal," which received attention from a national media association and placed her at odds with her own editor in chief. The catalyst: "Mind-Blowing Cunnilingus," a column she presented as a how-to guide for performing oral sex on a woman, including locating the clitoris and reading a woman's breathing and body language to determine her level of satisfaction. "Cunnilingus is one of the surest ways to sexually pleasure a woman," Payne wrote at the column's start. "And why wouldn't it be? Your tongue and lips are soft, warm, wet and gentle. Your tongue can twist and flick in ways your fingers could only dream of. Burying your face in a woman's vulva is about as intimate as relations get."[2]

The column, planned as the first in a two-part series, was accompanied by a "textbook-style" illustration of the female genitalia that covered roughly 20 percent of the newspaper page. In an interview more than two years after the column ran, Payne said she was still not sure whether it was the explicitness of the illustration or the topic under discussion, but the response to the column's publication "was loud, swift, violent, and kind of crazy." Angry telephone calls and "nasty letters to the editor" arrived by the dozens in the days following the piece's premiere.[3]

Comments on an online forum discussing the column deemed it pointless and "softcore porn bullshit." As Devon Wells, the newspaper's editor in chief, said at the time, "We're getting a lot of response on both sides, both for and against it. We get a lot of people rallying behind Kaya, saying, 'Yeah, it's a great thing, wonderful.' And we get some people who say, 'No, no, it's a detriment to society. The *Muse* is turning into a pornographic magazine.'" The criticisms divided editors in the *Muse* newsroom and led Wells to make a difficult decision one week later. As Payne recalled, "I went in for the Tuesday afternoon meeting, going into production night. My friend, who was one of the editors, came out and saw me and said, you know, with these really sad eyes, 'You've gotten hate mail. People are nervous. Devon's not going to run the second half.'"[4]

By chance, during the week the original column appeared in print, the *Muse* was hosting the annual national conference of the Canadian University Press. The CUP is a cooperative comprising more than seventy student newspapers across Canada that identifies itself as the "oldest student news service in the world." The "so-called cunnilingus controversy," in Payne's words, triggered immediate interest from CUP conference attendees, spurring a supportive letter-writing campaign from members of the CUP women's caucus specifically. It also caused Payne, a nineteen-year-old sociology major at the time, to become larger-than-life on campus, leading to rumors circulating that tagged her as "either a heterosexual sex fiend, a sexually frustrated lesbian, or a religious virgin."[5]

In the end, the second half of the column—dubbed by Payne as "the more important actually-getting-a-woman-to-orgasm-and-beyond part"— never ran in the *Muse*. Yet, stemming from the CUP backing, it appeared instead in two university student newspapers in Montreal, including the *McGill Daily*. In an italicized introduction to the piece, regular *Daily* sex columnist Denise Brundson wrote, "This week I'm giving up my space to a legend in the student press sex-column community." Payne's experience overall emboldened her to fight the squelching of sexual expression in any form. As she said:

It's just proof that sex really doesn't stop when you orgasm [an allusion to advice she included in the cunnilingus column's second part]. Sometimes there's controversy after it. You know, it's fun, positive, healthy when done right and it's a major, sometimes *the* major, part of students' lives and lusts and thoughts. . . . And yet, if we're judged to be just a tiny bit too explicit in discussing it, you know, it's treated as something dirty that should be hidden away. I don't want students to ever feel ashamed about it or be afraid to talk about it. We are having sex, so we should be free to discuss and dissect it in every way possible.[6]

Over the past decade, college newspapers throughout the United States and Canada have dissected every facet of student sex and relationships at a regular interval and with an astounding level of explicitness, most often in column form. Among the many recent studies, surveys, commentaries, and exposés focused on modern students' sexual and social interactions, college newspaper sex columns are the sole interpretations widely produced on a peer level by students. Through their pervasiveness, popularity, and uniformity of content and style, the columns provide a glimpse into today's college social and sexual scene that is unmatched in breadth or depth. As former *Pitt News* sex columnist Rose Afriyie said:

It [the sex column] is a cultural touchstone to a certain extent, absolutely, but I don't think it's a phenomenon. If anything, it's just an extension. I think it's something that's been happening all along. Sex columns have been written at colleges for years on Friday nights, at parties, before someone hooked up with someone else. . . . The style may be new, but the substance has been there within college life forever. I mean, I'd see people pick up the paper and turn to the column every week, and everyone told me they read it religiously and they'd laugh because it was basically a reflection of everything they'd gone through the weekend before. You know, it was, like, a reflection of their sex lives.

In its entirety, this self-reflection, or student-body-as-one-self reflection, displays nearly every element of what one columnist called the "moaning, groaning, panting, screaming, cursing, laughing, guffawing and grunting of sex." The columns also cover the more general campus social scene that another sex scribe described as "the hooking up, breaking up, making up and getting it on that, eventually, become a part of many . . . students' lives." Or as Chris Keegan put it more simply, in a piece for the *Good 5 Cent Cigar* at the University of Rhode Island, the columns encompass "love, lust and every kink in between."[7]

P's and Q's of PDAs

As *Post* staffers at Ohio University recalled, even the column's headline contained a hint of hesitation: "Vaginal, Um, Noises Worth Celebrating." Former *Post* opinion editor Laura Arenschield admitted, "We were nervous about this column basically more than anything else. I mean, it's more out-there subject matter than most people are used to seeing. We knew it would probably disgust some people. We weren't really sure if we should go with it or not. In the end, though, we just figured, why not?" The topic of the column: queefing, sometimes referred to as vaginal flatulence. As sex columnist Brynn Burton wrote, it is "odorless, spontaneous, virtually undetectable and unpreventable, but it produces a sound so vile, it has the ability to kill a night of serious lovin.'"[8]

An especially vile campus response greeted the column, including letters to the editor; critical personal e-mails sent to Burton; informal declarations of disapproval from school administrators; and multiple exclamatory phone calls to *Post* editor Phil Elliott that he said started with some variation of the shout, "I can't believe you let Brynn write about that!" Amid the initial frenzy, Arenschield said it was an impromptu debate about the column at a fraternity party two days after its publication that solidified her decision to run it. "A lot of the guys at the party couldn't believe it had been in the paper," she said. "They were just mortified about it. Some girls were also like, 'I thought that was freaking gross.' But a few of them were like, 'You know, it's great she wrote about it, because I'm glad I'm not the only one it's happened to.' So people were coming down on all sides. . . . That was what we hoped the column would do in the first place. I mean, like it, love it or hate it, it was being talked about all over campus. In fact, it's still talked about occasionally, years later, from what I hear."

Columnists' principal goal has long been to jump-start sex talk among readers, in hopes of breaking what the *Tiger* at Clemson University termed the "phenomenon of silence" surrounding student sex. As Alexis McCabe wrote in her first column for the *Oracle* at the University of South Florida, "Sex. It's everywhere—on the T-shirts we buy, in the magazines we read and in the music videos we watch. Why is it, then, in a society overflowing with sex, our voices still tend to drop a few octaves whenever we start to talk about, you know, 'it'? It's as though we're being told, 'Look at it, buy it, wear it, listen to it—but whatever you do, don't talk about it!' It makes no sense."[9]

By comparison, sex columns are fearless in talking about the subject frankly and from all angles. From the beginning, this talk has followed four main formats: first-person narratives of students' own sex and relationship adventures; more traditional op-eds that cite sources and present social commentary; the question-and-answer approach; and basic how-to guides or educational articles that one news report equated with "an anatomy lecture." Overall, the editorials, confessionals, lectures, and Q&As possess striking similarities in subject matter, a reality that columnists acknowledge. In their view, the repetition of topics reflects the cyclical nature of the student readership. "It's understandable, because it's the same four years in your life," said former *Hoya* columnist Julia Baugher. "Try to talk to a woman who's having a baby. Do you think she's going to be talking about anything new? Probably not. It may be old news, but it will be new to her."[10]

The essence of the columns' old-made-new focus is in their wording. Columns are crammed with topics, behaviors, and beliefs identified by acronyms, colloquialisms, and invented expressions unique to their modern student audience. Entire pieces revolve around the p's and q's of PDAs (public displays of affection), the QGPs (questions to ask to get into an individual's pants), SMFs (serial monogamy fiends), and filibusters of fellatio (especially long oral sex sessions). Others focus on students'"pseudo-O savvy" (talent at faking orgasms), their "pre-cherry-poppin' state" (virginity), and the "big hurrahs" (periods of excessive student sex and celebration, such as spring break and Halloween).[11]

Campus landmarks are frequently named and ranked in columns for their suitability as stopping-points for "extra-mattressal intercourse" (sex outside the bedroom). Regular pieces are also run on "heading south" (performing oral sex on a woman) and "the jizz gut" (a reference to oral sex performed on a man). Separate instructions are provided on how to execute or avoid "the half-night stand" (leaving a sexual partner's bedside before morning), "backseat booty" (sexual activity in the backseat of a car), DUI (dialing under the influence, previously known as drunk dialing), and the new psychological affliction DIADD ("Do It" Attention Deficit Disorder, or an overwhelming obsession with sex). More serious sex talk touches on erectile dysfunction, feminine hygiene, breast enhancement, penis enlargement, vaginoplasty, sex during menstruation, abortion, rape, sexual assault, incest, and the prevention of sexually transmitted infections (STIs), which one columnist labeled bluntly "the world's nastiest acronyms this side of the U.S.S.R."[12]

Collectively, columns embrace a fiercely sex-positive tone. They express tolerance toward almost all sexual viewpoints, orientations, and experimentation, including polyamory, polygamy, homosexuality, bisexuality, hetero-flexibility (a middle area between being "straight" and "bi"), metrosexuals, transgender and gender-queer lifestyles, bondage and sadomasochism, sex toy usage, masturbation, casual sex, anal sex, oral sex, cyber sex, group sex, safe sex, and a range of common and rarer sexual fetishes such as attractions to overweight individuals and those of Asian descent.

For most columns, however, the "sex" part of their designations is a misnomer or only partially correct. Many pieces push well beyond the boundaries of the bedroom. They present stories and advice on a range of social trends and all relationship stages, including the "blind crush" (an unexplained attraction to an individual whom one knows nothing about), "fart compatibility" (the point in a relationship when true intimacy exists), "engagementringophobia" (fear of being engaged), the "world of white lace" (marriage), and the "fashion bump" (pregnancy).[13]

Bigger-picture issues broached by columnists in their sarcastic tone include sex and religion, sex and the environment, and sex and politics. For example, a November 2008 *Daily Campus* column at the University of Connecticut explained the impact of President Barack Obama's election victory on Americans' sex lives. "An Obama presidency means more education and more contraceptive use—so, with any luck, we'll have some smarter, less irresponsible guys running around and fewer 'whoops, forgot the condom' moments," columnist John Bailey wrote. "Obama [also] presents something different: a manliness that depends on smooth erudition rather than aggressive machismo. In the sexual market, we might be looking at a 'trickle-down' effect: nationally, we'll be seeing a little less blue jeans, a little more tux pants. Cut a few gallons off the hat and swap the six-shooter for a BlackBerry."[14]

The columns are especially straight shooters on sex and new media. They discuss the implications of online dating; online pornography; virtual sex in the fantasy worlds of *Second Life* and *The Sims*; and technosexual intercourse, an activity traditionally associated with phone sex but now embracing all manner of cyber-based connections such as "sexting" (sexually explicit text messaging) and erotic instant messaging. As *Old Gold & Black* sex columnist McLean Robbins wrote while at Wake Forest University:

> Technology has impersonalized our sex lives, has de-sensitized more than just our eyeballs and fingertips. We've all heard the stories—"he texted me like five times last night!"—"we IMed [instant messaged] for hours"—"he is no longer listed as single on Facebook!" . . . There's a hierarchy to such communication. It means more when he texts than when he sends an IM, and a personal e-mail means much more than a quickie . . . Facebook message. But really—how do such computer communiqués stack up to say, a phone call? And where does a phone call rate compared to a real, bona fide interaction?[15]

New Paltz Oracle sex columnist Robin Cooper at the State University of New York, New Paltz, wrote similarly that modern students' upbringing with new media has affected their yearning for sex, leading them to desire it as a means of attaining the physical intimacy missing from the rest of their lives. In a piece headlined "ED: Emotional Dysfunction," she explained:

> We were about five years old when the first Nintendo came out, we were born into compact disc mania, and by the time we hit puberty the Internet had taken over. We have never had to really talk to people. . . . Now that we are legal adults, American technology has flourished so much that all we need are our little iPods to "connect" us to the world. With such little interaction with people outside of an electronic box, it would be easy to understand why any emotional closeness might be intimidating. Sex, casual sex at that, is possibly the answer. What other way can one feel close to another person without emotional bindings. . . . We've been so distanced from the world and emotional closeness from such a young age, via technology, that sex has become a way for our generation to connect to each other.[16]

Columnists generally agree the most explosive topic areas are bestiality, erotic asphyxiation, post-oral-sex etiquette, and anal sex—the latter referenced in columns as "flying over the Black Sea," "the dirtiest of dirties," and the "last sexual taboo." Many columnists say anal sex pieces are the talk of their campuses for weeks following publication. Former *Nevada Sagebrush* sex scribe Erin Granat joked that at the University of Nevada, Reno, in the wake of a column she wrote on anal sex, "It was basically like hell had frozen over and it was like the biggest deal ever to happen on campus or something."[17]

Beyond delving into topics deemed controversial, columns also frequently focus on what one columnist called the "cesspool of weirdness" in the modern student social scene. Columns swirling within this cesspool include those focused on "man muff maintenance" (male pubic hair care), furverts (individuals who engage in sexual activity while dressed in animal costumes), sexual exhibitionism (sometimes called dogging), masturbating while asleep, and "sextra credit" (sexual activity between students and professors or teaching assistants). Other more peculiar pieces have addressed the cultural impact of the Paris Hilton sex tape; the act of becoming aroused while riding a motorcycle; a female student's phobia of the penis; and a range of sexual myths, such as the false beliefs that male ejaculatory fluid serves as a first-rate facial moisturizer and that Coca-Cola can double as a post-sex spermicidal.[18]

More humorous columns often involve stories of good sex gone bad, including the tale of a female student who vomited into her boyfriend's lap while performing oral sex on him. Another column recounted the saga of a young woman whose eyelid sealed shut after her boyfriend ejaculated onto it at the end of a particularly passionate sexual romp. Separately, the mysteries of sexual attraction are explored in a number of tongue-in-cheek pieces, including a *Dartmouth Free Press* column that compiled a range of responses from students answering the question posed in the headline, "What's Sexy, Dartmouth?" Some answers: "the belly button," "Paul Bunyan," "facial hair . . . on women," "freckles in the right proportion," "girls with braces," "biting of the bottom lip," and "Professor Susan Gordon, from the math department." Other columns turn to cheesy pickup lines for laughs, including one that shared zingers such as "Want to play construction worker? You'll get hammered and I'll nail you."; and the even more direct question, "How do you like your eggs in the morning, scrambled or fertilized?" For *Post* sex columnist Paul Shugar, it was not lines but lies that were mined for humor. At the start of one column, he shared the most common untruths male undergraduates tell women. The top five finalists: "5.) I really could care less about sex. 4.) I love you. 3.) I didn't know she was your sister. 2.) She's only helping me with my math homework. 1.) I have a huge penis."[19]

The columns' comic melting pot also involves columnists' sarcastic responses to students' sex questions, or at times simply the topic or wording of the questions themselves. As a female student wrote to sex columnist "Madame Vixen" in the *Acorn* at Drew University, "I'm a female sophomore and I think guys' penises look silly when erect and cute when not. Cute like a small kitty with its fur in tufts. . . . Well no, more like my own old senile cat after she's drugged with her tongue hanging out and drooling with most of her fur shaved off. Don't get me wrong, guys can look awesome, but when you get there it's kinda . . . wrong, or just makes me laugh. Is this normal?" Vixen's straightforward answer: "No."[20]

Overall, the columns' comedic tone is meant as an attention-grabbing way to inform. As Ohio University peer health educator Michael Burns said, "Some people learn from facts; others learn from reading something funny." Along with its educational value, the humor serves a significant secondary purpose in columnists' eyes: showing students it is acceptable to laugh at even the most embarrassing sexual situations, bodily quirks, and social faux pas. "I mean, we're people," said Janet Jay, a former sex columnist for the *Tartan* at Carnegie Mellon University. "We have bodies. They do weird things. I mean, I think if you're going to be having sex, you need to be able to laugh at yourself a little bit. That's the tone I try to convey in the columns. It's not just playing around because there are feelings and real health issues involved, but at the same time, it's like, 'Lighten up a little bit.' I mean, it's just sex." Paul Shugar noted similarly in a column:

> Sex is not something beautiful between two people—like most girls are taught to believe. Sex might possibly be the most absurd thing that can happen between two people. If you have never laughed out loud during sex, I wonder how you could miss the absurdity. Two people—faces contorted in a combination of pure joy and an Indian burn—fart as their two bodies writhe against each other. That sure doesn't sound like all those flowery romance novels, and it definitely isn't "Debbie Does Dallas." That is the real sex, which very few people know anything about. That is what this column is going to be about.[21]

Sex Is Sex Is Sex Is Sex

Jenna Bromberg called it "the case of the abandoned boxers." A pair of men's underwear was discovered one sunny Saturday morning during the school year in a residence she shared with five roommates near Cornell University. As she wrote in her first "Bedroom Eyes" column for the *Cornell Daily Sun*, the "ratty cotton evidence" became the chief catalyst for her roommates' real-life spin on the board game Clue.

In the game's first round, several residents denied the boxers belonged to their boyfriends or casual sex partners, only heightening the mystery. And so Bromberg awoke at noon to "the shrill overtones of energized girly voices" still debating the undergarment's origins. Soon after her arrival at "the crime scene," she wrote that her skewed hair and smudged makeup suddenly made her the prime suspect in her housemates' eyes, and with good reason. The owner of "the rogue underwear": Bryan, a Cornell senior with whom Bromberg had fallen in "lust-at-first-sight" during an alcohol-fueled party several weeks before and subsequently shared flirty text messages. She billed their encounter the previous evening as a night of "no-strings-attached, purely-for-physical pleasure sex." In the column, she admitted she was not seeking a relationship with him, he had not met her friends, and he "had never reached a level of importance in my life beyond his presence in my cell phone." She had not even asked him to spend the night after having sex, instead requesting that he "peace out" before dawn so she could enjoy a more restful slumber.

The morning after their "limited-time only" rendezvous, through the day-old mascara obscuring her vision, Bromberg wrote about the only proof of Bryan's existence still in the picture: a pair of blue boxers "bathing in the late morning sunlight at the bottom of the stairs," most likely left behind by accident. Were the boxers a negative symbol of Bromberg's promiscuity, a mark of embarrassment, a scarlet letter with a Ralph Lauren insignia? On the contrary, upon hearing her tale, Bromberg wrote that her friends' smiles "were bursting with the pride of a thousand Ivy-League mothers."[22]

In this sense, the "orphaned boxers," and the notch in Bromberg's bedpost etched after the pair came off, are symbolic of what National Public Radio's Tom Ashbrook defined as a larger "tectonic plate shift" in collegiate dating. Beyond their straight sexual health advice and quirkier sex toy and anal sex mantras, it is the columns' documenting of this shift that stirs the most press attention and heralds the columns as significant arbiters of the changes afoot in the modern student social scene. Specifically, as embodied by Bromberg's friends' pride in her sexual promiscuity, the columns regularly reveal a new brand of campus sex and socialization, one summed up within a *Daily Campus* column in seven words: "Sex is sex is sex is sex." As the column, "College Sex 101," continued, "Around these parts love and emotion have little to do with a 2 A.M. rendezvous evolving from rounds of beer pong and some bump and grind action on the living room 'dance floor.' . . . You don't even have to like the person."[23]

Along with "like," love is described as an increasingly un-collegiate sentiment. Dating, romance, and rampant monogamy are also depicted as scarce. In the columns, dating specifically is referenced as "almost obsolete"; a "largely fossilized event"; "in a coma of an indeterminate fate"; and, to students, "as familiar as an opera or a drive-in movie." In a piece for the *Dartmouth Free Press*, Valerie Arvidson wrote, "Throughout history there have always been rules about dating, courting, and flirting. But now, it seems to be a lawless territory, and anarchy has ensued. Rules and roles have shifted and there are no expectations or obligations. . . . In foregoing formality, chivalry, courtly love, arranged marriages, and punctilious adherence to the convention of 'going steady,' we are left with no idea what the hell is going on."[24]

Traditional romance is also referred to as a product of yesteryear, a "coffee shop and café scenario" and "so Bogey and Bacall, so *An Affair to Remember*." *Daily Mississippian* sex columnist Sumer Rose wrote, "The dinner and a movie era has ended. Boys no longer call girls in hopes of taking them out on Saturday night. Today boys call girls and let them know which bar their [sic] going to in hopes that the girl will meet them there. A beautiful evening with your crush consists of dinner and drinks with your friends, getting hammered at the bar, meeting at a late night [club] and hoping to go home with that person." In a *Columbia Spectator* column, Miriam Datskovsky similarly noted, "Gone are the 'good old days' when differentiating between sex and romance was as simple as telling light from dark, when you either saved yourself or had lots of premarital sex. . . . The lines could not be less clearly drawn if we tried: sex happens frequently and unexpectedly, making its meaning impossible to gauge."[25]

Within the columns, this lack of meaning leads to mystification. Columnists describe the social stage on which they tread as "a fucking roller coaster ride with six different kinds of loops," "a freak sideshow act," and "like a war zone filled with belly-baring shirts and cargo pants." Without pretense, columns offer more questions than answers about the way social and sexual interactions play out before them. As *Review* sex columnist Laura Dlugatch at the University of Delaware asked, "Is a real first date in college a myth? Is chivalry dead?" *Michigan Daily* columnist Erin Kaplan similarly speculated, "On a campus where we can fall in and out of love, relationships, friendships and beds without so much as a heads-up from our counterpart, I'm beginning to wonder: Is dating dead?" *Post* columnist Brynn Burton noted eight months before, "College dating isn't conventional these days; there are no dinner and movies, no drinks at 8 P.M. So how do you know when the person you are talking to or hooking up with may be a significant other? Honestly, I don't know." Or as *California Aggie* columnist Archie Garcia asked simply, "Where has the art of dating gone?"[26]

According to columns, the artistry is still present, but only at the extremes. Collegiate couplings exist, columns note, but they skip the courting period, rushing from straight sex to hardcore commitment at a blistering pace, typically accompanied by heavy drinking and sexual activity from a pair's first meeting. As *Cornell Daily Sun* columnist Kate McDowell wrote, "People here don't date. They either couple up and act married or do the random one night hook up thing." Julia Baugher specifically alluded to the loss of what she called "dating with a lowercase 'd,'" or the more casual one-on-one activities traditionally known as courting that "on the relationship spectrum . . . falls after hooking up but before monogamous commitment." Miriam Datskovsky likewise wrote, "Dating just isn't in our repertoire at Columbia. If I were to write a column about how many people you can date at once, or how many dates a week is too much or too little, no one would know what I was talking about."[27]

With the exit of "the lowercase 'd'" from collegians' relationship vocabularies, what are students not already paired off in "college marriages" involved in socially and sexually? "You cannot tell me that the rest of the students are celibate, sitting at home with a chastity belt locked around their waist, saving themselves until marriage," *Dartmouth Free Press* columnist Heather Strack wrote. "Enter the hook-up." The hookup is regarded in columns as the primary—and, at times, sole—means through which sexual interaction between students takes place. "It's becoming a trend, like big sunglasses and popped collars," *Maroon* columnist Nicole Wroten wrote at Loyola University New Orleans under the pen name Jodi San Lucas. Or as *Daily Californian* "Sex on Tuesday" columnist Mindy Friedman noted, "While academic standards are rising and free time is waning, your horniness is the only constant. . . . the logical solution is to have random, no-investment hook-ups."[28]

This solution is identified in columns as both a noun and a verb. It is described by many names and involves a variety of activities, including light kissing; more impassioned make-out sessions; and clothing-optional "below the belt" sexual behavior such as oral sex, dry humping, "just the tip" penile penetration, and full intercourse. "It covers all kinds of sins, all kinds of sexual acts and non-sexual acts, and it can even cover sleeping in someone else's bed, even if it's just sleeping," sex columnist Elizabeth Stortroen wrote while at the University of Colorado, Boulder. At California Polytechnic State University, *Mustang Daily* sex columnist Denise Nilan explained its perplexity further, noting without irony, "'Hooking-up' is the most confusing word to ever grace Cal Poly's campus. To most people it means kissing, to others it means a little more than that and to some it means sex. To confuse matters more, hooking-up can also be some sort of dating term, like a precursor to an official boyfriend-girlfriend title. Or it may be used to describe a past semi-relationship that was never titled i.e. 'Oh yes, we used to hook-up.' So how is a student to know the exact status of his or her hook-up?"[29]

Socially, its status is most frequently described under the heading of one-night stands (ONS), more prolonged flings, even more general "things," or simply "this." *Emory Wheel* sex columnist Haley Yarosh wrote, "'This' is what our generation has come to call hooking up. No, mom and dad, this does not always include sex and group orgies as you had first assumed. . . . 'This' fills the gap between lust and trust. It is the wonderful space between coincidental and consecutive kissing. It doesn't call for introductions to friends and family and certainly doesn't need to be in daylight hours. 'This' prevents makeups and breakups, or at least it tries to avoid them."[30]

"This" is a middle ground, a gray area filled with people whom students randomly meet, sleep with, and never see again, and individuals on students' cell phone speed dial lists available for commitment-free sex after a quick "booty call." An extended version of "this," columnists note, is another acronym: the PSR, or purely sexual relationship. Separate columnists dub it the fellationship, friends with benefits, the bed buddy, the fuck buddy, the luvah, and just "my sex." As columnist Anna Tauzin wrote while at Texas State, "Imagine hanging out with a guy or girl you find attractive and enticing. You spend time with them, laugh with them, drink and cajole with them. You have amazing sex with them. The catch is, the two of you will never commit to each other. You're not dating or looking for a long-term relationship. The annoyances that happen between boyfriends and girlfriends simply don't exist. Being sex buddies sounds like the perfect situation for many."[31]

The vague middle ground between bed buddies and committed coupling extends to a relationship's "end." It is a spurious term in columns, considering that all past sexual partners are not described as "exes," but as individuals with whom it may be convenient to soon hook up again. A majority of columns relate that jumping back into a union, however brief, with a previous lover is exponentially more common than calling things off with a person for good. "When you dated someone in high school . . . when the relationship was over, it was over," *Heights* sex columnist RJ Milligan wrote. "But in college, how things have changed. First of all, there are few defined dating relationships here, so it's tough to really 'break-up.'"[32]

Instead, "relapses" between partners are presented as commonplace, even laying claim to a special set of terms, including hate-fucking, "to ex," and goodbye sex. "It has become a phenomenon," *Johns Hopkins News-Letter* sex columnist Jessica Beaton wrote. "'Ex' used to just be a former lover. Recently, a combination of slang and relationship behavior has caused it to become a verb, 'to ex': to hook-up . . . with an old boyfriend or girlfriend." *Badger Herald* sex columnist Jenny Kalaidis similarly explained, "Sometimes breakups are only the beginning of relationships. Think about it: After spending a good few months, or even years, with the same person, doesn't it seem like a waste to just end things at the snap of the hand and move on? What about all that time you invested in that someone?"[33]

In the end, as outlined in the columns, the game play of student social behavior—the faux breakups, frequent hookups, friends with benefits, and "call of the booty"—is all a means to one winning end: sex, or what a columnist called "collegiate amounts of copulation." There is no behavior or communication carried out that can be taken literally within the college social scene, according to columns. Instead, all are part of a carefully constructed pantheon of symbolic actions and phrases only intended to bring the sender and receiver one step closer to some manner of sexual activity—and its subsequent conclusion. "Orgasm: That's the ultimate goal," Robin Cooper wrote. "All the liquor, beer, pressed powder, perfume, mascara, eye shadow, toothpaste, gum, tight shirts and perfectly slung jeans add up to that one final goal. Orgasm."[34]

Within this single-minded search for all-things-orgasmic, the lone requirement is simply that it occurs at all, and the more times the better. *Cornell Daily Sun* sex columnist Jessica Saunders called it the preference of "quantity to quality. Merely standing outside [the campus bars] . . . at the end of the night can show you that. It appears that the very act of going home with someone is far more important than selecting quality material." As she noted in a later column, "The goal of many college students is to avoid sexual droughts at all costs—to assure ourselves that each weekend night we will be found within the arms of someone." According to columnists, the only inferior sexual activities are those that students are not engaging in. "With all my friends pairing off like it's about to go out of style, it's hard not to notice that everyone is having ridiculous amounts of sex," *California Aggie* columnist Anna Ritner wrote. "In fact, if you're not doing the G-spot two-step with a significant other this winter, you are automatically demoted to a coolness level equivalent to that of Michael Bolton."[35]

In the spirit of this connection between sex and popularity, columnists have rechristened one of the most iconic campus events: the walk of shame. It has long been loosely defined as the morning stroll home from a hookup's residence while sporting the previous night's clothing, unkempt hair, and a self-conscious smile. In columns, this walk is no longer described as an act of which to be ashamed. It is dubbed instead the walk of fame, the stride of pride, the trophy stroll, the victory lap, and the post-sex swagger. As *Crimson White* columnist Elizabeth Stierwalt wrote, "I say to hell with the feelings of embarrassment after this infamous walk. Why should there be this overbearing conception that we have to feel ashamed after hooking up and strolling back to our respective vehicles? It's all propaganda, I say. From this day forward, I declare this long tradition among college students to be renamed the Strut of Infamy. . . . Strutters unite."[36]

A related rechristening focuses not on the strut, but the slut. Columns discuss at great length female students' desire to reclaim or rid the word "slut"—and its bedfellows "whore," "ho," and "promiscuous"—from collegians' sexual vocabularies. Slut is an anachronism, columns reveal, born of a time when men dominated universities, the double standard ruled the sexual universe, and unmarried women were expected to be proper ladies sporting closed legs and coy smiles. "The 'rules' of courtship, evolutionary behavior, and reproduction are not static or stagnant," Arvidson wrote. "With contraceptives as a tool and more choice than ever before, men and women are nearly sexual equals on the playing field. There is no reason why a woman who sleeps around as much as a guy does should be the one called a slut." Kate McDowell similarly beat this sexual double standard into submission, noting:

Women are supposed to be motherly and nurturing by nature, looking for that special someone to be a father for their child. We're supposed to be the ninnies who worry about things like love and commitment. We're the ones who apparently mistake sexual attention for genuine emotional affection. I'm no biology major, but I think, (ladies you'll agree) that the special feeling you get when you see a fine male specimen at a fraternity's after hours [party] is not your body telling you that you want a long lasting emotional commitment. It's your body's way of telling you, "Ooh yeah, I want that one!" Nonetheless, guys are players, girls are sluts. . . . If we're being safe and respecting our bodies, why are we labeled sluts and ho's? Can we help it if guys are easy? Let the women play too![37]

This embracing of sexuality and sexual promiscuity extends to columns' characterizations of female students overall. Columns depict a female sexuality bursting at the seams with assertiveness and experimentation, and built atop principles of pleasure much more than primness. These portrayals have proved popular and controversial in part because they are coming from the female columnists themselves. In general, the sex columnist position has been female-dominated since its start and throughout its pop culture ascendancy, making related interpretations of women's sexuality, shifting courtship rituals, and the gender divide especially significant.

What do modern college women want, according to the columns? They want sex, lots of it, preferably passionate, and mostly commitment-free. As *Daily Princetonian* columnist Rachel Axelbank wrote, "I have heard the same thing on the lips of practically every coed from Nassau Hall to Prospect Street: 'We wanna get laid tonight!'" *Dartmouth* columnist Abi Medvin quoted a female student similarly exclaiming, "I am a sexual machine, and I have sex or masturbate several times per day, every day. I sleep around as much as I can, because true freedom and pleasure does not know limits. I think this is pretty typical of a Dartmouth girl." Anna Tauzin at Texas State even addressed college males directly in one column, sharing, "Let me state this very clearly for you hetero XY chromosome readers: women are very capable of having sex without emotion. Sometimes a girl just gets an itch, and she needs you to scratch it."[38]

According to columnists, women are also scratching their sexual itch to an unparalleled degree without men, through activities such as pornography viewing, masturbation, and same-sex experimentation. "I love being a woman because I love being in control," *Daily Nexus* columnist Beth Van Dyke wrote. "And we are (almost) always in control of all our sexual functions. We are in control of when we get wet, where we get wet and what makes us get wet." Female students' pursuit of sexual enjoyment—through self-gratification especially—is even framed in a number of pieces as a means of embracing the spirit of pleasure *and* revolution. As *Diamondback* sex scribe Marisa Picker at the University of Maryland ended one piece, "Perhaps a purple, waterproof dildo that suctions to the shower wall wasn't exactly what Susan B. Anthony had in mind as a tool for female empowerment, but, hey, whatever works, right?"[39]

College women depicted in the columns espouse a brand of modern female empowerment that is not second-wave or third-wave feminism as much as it is a goodbye-wave (to) feminism. Female students respect the feminist movement and its history, columns say, but they are increasingly turned off by the contention that being openly, proudly, even promiscuously sexual is somehow a setback for women's rights or a disemboweling of a woman's full self. Within the columns, college women express confidence in their sexuality and physical beauty as extensions of their intelligence, personality, and ambition. They are aspects of themselves that they enjoy flaunting for the personal rush and power such behavior yields. To this end, columnists use phrases such as "boob power," "owning our miniskirt," "Slut Pride," and "let[ting] the inner slut out" to describe young women's utilization of their sexual selves to achieve whatever results they desire—whether it is a free drink, a bit of fun, or even a full orgasm. "I have and enjoy sex," columnist Stephanie Oliveira said while at the University of South Florida. "I have explored and enjoyed kink. I've watched, read and gotten off—by myself, no less—with pornography. I've owned several sex toys. I have a whole shelf of dirty books, and I'm published weekly talking about naughty things. I'll tell anyone within earshot that if it keeps you mentally and physically healthy and feels good, go for it."[40]

In a separate column, Miriam Datskovsky recalled attending a journalism conference featuring celebrity advice guru Dr. Drew Pinsky and Ariel Levy, the author of *Female Chauvinist Pigs*. In her book, Levy argues that women have tricked themselves into believing their über-sexual lifestyle is empowering when it is really nothing but a confirmation of their long-held status as playthings for men's lust-filled eyes. "Alongside with her [Levy], he [Pinksy] argued that he believed women, especially those in college, live in a world where they feel obligated to act like a man and have sex frequently and without attachment," Datskovsky wrote. "According to Dr. Drew and Ariel Levy, women get nothing out of this new world. Neither of them leave room for the possibility that women might choose to have sex without attachment and may be happy and emotionally healthy doing so."[41]

In this respect, columnists argue that critics are missing the point. Simply put, women may still be playing into certain male fantasies or objectified female stereotypes, but they could care less. The once pervasive "power of the penis," as described in one column, has shifted to a societal "vagina envy" of empowered women enjoying themselves outside of any misogynistic frameworks or feminist agendas. "Women can become their own inventions," Arvidson wrote. "With their creative powers they can be whatever they want to be. They can define themselves any way they please. No one should feel like they have to deny their sexuality. Whether it is distinct, ambiguous, high libido, or low libido: we are all different and we don't need to conform to one chosen sexual role."[42]

Additionally, the columns describe a campus landscape in which stereotyped gender roles have flipped. In the new millennium, women rule the sexual universe—and university. The men are just visiting—emasculated, metro-sexualized versions of their former selves. The "authentic cowboy" machismo of past male students has vanished. It has been replaced by indecisive fashionistas who moisturize, shop, cook, clean, gossip with glee, call sexual partners repeatedly and annoyingly, and drop everything for female partners who are fully aware that they hold absolute sexual sway. *Red and Black* sex columnist Lauren Morgan at the University of Georgia compared the modern college male to a neutered dog, vainly left to lick "the empty place where its testicles once were." As she wrote, "I wonder, what has happened to the male race? . . . Is it possible that a form of social castration has occurred and women not only wear the pant[s], but also have balls?"[43]

In place of the traditional male suitor, young women are described within the columns as embodying a commanding persona, stepping into the role of sexual and relationship aggressor. Overall, columns describe a female student body whose sexual desire is coupled with a more general awareness of the media's flawed messages about romance aimed at them since childhood. "As little girls, we grew up watching Disney movies about a princess being rescued by her handsome prince and living happily ever after," *Daily Reveille* columnist Jessica Pivik wrote while at Louisiana State University. "Our arrival at college demolishes our fairy-tale life." Or as McLean Robbins wrote, "I had always thought sex should be special—something only to be shared between two individuals in a loving, committed relationship. But was it possible that sex could be just . . . sex?"[44]

Carpe Datem

The columns' depictions of students' sex-heavy, monogamy-light socializing have triggered one of the longer-running debates among critics, skeptics, and supporters: Is column content promoting promiscuity or reflecting reality? Within this critical sphere, columns are deemed presumptuous, in part for giving off the impression that sex is occurring among undergraduates at a higher rate than some studies indicate. As separate reports have found, modern college students may be having slightly less sex and are becoming more passionate about publicly acknowledging their virginity or abstinence.[45]

Yet according to a 2008 American College Health Association national survey, even while engaged in less sexual activity, collegians estimated their fellow students boasted three times the number of sexual partners as they themselves had in the previous year. It is a miscalculation that experts say could lead students to have sex simply to keep up with their peers. Among the highest-profile culprits behind this sexual overestimation, according to critics, are college newspaper sex columns. A *San Jose Mercury News* report noted, "Critics . . . warn that the freewheeling content of the sex columns could unintentionally increase pressure on students to engage in behavior for which they are not emotionally prepared."[46]

The critical demonizing of the columns as über-sexual provocateurs is convenient, given their high-profile status, but ill-informed. The columns make no unfounded claims about the incidence of sexual activity on particular campuses or among young people nationwide. They are simply cognizant of the fact that, regardless of specific studies' findings, sex is happening en masse. Over the past decade, there have been lots of quantitative and qualitative studies on student sexual activity. They use different sample sizes. They focus on different swaths of the student population. They ask different questions, and define sexual activity in different ways. And, unsurprisingly, they report different results and reach different conclusions. Wading through them all at once is dizzying and leads to only one solid conclusion: In the end, the numbers do not really mean much at all.

Regardless of relative percentage gains or dips, the larger reality is that many students on every campus are engaging in all kinds of sexual activity in and out of their dorm rooms and at all times of day and night. To deny or diminish sex's importance in the collegiate sphere—and by extension the columns documenting it—based on sampling data or the emergence of a few high-profile student abstinence clubs is either shortsighted or downright dishonest. As former *Daily Evergreen* sex columnist Erin Thomas confirmed, "Students are doing it. They're doing it good, some bad, a few early, and lots often. You know, we're college kids. We have three interests: passing school, beer, and sex."

In respect to that latter interest, even amid their popularity, the columns do not exert the amount of influence critics allege. "I think that people are having sex, and it's not because of a newspaper article," said Jessica Saunders. "No one's going to not be monogamous or have casual hooking-up situations just because of something I say. It just is what it is and it exists and anybody who denies that it exists is crazy." A 2005 *Chicago Sun-Times* series, "Sex on Campus," found that students, school officials, outside health experts, and other researchers agreed with the columnists in their descriptions of "a booze-fueled, sexually charged campus environment marked by emotionless, too-cool-to-care hookups, low self-expectations and high pressure to 'be normal' by sleeping around. Not everyone takes part. But the culture influences even those who don't." In the game of chicken versus egg, the larger culture is the cause of the student sex craze and resocialization, not student sex columns. They are merely the outlets chronicling it. And in this role, their conclusions have proved inviolate.[47]

Along with the *Sun-Times*'s findings, numerous research studies, news reports, and experts have verified the general relationship and lifestyle patterns appearing in the columns. For example, to complete his 2005 book *Binge: What Your College Student Won't Tell You*, veteran journalist Barrett Seaman carried out a rare long-term investigation into the underbelly of campus life so often hidden from educators' and parents' view. Seaman spent two years living and socializing with students at a dozen colleges in the United States and Canada. His findings are in absolute lockstep with columns' conclusions, recounting a similar "nondating scene" and "hanging-out/hooking-up culture" in which women act much more often as sex and relationship initiators and "students are having a lot of sex." After years of research for his book *I Am Charlotte Simmons*, Tom Wolfe also described a "sexual carnival" very similar to the columns' depictions, albeit in much more flowery terms. According to Harvard University psychologist Mark O'Connell, "There's always been a lot of sex in college. It's the quality of sex that's changed. It's increasingly disconnected. It's a whole different mindset: 'I had a beer last night, I hooked up last night.' Sex just isn't a big deal any more." The appraisal is a vivid echo of the columns' mantra: "Sex is sex is sex is sex."[48]

Even those ideologically opposed to the columns and the sexual culture they represent confirm their basic tenets. The most prominent example is twentysomething social conservative Ben Shapiro. In his highly publicized book *Porn Generation*, he rants for more than two hundred pages about the rampant sexualization of everything in the postmillennial United States—from the government, advertising, and the Internet to celebrity culture and modern collegiate life. Yet couched between his impassioned critiques are personal observations and assessments by college students and recent graduates that confirm the columns' portrayal of this generation's dating-free, sex-saturated lifestyle. For example, he quotes a young Princeton University alumnus saying, "Dates, and, for the most part, love affairs, are passé. Why bother asking someone to dinner when you can meet at a party, down a few drinks and go home together?" Shapiro separately notes that the mottos of today's universities are "do whatever or whomever you want" and "if it feels good, do it."[49]

With respect to these maxims, the most off-base criticisms are those saying the columns are singularly glorifying risky sexual behavior without stressing potential dangers, downsides, and larger implications. "The columns . . . hint at a fantasy lifestyle filled with hangup-free sexual encounters, without the torment and awkwardness that usually accompany college relationships," an *Atlantic Monthly* report noted. "After scanning columns from schools across the country, it's easy to come away thinking that torment and awkwardness went out with shoulder pads, and that America's college kids are busy vibrating and videotaping themselves into the stratosphere."[50]

It is a cute sentiment, but like calling the Atlantic the Pacific, it is completely opposite of the truth. A bevy of similarly shortsighted critiques exist that focus on a small number of columns on more extreme topics such as BDSM and anal sex, without an accompanying evaluation of the content within columns overall. A few columnists use the phrase "blinded by the sex" in reference to critics who are unable to get past the salacious nature of the topics promoted in headlines and see the actual treatment of such topics. Former *Daily Nebraskan* columnist Timaree Schmit equated it with looking at the skin covering an apple but not seeing its core. Although the columns arguably lend legitimacy to students' new brand of sex and socializing simply by identifying it and placing it in print, a deeper glimpse at their core reveals an editorial conflict that the more vociferous critics miss. The supposedly fantastical, sex-only-and-often lifestyle that critics claim the columns are celebrating is actually tempered by tons of critiques and questions that border on interrogations. Simply put, columnists do not always advocate what they observe.

For example, in a move that is quite fantasy-free, columnists endlessly preach sexual protection, in the form of condoms, dental dams, "safe words," and open dialogues with partners about individuals' sexual histories. Protection, communication, and knowledge are the three most repeated words in columns overall. Columns also do not simply discuss and celebrate sex, but also every aspect of sex's foil, virginity, including religious-based virginity, virginity of circumstance, born-again virginity, mental virginity, anal virginity, oral virginity, the social and health issues surrounding the losing of one's virginity, and even the difficulty of defining virginity among modern students. Similarly, occasional pieces explain and tout the relative merits of asexuality and purposeful or accidental abstinence, based on columnists' contentions that abstinent and sexually active students are not inherent enemies or living in separate sexual worlds.

Even more, while describing the new female sexual empowerment, many columnists describe a yearning for "the days of the gentleman." They express their desire for the return of the male who will make decisions, boldly initiate conversation, hold doors open, pick up dinner checks, grunt, spit, rev up for talk of football instead of a recap of *American Idol*, and just more generally embody a sexuality that is virile, feral, and over-powering instead of clingy and comfortable. "Women want men who are assholes," *Daily Nexus* columnist Beth Van Dyke wrote. "We want a dick in both senses of the word. We can't stand Honey Bunches of Oats because they don't present a challenge. . . . We want to tame the untamable. We want a guy we'd never show Mommy until he's properly trained. It sucks, but it's true. Nice Guys are cute until they talk. When we want them to say, 'I just want to ravage you in this bathroom stall!' they say, 'Do you need any toilet paper, honey?'"[51]

In addition, while documenting the current collegiate sexual chaos, many columnists simultaneously support the return of more defined dating prac-tices—specifically monogamy, emotional intimacy, and love as the means to the happiest end. McLean Robbins called it "carpe datem." *Rebel Yell* colum-nist Lindsay Johnson explained, "Because there can truly never be absolutely no strings attached to any kind of sex-only relationship, and because booty calls lack love and caring, they'll never be quite as rewarding or as healthy as a sexual relationship between two people who are actually dating or in a committed relationship." Not every columnist supports such commitment. For example, *Lumberjack* sex scribe Claire Fuller at Northern Arizona Univer-sity wrote, "I think the concept of 'The One' is on par with what swirls down my toilet in the morning." Yet overall, the much more common sentiment echoed among columnists is one of hope for the reappearance of traditional romance and relationships. As *Carolinian* columnist Brook Taylor wrote, "What I want is exactly what I've spent my entire life observing: the kind of love my parents share." *Yale Daily News* columnist Natalie Krinsky noted similarly, "I merely ask that every once in a while, when you are getting laid, or thinking about getting laid, or hoping to get laid, you think about love. And when you find it, you clue me in on how exactly you were able to do so."[52]

Clash of Cultures
Outside Criticism and Censorship of Student Sex Columns

6

> One man, a father who had been on campus to scout the college for his daughter . . . said he was loving the school and it was so pretty, and then he happened to pick up the newspaper and . . . got to my column, and his impression became that if girls like me went to the school he refused to even let her apply.
>
> ERIN GRANAT
> *former sex columnist,* Nevada Sagebrush

In fall 2003, the *Mustang Daily* at California Polytechnic State University launched "Battle of the Sex Columnists." The feature had the flavor of a mini *American Idol*, with a sexual twist. Two sex columns were run side by side, along with a prompt from the newspaper asking readers to select their favorite student sex writer and e-mail editors with a vote. One of the columns published in the premiere battle, headlined "Nothing Fresher Than Freshmen," offered undergraduate males advice on how to attract freshmen women, whom columnist James Whitaker referred to as "prized jewels, like diamonds scattered across campus in a great scavenger hunt." As he wrote, "When talking to a freshman chick you only need to remember three things. Your first name, where you're from, and your major. At a party these are the only things you will say before giving her a stiff red cup of jungle juice and offering to show her your collection of beer cans upstairs in your room."

Immediately after its publication, critics denounced the column as misogynistic and called it a potential date rape "how-to." The campus police chief publicly linked it with a concurrent increase in sexual assaults in the greater campus community. School administrators, representatives of the university Women's Center and Counseling Services, area mental health professionals, and the San Luis Obispo police chief also criticized the newspaper for printing the piece. Student editors were summoned to condemnatory meetings and advised to attend a sensitivity training session. Protestors threatened a boycott of the paper, but it was not carried out. As the newspaper's faculty adviser told *College Media Review*, "I tried to do what I could, but it was like fighting back the heathens." Or as the paper's editor in chief said near the end of the academic term, for better and worse, "the sex controversy ended up defining our year with the *Mustang*."[1]

Along with sex, the defining element of many students' columns has been controversy. Most columns spark disagreements, denouncements, and attempted censorship in various forms—from everyday battles fought via e-mail and private chats to what one columnist called "full-blown wars" aimed at stopping sex in the student press. The most common cause of these conflicts: a startling overreaction by individuals and organizations beyond the student readership.

Student response on a national level is generally muted or supportive of the sex columns. It is those outside this targeted audience who have been the principal triggers behind the most significant, publicized sex fights, including university faculty, administrators, alumni, major donors, area politicians, law enforcement officers, religious officials, regional and national conservative and family groups, parents of current and prospective students, and the professional press.[2] "The kids aren't offended by the sex columns," said Tamara Kreinin, executive director of women and population at the United Nations Foundation and a former president and CEO of the Sexuality Information and Education Council of the United States. "Adults get nervous talking about sex. Kids realize it is everywhere, and they have to talk about it." A Middle Tennessee State University student similarly said in response to a controversy over a sex column in the campus newspaper, "The people who are surprised by it are not the students, but the parents, the faculty, and people not privy to student conversations." According to Ron Johnson, director of student media at Indiana University, the recurring hostile response from outside readers relates to a "clash of cultures." In his words, "Out of one side of our mouth we coach our students to experiment and provide their readers with content they can relate to—including relationship issues, dating and sex. [The problem is] most college publications are being read and criticized by those outside the campus community."[3]

While outside critics swear their anger stems strictly from the columns' sexual content, the real motivations are much more varied, ironic, and disturbing: academics deciding they know what is best for students and attempting to reinstate failed "in loco parentis" efforts of the past; individuals not grasping the law or spirit of an editorially independent campus press; shortsighted school staffers seeing any potential sex scandal as a financial blow for their universities; and politicians, administrators, and religious officials unfairly using the columns as ammo in much larger fights against societal sex-ification to appease backers, constituents, and congregations. Mainly, the culture clashes are about adults who simply do not get it. They do not get why students are willing to attach their names and head shots to writings on issues so private. They do not get why the columns are so popular among student readers. And they do not get that while they may read the columns and react to them, they are in no way the intended audience and their opinions carry about as much appeal to student columnists and editors as an 8:00 A.M. class.

The columns are not about them, the outsiders, and are not published as insults to their churches, their states, or their schools. They are meant to serve as prime examples of campus newspapers' student-first editorial philosophy. As Nicole Wroten, a former sex columnist for the *Maroon* at Loyola University New Orleans, told *Playboy*:

> I did a column called "Wedding Nights Are Overrated," which was not well received at all. It was advice to a girl on how to lose her virginity: Okay, you need to be ready for the mental aspects and the physical aspects, and you need to know who you're going to do it with. . . . Normal stuff, nothing very risqué. I wasn't writing blow job every other word. The worst word I used was hymen. . . . The responses I got were ridiculous. We had alumni from, like, the 1940s coming into the offices, saying, "How dare you write this?" Other faculty members gave my advisor a hard time, saying, "What are you letting these kids

do?" I was working at a magazine then, and when my boss read it she threatened to fire me. The old geezers didn't like it, but I didn't care. I wasn't writing it for them.[4]

Behind-the-Scenes Forces

A professor at the College of William & Mary had a problem with Kate Prengaman's sex column in the *Flat Hat*. From its start, he lectured against it in his classes. According to Prengaman, he also urged *Flat Hat* editors to replace her with a married columnist. And two months after it debuted, he mailed a critical letter to her parents, along with copies of what she admitted were three of her more scandalous columns, headlined "Bondage Definitely Worth Trying," "Masturbation Shouldn't Be Secret," and "Halloween: Excuse for Fantasy." As she recalled, "He found my address in the campus directory. He sent them to my parents with a note saying that there were predators on our campus and that I was putting myself in danger and that I needed to be taught that love should come first. . . . That freaked my parents the hell out, because I had not told them I was writing a sex column . . . so that was their introduction to it." Prengaman's mother and father first telephoned her boyfriend's parents, then her boyfriend, and finally her, demanding an explanation and expressing concern about her academic future. "It was a low, sneaky blow in the fight to stop this column and this sex-positive dialogue, and it almost worked," Prengaman wrote in her final *Flat Hat* piece. "My parents flipped out and I fumed with rage that a professor could behave so childishly as to tattle to my parents."[5]

While most professors and administrators unhappy with sex columns avoid contact with columnists' families, they are similarly vocal and at times tenacious in their criticisms. These university-based, non-student readers constitute the most common challengers to student newspaper sexual expression. The twisted rationale behind their column interventions: They think they know what is best for columnists, their editors, and student newspapers as a whole. The most frequent, yet least reported, method of administrative critique and implied censorship occurs via not-for-publication e-mails and off-the-record sit-downs initiated by school personnel as high up as the university president. In these exchanges, the aim of content suppression normally is expressed in the spirit of parental-type advice, but the motive is either implicit or at times stated outright. Former *Pitt News* sex columnist Rose Afriyie called them "the behind-the-scenes forces . . . whether they were faculty or the administration, someone always had something to say about my sex column every time it came out."

During an interview, Phil Elliott, former editor of the *Post* at Ohio University who oversaw a pair of sex columns, shared an example of the messages columnists and editors report receiving. The e-mail from a university administrator in September 2002 began with the words, "This is not for publication." It continued:

> Why did the *Post* feel compelled to promote promiscuity by [former *Post* sex columnist] Brynn Burton's lurid revelations? If you only knew how much damage this was doing to the *Post*'s credibility, you would pull her nonsense from your pages. I've heard such phrases as "The *Post* is taking the pissing for a tart" to "It reads like a porn sheet to me" to "I will speak to the advertisers I know." Yeah yeah yeah, it's your First Amendment rights to say anything, yada, yada. But with rights come responsibilities. . . . Of all the important topics the *Post* should be covering, you devote a significant amount of space on the opinion page to one student's sexual escapades and immature ranting. . . . Let me be blunt. This is my eighth year at Ohio University. For seven years I've defended the *Post* at EVERY turn and refuse to bash it in public. I don't know how much longer I can defend it if this waste of space continues.

At times, school officials make their messages public. For example, in October 2007, Lyndon State College student Jordan Royer received an e-mail calling for his expulsion, although it was not addressed to him. The message, written by Lyndon State professor Elizabeth Norris, was sent originally to all faculty, students, and staff at the school *except* Royer. A classmate soon forwarded it to Royer's school e-mail account. He learned that the object of Norris's ire, and the reason for her recommendation of his expulsion: "Holy Sheet," a sex column he wrote for the *Critic* student newspaper.[6]

Royer first pitched his idea for the column to *Critic* editor Keith Whitcomb Jr. near the start of fall semester to prop up sagging reader interest. "Our newspaper here was, to say the least, pretty slow off the presses. . . . Not many people were picking it up," he said. "It was becoming garbage around campus basically. So, we were looking for something to spark curiosity with kids on campus." In early pieces, Royer wrote sarcastically about the dangers of having sex on a top bunk bed; the advantages of flirting through online programs such as AOL Instant Messenger; and the importance of using condoms to avoid STIs, accompanied by the adage, "Speed bumps are for parking lots, not for your genitals, so wrap it up." In a separate column, Royer humorously solicited students to determine the "one thing you don't want to hear from someone from the opposite sex," noting that male students' top responses were "I'm pregnant" and "Are you in yet?" In the column that most disgusted Norris, Royer outlined the evolution of his interest in pornography—from stumbling on his father's pornographic magazines as a child to downloading sexually explicit Internet videos as a young adult. "Porn does more than speed up how long it takes to ejaculate when I stimulate myself," he closed the piece. "It strengthens my sex life. Call me crazy, but if watching porn makes me better in bed, I think I will have the occasional peek."[7]

In her campus-wide e-mail—which carried the subject line "An Open Letter to Jordan Royer"—Norris wrote that her long-standing frustration with "Holy Sheet" peaked with what she described as its support for the dissemination of pornography. In her opinion, this stance left Royer in violation of the principles of student conduct outlined in the college catalog. "Through your articles, you have demonstrated a disregard for personal and social responsibility, a complete lack of common sense, a disregard for personal and academic integrity, and a dangerously flippant and misogynistic attitude toward human relationships," she wrote in the message, which ultimately failed to trigger any administrative action against Royer. "Your words represent all of us . . . Therefore, since you have violated the basic principles that hold us together and structure the foundation of our institution, I am calling for your immediate dismissal from Lyndon State College."[8]

In spring 2009, University of Montana assistant law professor Kristen Juras likewise went public with her efforts to stop the sex drive of the *Montana Kaimin*, specifically its publication of the first regular sex column in the newspaper's more-than-one-hundred-year history. Labeling the feature "inappropriate, unimportant," and "embarrassingly unprofessional," Juras sent multiple messages of disgust to the *Kaimin*, the university president, the dean of the journalism school, and several state government officials, threatening to contact the university publications board, the board of regents, and even the state legislature if her concerns were not placated.[9]

The following fall semester, more than two thousand miles away, Towson University president Robert Caret expressed similarly bold criticisms and roadblock intentions for a sex column in the *Towerlight* campus newspaper. "The Bed Post" debuted in September 2009, penned by a student writer known only as "Lux," who touched on topics such as phone sex, one-night stands, and solitary and mutual masturbation. The "Post" that notched an especially unfavorable place in Caret's heart implored students to thoroughly explore their genitalia and expand their self-pleasure routines. "Boys—try jerking-off standing up or on your knees," the piece advised. "Girls—try pleasuring yourself with a feather or bring a toy into the bedroom. For all of you newbies—use your hands. Mess around with location, pressure, speed and direction until something feels good. The better you know yourself—the easier it will be for someone else to please you!"

Caret soon thereafter wrote a letter to the editor expressing his displeasure, noting, "This is not about first amendment rights or freedom of the press. It's about misjudgment of the range and disposition of your audience and its expectations about what they will find in the *Towerlight* and what they might be appalled at seeing there. Last Monday your columnist wrote a 'how to' sex column whose appropriate place was not Towson's student newspaper but a sex manual or the type of sleazy magazines one finds sectored off in drugstores." Six days later, he sent a personal e-mail to the newspaper's editor in chief that she described in a public statement as "intimidating, patronizing and bullying," spurring a quick response from her that she greatly regretted and caused her to resign from her position. Caret also informed *Towerlight* staffers "he would do everything in his power to disassociate the university from the column if it continued appearing," including possibly removing university advertising from the entire publication. Considering that the university accounts for 40 percent of the newspaper's advertising revenue, the threatened move would have severely undercut its bottom line. "Please understand my strong feelings," Caret implored staffers at the close of his initial letter to the editor. "As your President I stand in a relationship to you that has a teaching obligation as one component."[10]

Strong feelings aside, Caret is Towson's president, not *Towerlight*'s publisher. The newspaper is independent of the university, aligned with the school solely through distribution privileges, advertising arrangements, and a lease agreement for newsroom space. Staffers also did not ask for Caret's counsel—and in its public form his advice undoubtedly caused more harm than good. With the letter, he was not standing in a relationship with the newspaper; he was standing in its way. As the *Baltimore Sun* declared in an editorial condemning Caret's actions, "The first lessons student journalists in a democracy learn should not have to be how to survive under the censor's arbitrary fist. . . . The whole purpose of student publications like Towson's is to train students to become responsible journalists, and for that to happen, they need the experience of learning on their own what is and what isn't appropriate. Heavy-handed intervention doesn't accomplish that."[11]

The stunning arrogance of individual critics like Caret, Juras, Norris, and many other outsiders is almost perversely super-heroic—a belief that one person can and should possess the power to proactively save a sex columnist, a student newspaper, a school, an entire state from themselves, even when they are not asking to be saved. Additionally ironic, and arrogant, the columns' most critical outsiders do not tend to have any professional journalism experience, sexual health or relationships training, knowledge of the student newspaper production process, or direct association with the publications themselves.

The vitriol and vigor of outsiders' personal stop-the-column quests also raise questions, the principal one being: If you do not like it, why are you reading it? Strangely, the critics are often the columns' most passionate readers and responders. They exhibit in communication with newspapers' editorial boards a shockingly thorough knowledge of the columns' language choices, base arguments, and deeper themes, albeit in most cases so they can deconstruct them. Columnists joke in interviews that they wish their more ardent admirers and everyday student readers examined their work with such impassioned scrutiny. As one columnist said anonymously about a history professor who sent her regular, often disparaging e-mail reviews of her pieces, "He treated my work way too important[ly], like it was the next *Harry Potter*. After I got over being vilified, it always made me laugh. He probably spent more time on the messages telling me why they [the columns] sucked each week than I did writing them. Why he didn't just let it go and stop reading them is beyond me."

The columns are often clearly labeled as sex and relationship features and at times even carry tag lines informing people about the explicit content to come. Their regularity also acts as a fair forewarning, typically appearing in the same spot of the newspaper on the same day each week or month, making most students, faculty, school officials, and members of the greater campus community aware of when and where they need to read or skip. In addition, the headlines serve as caveats. As one editorial defending a column noted, "Anyone who read the headline, 'Good oral sex skills add fun, take away fear,' probably could have guessed what the column was about before reading on. Not only is there freedom of the press and speech, there is also a concept called choice."[12]

Some outsiders do not respect that concept, as evidenced by their words *and* their actions. The most definitive set of column controversies are those that stir administrative attempts to censor content they find offensive. For example, administrators at New York City's Wagner College once attempted to preempt what they feared would be parental backlash over a sex column sidebar by confiscating copies of the campus newspaper's offending issue. The column, run in the *Wagnerian*, focused on faking orgasms, under the headline "The Big Bang." It contained a sidebar with quotes from students identified by their full names and accompanying head shots. Each student responded to the question in the sidebar's headline, "Orgasms: Do You Fake It?" Although the students were all of legal age and were quoted and pictured voluntarily, administrators became concerned that their parents might be angry enough about their children's partici-pation to sue the school. Four days after the issue containing the column was published, officials removed all remaining copies from racks around campus. Administrators also threatened to fire the publication's longtime adviser, required editors to submit the following issue of the newspaper to the dean of students for pre-publication review, and demanded the creation of a publication mission statement.[13]

The incident prompted press coverage and the involvement of the Student Press Law Center (SPLC). It also spurred the creation of a pair of petitions, which were signed by nearly sixty Wagner professors and more than seven hundred students in protest of what the faculty petition called "blatant restriction of free speech at Wagner." The most inexplicable, unforgivable aspect of the entire mess: All students featured in the sidebar said they suffered no family fallouts or other problems of any kind from the exposure. This means the only actual problems stemming from the column's and sidebar's publication were those caused by the Wagner administrators themselves, specifically their decision to assume the worst, overreact, and view censorship as a viable solution to ease their fears.[14]

The efforts of these administrators and others like them would be comical for their misguided earnestness if the censorious undertones were not so serious. As exemplified by the Wagner case, university higher-ups often cite the need for student press oversight only after controversial sexual innuendo appears in print, ignoring the trust they had placed in student staffers up to the point they did not like what they were reading. They also generally cannot cite a clear law or school rule that the columns break, instead offering vague explanations about what is best for the university and journalism as a whole, which make free speech advocates both laugh and cringe. Finally, angry administrators often ignore the obvious: Avoiding oversight of the campus newspaper is actually a benefit when defending it to angry parents and alumni. A simple statement citing noninvolvement in student presswork out of respect for free speech is much less burdensome than demanding and subsequently assuming greater responsibility over the content students produce every day, week, or month.

One of the more dramatic examples of the burdensome route unfortunately favored by many administrators occurred at Craven Community College in North Carolina, where attempted administrative censorship was triggered not by a full column but a single word. College president Scott Ralls first publicly called for administrative overview of the school's student newspaper, the *Campus Communicator*, after the debut of the sex column "Between the Sheets" in March 2005. The premiere piece, written by student Amanda Worley, appeared in a single column on page 7 of the eight-page monthly, under the headline "Fantasy Play Can Jolt Tired Sex Lives." In the column, she offered a top-ten list of tips tied to rejuvenating students' sexual routines, including role-playing, aroma setting, strip poker playing, and moving sex from the bed to a car or pool. After its publication, complaints poured into the *Communicator* newsroom and the college's administrative offices. Corey Friedman, the newspaper's top editor, said a Craven student life coordinator informed him that Worley was even receiving personal threats. A majority of criticisms centered not on the column as a whole but on a sex toy mentioned once in parentheses. "Go with your partner and pick out a couple of adult toys," Worley advised in tip number seven. "Start cheap and soft (no hard dildo)."[15]

The large amount and impassioned nature of the complaints prompted Friedman and managing editor William Toler to cancel the column and pen an apology, which acknowledged the feature was a "bad fit for the newspaper's readership." Friedman noted in an interview that roughly half the school's student body is composed of nontraditional students aged twenty-five or older, a statistic confirmed by the college's *Institutional Fact Book*. "I thought on balance we would only lose readers," he said. "We didn't want to antagonize our readers. I mean, why were we publishing the newspaper? It's for them. It's their paper. If they collectively decided a vast majority of them didn't want this in their paper then we were going to pull it. But then the administration got involved and the controversy hit a bigger second wave."[16]

The wave began with a handshake and a private meeting between Ralls and Friedman two days after the column was published. According to Friedman, the conversation quickly became heated, with Ralls calling the column obscene, referring to outside calls of complaint he had received, and stating the need for administrative oversight of newspaper content. Ralls later told *Communicator* staffers at a meeting, "Our position as a college is you cannot have an independent and open forum." Soon thereafter, school administrators introduced a "prior review process" that included an advisory board charged with examining all newspaper content before it was published and guidelines designed to eliminate potentially offensive material from being printed in the future. *Communicator* staff writer and deputy managing editor Mitzi Ponce called the policy "a draft document for censorship," echoing fellow student staffers' assertions that the accompanying advisory board was little more than a "censorship committee." Friedman, Toler, and Ponce fought the committee with the help of FIRE

(Foundation for Individual Rights in Education). Legal representatives from the organization sent a letter of condemnation to Ralls, providing him with what a news report called "a graduate-level education in the pitfalls of stepping on the First Amendment."[17]

Specifically, FIRE underscored what media scholars and constitutional law experts have continually asserted since the column phenomenon's start: No student sex column content comes close to meeting the legal definition of obscenity or even the classic definition of pornography. It is also generally tamer than what is publicly on display in material such as "Savage Love," *The Starr Report, The 40-Year-Old Virgin, Californication*, and even some works housed in university libraries, an assertion Ponce playfully mocked one afternoon in the *Communicator* newsroom with the help of a college textbook containing a sexual expletive. "It was a text that was required for a class at Craven and it had the word 'fuck' in it twice," Friedman recalled. "Her little catch line was, 'Apparently, the college's two 'fucks' trump our one 'dildo' any day.'"

Ultimately, the efforts of the editors, FIRE, and the SPLC, and the media attention that came along with them, trumped the college's attempt at administrative control. In July 2005, Craven's board of trustees approved a two-page memorandum of agreement created by administrators and student newspaper staffers affirming that the *Communicator* was "editorially independent." According to Friedman, "From the beginning, they tried to frame the issue about sex, but the real issue was censorship. It was . . . a battle for the independence of the student newspaper to decide what to publish. Fortunately, it was a battle we won."[18]

Blow Job Backlash

While faculty and administrators are the main participants in the skirmishes over student newspaper sexual expression, they confront a range of outside pressures themselves. Many of the most impassioned criticisms emanating from beyond the college gates focus on the newspapers' growing availability off campus. Student newspapers boosted their readership in the communities surrounding their home campuses and also built widespread alumni mailing operations beginning in the early 1980s. Starting in the late 1990s, the placement of content online expanded newspapers' reach even further, to the point that, as the *Daily Californian* noted in 1999, "any person, on any computer, anywhere in the world, can access the latest [sex] column by logging onto [a] paper's Web site." In respect to this near-universal access, student sex columnists and their editors at times receive angry telephone calls and e-mails from alumni, community residents, prison inmates, and even international readers with no university affiliation, many of whom read the columns online, in certain cases only happening on them because of a blog post or after a Google search gone awry.[19]

As a parent of a student at Muhlenberg College wrote in opposition to a sex column in the *Muhlenberg Weekly*, "If this publication stayed within the confines of the school, that would be one thing, but it does not. It goes into homes where there might be younger children who are not ready for this kind of information and older people who might be offended. . . . Obviously, the paper's staff needs to learn a little more about discretion before venturing out into the world." One example of the controversy such venturing causes occurred in Kansas. According to news reports, while a sex column run in the *Daily Kansan* at the University of Kansas "was accepted and even applauded on campus, high schools kicked up a fuss." A former *Kansan* editorial page editor confirmed, "High school principals from around the state . . . started calling in. . . . They basically said they thought it was pornographic. Mostly they were calling saying they wanted to cancel their subscriptions. What we ended up doing was deciding not to mail out the *Kansan* on Thursdays [when the column ran]. That seemed to help a bit."[20]

Meanwhile, in February 1999, the editor in chief of the *Daily Barometer* at Oregon State University canceled the sex column begun in the news-paper the previous fall because of a single parental objection. A father in the surrounding community of Corvallis phoned the newsroom to complain that his six-year-old daughter had said "blow job" to him, repeating the words she heard from an eleven-year-old child who first read it in the *Daily Barometer* column "Ask Dr. Sex." Like many college newspapers, the *Barometer* is available for free in a number of off-campus locations, including a local grocery store where the older child had picked it up. In the column, Kathy Greaves, who at the time was an OSU doctoral student and an instructor for a popular human sexuality course, responded to a question submitted by a female student centered on the student's desire "to know how to give her boyfriend a good blow job." As Greaves recalled, in the wake of the child's sexual wordplay in front of her father,

> The proverbial shit hit the fan and the dad was livid. He called the president of the university. He called the mayor of the city [Corvallis]. . . . He flipped out. He wrote the editor of the *Barometer*. . . . He was going to go to a city council meeting and say either the newspaper shouldn't be distributed in the community or should be canceled altogether. And the newspaper gets a lot of money from advertisers in the community. In retrospect, I understand why she did this, but the editor at the time with no real guidance about freedom of speech and those sorts of things, her solution was just to cancel my column.

New editors reinstated the column the following term and it continues to run in the newspaper. As an OSU official said at the time about the top editor's decision, "Here's a student who's learning in very real terms the balancing act that an editor of a newspaper has to perform."[21]

What outside critics do not understand: The balancing act is ultimately impossible. Even when limiting newspaper distribution off campus, alumni, prospective students, and prospective students' parents often come across the columns while visiting the school. For example, in March 2009, a father of a prospective student at the University of West Florida—a man who considers himself "no shrinking violet and certainly not a prude"—wrote a letter of moral outrage to the university's board of trustees about a sex column in the *Voyager* student newspaper. The man stumbled on the column, penned by "Pixie Gonzalez," in a campus cafeteria while taking his high school senior son on a school tour. He started the letter by claiming he had not written anything like it in the past. "I DON'T DO THIS!" he wrote. "But I was so shocked and disgusted by what your newspaper chose to publish." He subsequently noted:

> What possible editorial and journalistic motive was there for printing such trash—was this opinion piece meant to elevate the discussion on sex, excess drinking, drug use or STD's on college campuses? . . . [Readers] learn from this enlightened young lady that . . . girls at

UWF want what Pixie wants—"a belly full of beer, a taquito from Whataburger and an orgasm." UNBELIEVABLE!!! . . . My eighteen year old obviously was shocked but more concerned that his mother and I would never allow him to attend a University that would publish such trash. Please help explain to me, and my wife and son, how we can look him in the eye and support his decision to attend your "institution of higher learning." What can we learn about your university through the publication of this opinion piece? What does it say about the competency, oversight and caring of your faculty and staff?[22]

The latter portion of the letter represents the misperception most commonly held among outraged outsiders and most feared by university administrators—namely that the publication of a sex column in the student newspaper somehow implies the school's endorsement of the lifestyle or activities the column describes. At the very least, administrators worry that critical alums, donors, or parents see a connection between a sex column and the school, which often has little to no editorial control over the student newspaper. An alumnus of Indiana University of Pennsylvania made this connection in a letter to the editor in the *Penn*, while blaming the student newspaper's sex column for single-handedly ruining his homecoming weekend:

I love to take my children back to the scene of it all, stand and watch the parade and take in all the camaraderie of being at IUP. My 10-year-old, Carmen, loves to go back, and I bet he will go to IUP someday. It all went well until after we left the Co-op store with new sweatshirts in hand. He opens the Indiana *Penn* and turns the pages to page 19 and goes wide eyes over the "Sex Toys Require Proper Care" article. Now, why would you put an article like that in this issue? . . . I don't feel it was responsible on your part. . . . It gave the wrong impression to my kid and gave the message that at IUP, we make sure our sex toys are operating and clean.[23]

Some columnists do adjust their column topics or general level of explicitness in deference to events or times of year that bring an especially large number of older or young readers onto campus. "You can always tell when it's parent's weekend, because I'll have certain columns that come out for that weekend and then accepted-students' weekend and alumni and homecoming weekends," former *Flat Hat* columnist Kate Prengaman said. "I try to be careful on those dates, because I got in trouble once when a column on S and M came out during homecoming weekend. That was bad news." As a letter to the editor critical of that particular column noted, "Leaving the University Center during Homecoming, I noticed an elderly alumnus picking up a copy of the *Flat Hat*. I tensed. I thought, 'please, don't read the sex column.' I could only imagine what would happen when this poor man learned all about 'S&M.' Heart attack? Cardiac arrest? What would he think of his alma mater now?"[24]

The ultimate deal breaker behind many administrative, parental, and political concerns is money. Specifically, anxieties abound about the loss of financial support universities might face from appalled taxpayers, parents of prospective students, donors, and lawmakers with control over public school budgets. For example, the iconic moment of Timaree Schmit's sex columnist stint for the *Daily Nebraskan* at the University of Nebraska, Lincoln, stemmed from the disgust of an influential school contributor. The donor's indignation was directed at a column Schmit wrote to students interested in having sexual intercourse for the first time. In the piece, headlined "Get into Rhythm, Learn Technique," she offered advice on the safest time in a woman's menstrual cycle to have sex without fear of pregnancy. As Schmit recalled:

I don't know whether it was a visceral reaction to me implying to a virgin it was okay to have unprotected sex or if it was just the topic of sex in general, but this woman, a big donor, happened to be on campus the day that column was published and saw it and then threatened right then and there to pull, like, six figures of a donation to the journalism school. Interestingly enough, I was doing a free HIV-testing drive that day, you know, helping ensure people were safe, and all day I kept getting interrupted with these frantic phone calls from my editor, who was like, "Okay, so they're throwing this emergency meeting with a couple of regents, a bunch of administrators and some faculty and this woman is disgusted and threatening to pull the money."[25]

The woman's concerns were ultimately placated and the donation went through, but the situation highlighted to Schmit the ever-present connection between sex and school funding. "The whole time I wrote the column, there were so many people who threatened in letters that people were going to pull money from the school," she said. "You know, someone was going to come, see the column, and envision the school for the Sodom and Gomorrah that it is and no more money will flow our way because of my dinky sex column." As a Lincoln attorney wrote in a *Daily Nebraskan* letter to the editor, "The public is increasingly being asked to provide financial support to the university. It would serve you well to remember that your constituency and readership are not limited to students. Adults, parents of students and prospective students, as well as members of the community read your paper and will make judgments about the level of support they are willing to provide based upon what attitudes and values they see represented in your paper."[26]

Political and religious representatives are among the outside groups expressing the most vociferous howls of disgust about what they perceive as the columns' lack of values. In general, related controversies involve not only name-calling but full-scale verbal attacks and organized protests against columns viewed as disrespectful or defiant toward various churches' or political parties' doctrines.

Condemnations with a uniquely religious fervor or focus emanate mainly from staffers at religious schools and outside organizations with varying levels of religious affiliation, such as those promoting abstinence or opposing abortion. "Anytime I write anything that has to do even a little bit with religion it becomes a big controversy," former *Carolinian* sex columnist Brook Taylor said. "Oh my God, religion and sex: Don't mix them." Lara Loewenstein, a former sex columnist for the *Daily Bruin* at UCLA, called related negative feedback the "Jesus doesn't like you" responses. For example, Sari Eitches, a former *Daily Californian* "Sex on Tuesday" columnist, said she received a particularly nasty reaction after a conservative religious parents' movement placed one of her columns on its website with a critique. In the accompanying comments section, readers censured her as an individual with no morals and a model for why parents should homeschool their children.

Meanwhile, throughout the year she wrote a sex column for the *Heights* at Boston College, Anna Schleelein was told she was destined for damnation in hell. Periodic student concerns were overshadowed by more frequent, vocal admonitions from college faculty, administrators, alumni, and religious officials in Greater Boston who felt her "Sex and the Univer-city" column went "so far as to assault the values of the Catholic Church." Critics specifically viewed Schleelein's sex talk as a rebellious gesture toward the conservative social and sexual policies of the college, one of twenty-eight U.S. schools affiliated with the Catholic-oriented Association of Jesuit Colleges and Universities. In what was considered her most controversial piece, she expressed support for contraceptive use, while sounding her disgust at the college's apposite, abstinent sexual stand. The column opened, "Condoms. Condoms. Condoms. I know this is a Jesuit university, and I know that means that pre-marital sex is supposed to be something akin to the Tooth Fairy. . . . Be that as it may, I cannot stress this enough here, people: a condom in hand is not worth two in the bush. They only protect you from diseases when you use them. Every time."[27]

Schleelein said she was prepared for some negative feedback, but not for the large amount and fervent tone of what she ended up receiving. "The upper-level administrators who were priests went ape-shit over it," said Larry Griffin, a former *Heights* editor who oversaw her column. Schleelein was invited to speak with one Jesuit priest during his office hours and told that he was praying for her soul. In e-mails, she was charged with blaspheming the newspaper and dubbed "Satan Mistress Schleelein." As one message began, "Apparently, this 'Catholic' college now has a sexologist . . . writing a sleazy sex column in the student newspaper. Shame on the College! The Mother of God showed Sister Lucia the many being thrown into the fires of Hell for such."[28]

Julia Baugher faced a similarly harsh set of critiques during the fifteen months she served as "Sex on the Hilltop" columnist for the *Hoya* at Georgetown University, also a member of the Association of Jesuit Colleges and Universities. A major set of criticisms centered on the column's symbolic status as an arbiter of the institution's apparent shift from the central tenets of the Catholicism on which it was founded. In a *Hoya* column headlined "So-Called Peer Wisdom Normally Anything But," Reverend Ryan Maher, a Georgetown associate dean, equated Baugher with "a monkey playing with sexual matches." He advised students to eschew her "mindless ramblings" and instead "seek advice about sex from people who are smarter, wiser and more mature than you. . . . A good way to begin that process is to delve deeply and seriously into your religious tradition." Father Rob Johansen, a Michigan-based priest featured in *National Review Online* and *Catholic World News*, wrote more sarcastically, "In place of the Catholic Faith, in the name of 'inclusivity,' Georgetown provides for its students things like a sex columnist in its official newspaper. . . . Go Hoyas! Embrace that Lust!"[29]

Religious anger similarly swirled around a sex column in the *Maroon* at Loyola University New Orleans, also a Jesuit school. Negative reactions reached a fever pitch in spring 2007 following the publication of a piece that approved of a student's interest in losing her virginity prior to marriage—advising her to "go forth and fornicate" safely and after mental and physical preparation. "It was the most read article on the Loyola Maroon's website ever, including Hurricane Katrina coverage," columnist Nicole Wroten noted nearly two years after the controversy erupted. "Alumni pulled funding [from the university] and I had several alumni confront me personally." As an older alumnus wrote at the time in a letter to the editor, "If this article is how the *Maroon* represents Loyola as a Jesuit Catholic University, I suggest Loyola save the resources spent on the *Maroon* and use them to have Catholic theologians straighten out erroneous understandings of the Jesuit tradition. What garbage." A separate alumnus publicly asked, "Is Loyola still considered a Catholic university? After reading [the column] . . . I will certainly include our alma mater in my prayers at daily Mass and Communion. . . . I am shocked that this column was published in the *Maroon*. Satan must be very proud of the *Maroon*. I am ashamed."[30]

University of Mississippi student Jessica-lynn Sumer Rose unintentionally sparked not just a school-wide, but a state-wide storm of religious-tinted protest with her suggestion that her fellow students enjoy a quick daily sex romp. In April 2003, the *Daily Mississippian* published a sex column by Rose headlined "Morning or Afternoon—Any Time's Good for a 'Nooner.'" It advised students to take part in a "nooner," which she defined as "a quickie with your significant other at lunchtime, or anytime for that matter." As she wrote, "Sex instead of lunch makes it a little easier to return to work for the rest of the afternoon, not to mention you burn calories rather than consume them. . . . So screw class, go home and screw instead." The column led to a telephone-and-e-mail protest organized by the head of the American Family Association, a regional Christian group based in Tupelo, Mississippi. The association, which declared the column a promoter of "reckless and illicit sexual relations," aimed its complaints at the University of Mississippi chancellor, members of the state's college board, and the governor, an Ole Miss alumnus. The *Daily Mississippian* received more than two thousand e-mails containing a form message of protest created by the association. It called for Rose's firing from the newspaper and the canceling of the sex column. One woman confessed that upon learning of Rose's column, "I didn't know whether to cry for the death of a civilized society or scream out in helplessness. What has this society become? How did we descend to such levels of decadence? What happened to morals and values? Who is in charge of our universities? . . . It is time for society to wake up. The inmates have taken over the institution!"[31]

Politicians and political institutions also at times publicly criticize the columns. For example, in late 2002, Illinois state senator Dick Klemm condemned the publishing of the sex column "Love Monkey" in the *Tartan*, the monthly student newspaper at McHenry County College in Illinois. The debut column, billed as a provider of "answers to monkey-business issues," touched on impotence and unprotected sex. "I don't think I want a *Hustler* magazine supported by the taxpayers," Klemm said after the column's premiere. Roughly six months later, Kansas state senator Tim Huelskamp expressed similar outrage at Meghan Bainum's *Daily Kansan* sex column. In an online newsletter, he wrote it was "better suited for the brown-paper covers of X-rated magazines" and called it "a morally repugnant action, funded by taxpayers."[32]

Often the press statements reek of easy plays for the moral high ground and older voters' affections, unaccompanied by any attempts at stopping what the politicians deem so repugnant. State legislators in Arizona are a dubious exception. In May 2005, the state budget for the following fiscal year was signed into law, including a footnote that prohibited funding for student media at Arizona's three public universities. The legislative action stemmed in part from officials' anger at a sex column in the *Lumberjack* at Northern Arizona University. The pre-Valentine's Day piece by student Claire Fuller offered advice on both fellatio and cunnilingus. It began with an observation that continues to stand as the most famous college sex column lead sentence: "On Valentine's Day, nothing says 'I love you' like oral sex."[33]

According to one press report, "As soon as it was published, a whole mess of people were up in arms over its vulgarity and inappropriateness. Top university officials had meetings to deliberate consequences [and] hundreds of people posted comments on the newspaper's website." A deluge of correspondence also arrived in staffers' e-mail in-boxes and in the newsroom. An open letter of condemnation by university president Jon Haeger noted, "I am going on record to note my own—and evidence suggests the broader university community's—disappointment and embarrassment at the publication of this article." A number of angry readers even argued that not only should editors discontinue the column but the entire newspaper should stop publishing as well. "Perhaps with enough protests over such trashy journalism they will totally eliminate the *Lumberjack*," Northern Arizona engineering professor David Hartman wrote in one such letter, which he sent to the newspaper's editor, Haeger, and the Arizona Board of Regents. "That would be my recommendation. You have betrayed the public trust and have thus lost the right to be allowed to continue in the publishing business."[34]

This "blow job backlash," as the media dubbed it, was followed by a controversy at Arizona State University centered on *State Press Magazine*, a weekly student newspaper supplement. The main item in the magazine considered offensive by state legislators: a report on "extreme body modification" such as genital piercing, promoted by a nearly full-page cover photograph showing a woman's bare breast with a pierced nipple. In response to Fuller's column, the *State Press* pierced-nipple cover, and other student press content deemed sexually explicit, state representative Russell Pearce, co-chair of the Arizona legislature's House Appropriations Committee, introduced a footnote into the budget calling for "no state funding for university student newspapers." He said he inserted the footnote after being approached by a number of irate fellow legislators. "If you want to be a free press, be a free press," he said, "but we're not going to subsidize articles that are over the top, and there were a lot of folks that felt it [the sexual content] was over the top."[35]

The irony of the legislation: Its only financial impact was the cost of the paper on which it was printed. The *Lumberjack* and the *Arizona Daily*

Wildcat, the student newspaper at the University of Arizona, are financed primarily through advertising and receive no state funding. The only other major university student newspaper in Arizona, the *State Press* at ASU, is mostly self-supporting. It receives only 10 percent of its subsidies from the university, but through tuition money, not state funds. Simply put, no student media budgets were affected. But the footnote is not just economically irrelevant; it is also ignorant of the First Amendment. As a consistent body of case law, constitutional scholars, and press experts have confirmed, school funding does not and should not come with editorial strings attached. The Arizona legislature, by contrast, basically declared that legal adults should not receive assistance any time they dare to produce content that offends lawmakers and a portion of the population. The footnote is a slippery slope toward a level of state control that is scary and anti-American. But it did get Pearce's name in the newspaper, highlighting one last important outside participant in student press sex fights.[36]

Amid the culture clashes causing column controversies, the media are not just intermediaries. Professional news outlets at times set the agenda, triggering debate and related trouble by deciding on their own or after only scant public complaint that the content is controversial enough to feature in print, online, or on air. The end goal in these endeavors is clearly not to present actual news so much as to create buzz and secure higher readership, web hits, ratings, and advertising revenue. One student newspaper editor calls these media-created fights "artificial uproars."

For example, in late February 2004 at South Dakota State University, a brief controversy erupted over a sex column focused on oral sex that ran in *Juice*, a regular supplement to the *Collegian*. The column answered a question from a female reader identified as "BJ Challenged," who wrote, "My friend told me when she gives her boyfriend head it takes him under five minutes to get off. It always takes me at least a half hour! What am I doing wrong?" Columnist Kara Lindquist recommended varying the sucking technique, but cautioned against engaging in the activity for too long. As she noted, "Having a girl bobbing around for hours, and only ending up with a giant hickey on his dick to show for it does not sound like a good time."[37]

Roughly forty-eight hours after its publication, administrators began lodging complaints and outside readers sent critical e-mails and letters to the editor. According to a *Collegian* report, angry telephone calls were even directed at the university's Department of Journalism and Mass Communication, including from "parents planning to send their children to SDSU but reconsidering due to the material the *Collegian* published." Yet a majority of complaints did not emanate from individuals who actually read the column, "Blow Job Should Be Quick." Instead, most critics said they only learned about it from one of two evening television news programs in Sioux Falls that aired stories about the content's possible over-the-line explicitness. "When an SDSU student who works at KELO [a Sioux Falls television station] showed his or her bosses that column, they smelled a story," a *Collegian* editor wrote a week after the column's publication. "Did they manufacture a controversy? I think so."[38]

Meanwhile, at Middle Tennessee State University, a lone parent's anger over a sex column in the *Sidelines* student newspaper stirred school-wide controversy mainly because of the press coverage her protest received. The column, "Anonymous Women's Perspectives Give Ways to Spice Up Your Sex Life," provided a range of "secrets" shared by female students aimed at helping men better understand their sexual desires. For example, under a secret titled "Toys Are Not the Enemy," columnist Callie Elizabeth Butler wrote, "Many men consider vibrators and dildos threatening in some way. This simply isn't so! . . . A nice dildo or butt plug can make double penetration a reality for your duo without bothering with a third partner. Nipple clamps can provide added sensation. A cock ring can keep you harder for longer. Toys, while not essential to an electric sex life, can be a great enhancement."[39]

Debbie Mayfield, the mother of a Middle Tennessee State student, told the *Tennessean* she was "shocked and offended" by the column, which she read online. She sent an e-mail of disgust containing the article and her critique to more than ninety Middle Tennessee State administrators, area politicians, local and national media outlets, and well-known conservative media personalities, including Bill O'Reilly, Sean Hannity, and Tennessee radio talk show host Steve Gill. Her message—in which she called the column "nothing but a How-To manual for sexual perversion"—prompted numerous media reports and sparked a campus-wide debate about the column's explicitness and the free speech protections allowing it to be published. While confirming the column would continue to run, Matt Anderson, the newspaper's editor in chief, said Mayfield was the only individual to register an objection prior to the media coverage she sparked. "Let's not lose sight of the fact that it was one e-mail from one woman," Anderson said a week after the column was published. "This issue . . . came and went without incident, but once there was a little outrage it was the talk of the campus." Literally, while the original column ran in the Living section on page 5 of the newspaper, an article six days later addressing the controversy appeared on the newspaper's front page.[40]

A column on oral sex in the *Spectrum* at North Dakota State University also garnered no attention when first published. The piece, "Just a Spoon Full of Sugar Helps the Medicine Go Down," began, "Over the lips, past the gums, look out stomach, here it comes. . . . By giving a guy a blow job, you are quite possibly paying him one of the biggest compliments to his manhood." The controversy encircling the column began to percolate on campus after the press operator in charge of the newspaper's print run alerted the *Forum*, the daily newspaper in the surrounding city of Fargo, about the content. The *Forum* ran a related story and, according to *Spectrum* editor Matthew Perrine, "it was off to the races from there." As one press report confirmed, "The just-launched column by 'Allison Moorhead,' the pseudonym for the female writer, was barely noted by the school's twelve-thousand students. But the column about oral sex outraged the larger campus community, and many adults bombarded the paper's editor with angry phone calls."[41]

The university's Board of Student Publications publicly stated it did not support the column and compelled editors to develop written guidelines for similar features in the future. The column ultimately was dropped by the paper at the discretion of top editors and the newspaper adviser, subsequently appearing in the *High Plains Reader*, a weekly alternative newspaper in Fargo. Perrine said he became scared to answer the newsroom phone during the controversy. He wrote in a *Spectrum* editor's note ten days after the column's publication, "People statewide are still calling for a public crucifixion of yours truly." As he recalled in an interview more than two years later:

The press operator saw it and decided to alert the editor of the paper in Fargo. . . . The *Forum* then picked up on it after that, and it became more a media thing. We still didn't really have anyone on campus complaining about it, which was really shocking. It was all the media in the town and then the state, and I did an interview with Fox, the local affiliate, and that was broadcast in like Wisconsin. And then I was interviewed in the *San Jose Mercury News*, and I believe that was the one that was picked up by some UK news services. . . . It went from just kind of being ho-hum on campus and no one really talking about it to this big explosion. Like the news reports wouldn't even quote students, it was just all the talking heads. It was just kind of taken out of our hands and brought somewhere else by the press.[42]

Thanks for the Controversy

The ultimate irony of the outside criticisms and acts of censorship centered on college newspaper sex columns is that they often bring more attention to the columns they are attempting to discredit or suppress. While the columns are popular and well read in their own right, the public censures and attempts of suppression typically generate an even higher level of interest, debate, and intervention by students, the media, health professionals, and journalism scholars.

For example, at Lyndon State, Norris's expulsive e-mail led to an explosion of attention, to the point that one news report declared, "Sex has overtaken the conversation at Lyndon State College." As the student newspaper's editor in chief confirmed, "I don't remember the *Critic* ever getting so many letters about anything, including students being physically harassed at drinking parties, hazings, and the much more recent arson attempts in the Rogers dormitory building. You know, the one where two people attempted to force their way into a student's room while he was asleep, and then *lit a trashcan on fire*? Not to blow a minor incident out of proportion, but the possibility that a dorm filled with students could burn down does exist, yet all we can seem to talk about is the sex column in the student newspaper." Local print and television news covered the controversy. Discussions were held in classes and a school-wide forum on free speech was staged. Students even started a group on Facebook called "Save Holy Sheet" to ensure columnist Jordan Royer was not dismissed from school. A student at a nearby college monitoring the controversy wrote, "To the professor calling for his [Royer's] expulsion: Lay off! Quit making this into a bigger deal than it is. Because you had to call for an absurd crusade against this guy, he's getting all sorts of press and support!"[43]

Along with stirring greater attention and support, the critics also unwittingly place columns in the spotlight as leaders in the continuing fight for freedom of speech and the press on campus. While columns are regarded by a majority of readers as entertainment, it has been their most vocal opponents who have lent them additional gravitas, elevating their work from mere sex and relationship advice to embodiments of the best of the student press.

For example, in Montana, Juras's attacks and calls for possible state control of the *Kaimin* prompted campus-wide debate and national media and blogosphere attention. Her public condemnations also upped the column's web views considerably and led to numerous high-profile statements of *Kaimin* and sex column support, most likely the opposite of what she hoped to achieve. In a related editorial headlined "Free Speech Is Sexy," a *Michigan Daily* columnist wrote, "While banning a sex column from a student newspaper may seem like a minor issue, any infringement upon a student newspaper's right to print the content it deems relevant to students violates not only the First Amendment but also the very foundations of ethical journalism. . . . [Readers] should recognize not only the relevance of sex columns to today's college students, but also the right for student newspapers to print them." Wagner College literature professor Pranav Jani separately stated in response to the *Wagnerian* sex mess, "We don't want the administration to run the paper. . . . We need to draw the line whenever free speech is attacked, even a little bit, because if we don't draw that line as soon as its [sic] attacked then they'll keep trying to take more of it away from us."[44]

For many sex columnists, controversy is not merely a right. It is also not simply a corollary or by-product of their efforts. It is the point. Columnists often utilize potentially shocking topics, terms, and descriptions as a means to an end: getting people to take notice of the sexual issues they discuss. "You know, I freaked people out occasionally and caused problems, but I made people talk about sexual issues," said former *Argosy* sex columnist Zoë Davé at Canada's Mount Allison University. "And that's the most important thing. If they're talking about it, then they read it. And if they read it, then they know more about that subject than they did before." Former *Muhlenberg Weekly* sex columnist Christina Liciaga similarly declared, "Since my first column debut, I've been questioned, prodded, cursed and thanked by people all over campus and the occasional parent or Board member. I have been glad to have those conversations, to have sparked conversations like those and most importantly to encourage sex as an appropriate topic of conversation."[45]

Along with sparking conversation, the controversies confirm that the columns are the most significant modern embodiments of the idealistic agitator role long associated with the student newspaper. Historically, the campus paper has often been cited as the entity with the greatest power to awaken a school debate, raise an issue, and weary an administration. As *Editor and Publisher* sarcastically stated in 1949, "It can raise more hell on a college campus than spiked punch at the dean's reception for freshmen women." New York University history professor and journalism researcher Jonathan Zimmerman said more seriously in 2003, "The administrators must be annoyed at the student newspaper, or else something is terribly wrong." Campus newspapers' sexual expression is an extension of this longtime annoying and hell-raising. "Why not publish a sex column in a college newspaper?" *Post* sex columnist Brynn Burton asked in one piece. "College papers are the only forms of media that can push the envelope. College papers are always questioning the establishment, expressing different ideas and essentially getting away with it. Why not question sex?"[46]

In her final piece, *Nevada Sagebrush* columnist Erin Granat even expressed gratitude to the readers who complained about her own envelope pushing. "Just know you couldn't have paid me a greater compliment than actually taking your time to write in about it," she wrote. "Not to mention how much you've boosted my future career chances by providing proof I did something during college that garnered attention and got people talking. Thanks for the controversy."[47]

7

Playboy for the College Set
The Rise and Influence of Campus Sex Magazines

> In the realm of sex, there is a tendency to do and not to reflect. For something that takes up a large portion of our under-graduate brainspace, there's very little serious analytical thought given to the subject. . . . The unexamined life, as Socrates says, is not worth living. So why should we be opposed to examining our sex lives?
>
> KIMI TRAUBE
> *"A Note from Editor Kimi Traube,"* Outlet, *December 2006*

Alecia Oleyourryk sat naked on a barstool. The continual click of a camera sounded around her. A photo shoot focused on her had just begun. She flipped through a copy of the first issue of *Boink*, the student sex maga-zine she started during her senior year in college. She looked into a nearby video camera recording the shoot. "I'm a Boston University student," she said with a smile. She flashed a thumbs-up sign. "Let me graduate, please." She laughed and glanced again at the magazine, tousling her wavy blonde hair back with her left hand. She then said more softly, as an afterthought, "Don't kick me out."[1]

The subsequent images on screen quickly cut from her bare buttocks to her breasts to a full shot of her doubled over on the stool and nearby table in laughter. A reporter was heard off-camera saying with a chuckle, "Just a typical Boston University student." Oleyourryk, twenty-one years old at the time, looked the speaker's way and broke into an open-mouthed smile, the sarcasm seeping in as another flash of the camera painted her with a burst of white light. The photo shoot, captured on video by an Italian television station, was staged in early April 2005, less than two months after *Boink* debuted amid controversy and hype in Greater Boston.

Hype has surrounded the start and early distribution of a majority of modern college sex magazines and journals of erotica. The beginnings were humble, with a single publication, *Squirm: The Art of Campus Sex*, premiering in 2000 at Vassar College in Poughkeepsie, New York, without any national media attention. But since 2004, the magazines have received more media coverage and at times stir more controversy than student newspaper sex columns. They have appeared for short or extended periods at more than a dozen colleges and universities in the United States and Canada, collectively earning labels worthy of a tabloid newspaper front page: "the sex pub orgy," "university sex rags," "X-rated glossies," "intellectual masturbation," "tit-and-lit mag[s]," a "dose of smut," and "the university take on student skin."[2]

Boink specifically, according to one news report, "has gained renown across the globe." Even prior to its release, reader interest and press attention transformed an idea for a simple student pornographic magazine into a media empire that at its height included merchandising, themed parties, a book released in February 2008, and a television production deal based on a show concept loosely centered on the magazine co-founders. *Boink* and its creators have been featured on MTV, CNN, National Public Radio, *The Tyra Banks Show*, *The Howard Stern Show*, *Inside Edition*, and in national publications such as the *New York Times*, the *Washington Post*, *Stuff*, and *Vanity Fair*. In 2005, the *Boston Globe* christened *Boink* as "*Playboy* for the college set."[3]

The connection of student sex magazines overall to *Playboy* is strong. The publication is the undisputed grandfather of modern student sex mags, accomplishing a significant feat few sexualized media products had before enjoyed: an embrace by mainstream America. During the 1960s, *Playboy* boasted a circulation of more than seven million and was read by one of every four college students. At the peak of its popularity and influence, college courses devoted whole sessions to facets of the magazine and parties were held on campuses each month to herald the premiere of the latest issue.[4]

Beginning in the 1970s, a new party of more explicit sex publications emerged, sporting titles such as *Gallery, Touch, Voir, Genesis, Dude, Cavalier, Viva, Coq, Hustler,* and *Penthouse.* According to historian Steven Watts, the magazines featured raunchier sexualized content, including toilet humor, startling images of women's pubic hair, and photos of "women fondling themselves, lesbianism, fetishism, threesomes . . . [and] kinky sexual adventures." At the same time, *Cosmopolitan* pushed similar boundaries, in reverse, although not so raunchily. The publication extended the notion that women could be sexually expressive and even lustful, with its most talked about portion being the nude centerfold featuring male models and actors. A naked Burt Reynolds posing for the April 1972 issue had the entire country abuzz. The next set of buzz-worthy sex magazines were the mid-1990s lad mags—most prominently *Maxim, FHM,* and *Stuff*—and their female counterparts *Bitch* and *Bust.* For a brief time, late teens and early twentysomethings viewed these media as the ultimate arbiters of what was hip, considering them the closest representations of sex and socializing as they knew them or imagined them to be. Then students began representing themselves, creating their own publications.[5]

According to news coverage and editor interviews, most issues of all campus sex magazines sell out or are grabbed up quickly. Students at the University of Chicago literally flocked to the first issue of the sex magazine *Vita Excolatur* "like free condoms at a state school." The premiere of *Sex Week at Yale: The Magazine* elicited a similar reaction on its home campus, with the director of the affiliated event stating publicly, "The magazine is all students are talking about." Meanwhile, the student co-founder of *H Bomb* at Harvard University said in the magazine's early days, "*H Bomb* is the only Harvard magazine that gets stolen out of mailboxes."[6]

Often stolen and never shy, the magazines spout an open, mainstream, and raunchy brand of sex talk that has never before existed in full campus publications of students' own making. While they are occasionally viewed more as curiosities and media phenomena than groundbreaking ventures, the magazines' initial popularity and continued existence in a down and print-unfriendly economy is proof that they are presenting a modern style of sexual expression that students want to peek at and read. As *Boston Magazine* stated in 2006, "College porn—by students, for students and the dirty old men who like them—is a notion that has come of age."[7]

One Hundred Percent *Zero* Experience

During the early part of 2004, Stephen Trevick had no idea what he was doing. The junior philosophy major at the University of Chicago had no previous journalism experience. He had no background in publishing. And he was not an expert in sex. He simply wanted to jump-start a discussion about sexual issues among college students and thought the most feasible, popular forum for that discussion would be in magazine form. According to Trevick, the initial idea for *Vita Excolatur* sprang to life at Medici, a restaurant popular among University of Chicago students. As he recalled:

> There were three of us sitting around together after a meeting for the Gay-Straight Alliance [a student group to which Trevick belonged]. Somebody brought up . . . that some other places had started these sorts of magazines. . . . All three of us were just kind of like, "University of Chicago should have this." And you have to understand, I actually had one hundred percent *zero* experience in editing or running a magazine or any of this at that point, but I just thought "Why not?" So, I was like, "Well, I'll do it. I'll take the reins." And then, you know, before we knew it, *Vita* was born.

Prior to publication of the first issue, Trevick oversaw only two meetings, a flurry of e-mails, and a lightning-fast production schedule with a team of approximately ten student staffers. Three students quit after he insulted the quality of a story submission at the first meeting. The story, he later learned, had been written and sent in anonymously by one of the students present, and she resigned angrily with two of her friends after the meeting. "It was good to learn that making fun of the staff wasn't a good idea," he said. "I wouldn't say it all went smoothly at first."

He supervised four photo shoots furtively assembled in campus dorm rooms and, with permission from school officials, shoots in the university chapel and the school's Regenstein Library. The latter shoot resulted in the two-part photographic spread "Love in the Stacks," which separately displayed a gay and lesbian couple making out and undressing in various parts of the library. Administrators granted permission for the library shoot specifically, Trevick admitted, because "we didn't *really* tell them what we'd be doing." The methods of solicitation for writing samples, artwork, and models, meanwhile, were scattered and often came down to personal contact. "My friends started calling me Larry [Flynt, the controversial publisher of *Hustler*], because I was just trying to get people to pose all the time for me," said Trevick. "I'd just go up to somebody and say, 'So I'm starting this magazine,' and they'd always respond at first, 'Oh, I could never be in that.' And I'm like, 'Well, I didn't really ask you to be, but now that you mention it . . .'"[8]

At the end of the magazine's harried production schedule, Trevick went into hiding. He locked himself in a room for two days with a friend to design the magazine on a self-imposed deadline, attempting in fits and starts to learn layout software he had never before operated. His parents fronted him about seven hundred dollars to publish the first thousand copies, with plans to sell each for a dollar to make a tiny profit. Yet the printer waffled, at first not printing anything, and eventually sending Trevick only two hundred copies, resulting in a drawn-out lawsuit that Trevick said he ultimately won. The full set of one thousand was finally printed and sold in December 2004 on campus, according to the *Chicago Sun-Times*, where it was "a hit . . . [its entire press run] eagerly grabbed up by curious students." By that time, Trevick was studying in India, where he received word of the sales success by e-mail. Nearly two years later, he laughed at the recollection. "I guess you could say it started off very ad hoc . . . and really none of our board [of student staffers] had experience with what they were doing," he noted. "But in the end, you know, it turned out not to be that hard."[9] Founding editors at a majority of campus sex magazines echo the story of *Vita*'s start. The most common characteristics shared: a quick publication process; an admitted lack of professionalism during the initial proceedings; and a small, passionate, unpaid group of students with no idea how their efforts were going to turn out.

In upstate New York, the founding of *Squirm*, the first campus sex magazine, was inspired by readings of erotic fiction and an annual Vassar College student gathering called "Homo Hop." In fall 1998, co-founder Barnett Cohen and a small group of Vassar undergraduates began enjoying periodic, informal get-togethers on campus to read bad literary erotica aloud. According to Cohen, at one point the group broached the idea of starting a literary erotica magazine of their own, instead of reading the works of others. He and his friends wanted the publication to embrace the spirit of what the *New York Times* called Vassar's "biggest campus dance of the year."[10]

Through the late 1990s, each fall more than one thousand students had flocked to Homo Hop, an event peppered with erotic photographs, alcohol and illegal drugs, strippers, a sadomasochism room, and numerous students who either went topless or dressed in drag. "It started out as a dance just for gay men, but over time it morphed into a kind of drug binge for everyone," said Cohen. As he recalled:

> The joy of it was that it was an evening for everyone, probably with the aid of drugs or alcohol, to simply be themselves and do whatever they wanted. If it meant having an orgy, that's fine. If it meant hooking up with someone of the same sex, even if you normally wouldn't do that, that's fine, too. It was an anything-goes mentality. . . . That was the same thing we wanted to do with *Squirm*, you know, push this idea of being free to be whoever you wanted to be or discuss whatever you wanted. It was basically saying, "It's okay." You know, it's okay to talk about sex toys. It's okay to write about erotica. It's okay to talk about being gay or straight or a little bit of both.

As Cohen's *Squirm* co-founder Deva Kyle said, "It was really just a bunch of friends doing something silly. We had all these ideas, but everybody was sort of on the same page and really just wanted to do something that people would see as fun and open and that they'd want to be part of."[11]

Camilla Hrdy, one of two founding editors of *H Bomb* at Harvard, similarly described the magazine's start as "a lot of fun, kind of slapstick, and definitely mad dash." As she recalled, "There was no professionalism to it at all. We were always kind of confused. We were always doing failed photo shoots. We would get all these people together and think it was going to be great, and then we'd look at the photos and be like, 'This is ridiculous.'" For example, Hrdy referred to what she termed "the Abu Ghraib photo shoot," in which staffers attempted to sexually reinvent the space in which the infamous 2004 scandal involving American military abuse of Iraqi prisoners had taken place. The images specifically strove to explore what Hrdy called "some dominatrix themes" related to the photograph of U.S. soldier Lynndie

England holding a leash tied around the neck of a naked detainee. "As you can imagine, the project was much more difficult than we thought," she said. "We had already done two shoots and somebody was just like, 'Why are we doing this? What's the goal?' And we were all scrambling through our notes trying to say something meaningful. . . . We were just trying to cross some line, I think. We realized the project was fun but it had no business being in a sex magazine and might even get us arrested."

For many publications, this early slapdash approach extended to basic staff hierarchy, at times even including seating arrangements. For example, at *Squirm*, staffers asked Cohen, the first editor in chief of the magazine, to refrain from sitting at the head of the table in the room where meetings were held, so he would not metaphorically assert any control over decision making or the staff sitting nearby. "I've worked at magazines and interned at magazines and so have some sense that there is a chain of command in place, but at the time that was decided to be antithetical to the nature of what we were all about," said Cohen. "Every editorial meeting was a free-for-all. . . . It was very much on the fly." Alecia Oleyourryk said the free-spirited staff structure at *Boink* built on the relaxed tenor of the start-up overall. As she recalled about first meeting co-founder Christopher Anderson, "It was one of those things where it was like, 'So, you wanna do this sex magazine? All right, what should we call it?' It was really just step by step. There was no huge game plan."[12]

Early issues of most publications were produced by about a dozen student volunteers, and sometimes much less. *Sex Week at Yale*'s founding editor Soren Sudhof said, "The whole magazine was basically three people who put it together within two or three weeks." Hrdy similarly noted that the final layout of the first *H Bomb* was completed in roughly twenty-four hours by her co-founder, Katharina Cieplak-von Baldegg, and one other student, in part because most staff members had no experience in design. "We didn't have the infrastructure to do it the way we wanted because everyone was so busy, and we weren't like the *Crimson* [Harvard's student newspaper], you know, we weren't paying anyone," she said. "It was really hard to get people to work for us or do any work in a timely fashion."

The main problem editors have in sustaining staff involves the letdown between the perceptions students hold about working for a sex magazine and the reality. "Students don't seem to understand that it's not all naked girls or a big swinging party and that there really is actual work involved," said Christopher Anderson, a professional photographer and one of the few non-students involved with these publications. "They think it's going to be this porn paradise." Or as his fellow *Boink* creator Alecia Oleyourryk explained, by mimicking an interested student, "Wait, wait . . . we're not going to have an orgy?"[13]

Instead of being orgiastic, editorial meetings tend to be extremely informal, normally held in editors' apartments, dorm rooms, or university student centers. For example, an early get-together for the short-lived erotica magazine *Quake* at the University of Pennsylvania involved "fifteen people crammed into co-founder Jamie York's living room. . . . There's a warm spinach dip on the table. Some nachos, brownies, salsa. Even pita bread. The prospective staff members wear jeans and t-shirts and sweatshirts." Meanwhile, early *Penitalia* production meetings at the University of Washington were often held in the student union building, with back-and-forths such as debating whether "blow job" was one word or two eliciting surprised or curious reactions from nearby students.[14]

According to editors, a majority of undergraduates interested in being involved with the magazines are looking to serve not as writers or photographers but models. Many editors of early issues said that students regularly approached them to ask if they could pose, without any prompting. For example, eighty-five students volunteered to pose for *Boink*'s inaugural issue. Approximately twenty were ultimately featured, including co-founder Oleyourryk, who appeared on the cover and on several other pages. As *H Bomb*'s Hrdy separately recalled, "We never sent out a public e-mail saying 'Come pose for *H Bomb*.' Just people who said they were interested, we put them on a list, and the list grew." Similar to the editorial staffs, all student models are volunteers, with one exception—*Boink* paid one hundred dollars to those who posed in its opening issues. Yet Anderson does not believe students choose to model for the money, a sentiment echoed by former *Boink* models. "Some people just think it's cool," he said. "There are other people who are looking for some sort of notoriety, and they want their fifteen minutes of fame. I have no doubt there is also a rebellious streak in other people who do it. Whatever the reason, the interest is there, and it's huge. People just really want to be naked, in front of the camera, and exposed to the world."

With models selected, photos shot, written content solicited and edited, and layouts nearing completion, one final question remained for most editors of early student sex magazines: Would university administrators support such overt sexual expression and exposure?

At Boston University, in respect to *Boink*, the answer was a resounding no. Prior to the magazine's release and without reviewing any content, the university's dean of students released a statement saying, "The University does not endorse, nor welcome, the prospective publication *Boink*; nor view its publication as a positive for the University community." The magazine was not allowed to be distributed on university property, even after Newbury Comics selected it for placement in its twenty-seven retail locations in Boston and throughout New England. Anderson said that eight U.S. printers also initially turned down the magazine, in part due to concerns about content, forcing *Boink* to be printed in Canada. "I have a couple of sweet memories of playing around with ideas and coming to a moment where we thought, 'Oh yeah, we can actually do this,'" he said. "And then we got a little bit of press in the BU school paper [the *Daily Free Press*] and suddenly we were inundated by local and national media and it felt like we were targeted and in over our heads. Then the BU administration hunkered down with this, like, bunker mentality. It was like they were preparing for an invading army. It was pretty overwhelming to be quite honest."[15]

In general, the *Boink*-BU battle has been isolated. Universities overall have adopted a surprisingly hands-off policy toward content. Most also provide magazines with partial or full financial support, and official administrative recognition as student publications or as part of larger student organizations. For example, *Squirm* received approximately two thousand dollars from Vassar when first founded, an amount that has grown to five thousand dollars annually, supplemented by fund-raisers such as a sex toy auction. *Open* sex magazine enjoys similar support at Rice University, including a school-sponsored grant that covered the roughly three-thousand-dollar publication costs of the premiere issue. By comparison, during its short run, *Quake* at Penn received recognition as an official student publication and funding for three-quarters of its expenses from the university's Student Activities Council. Former editor Jessica Haralson said that school administrators stuck by the magazine even after the Campus

Crusade for Christ criticized her and a *Daily Pennsylvanian* columnist attacked her as a "heroin peddler" for supposedly feeding students' sexual addiction. "That was a shock for me," she said. "I really anticipated having issues with the university."[16]

University of Chicago administrators have played both the parental and carefree cards with *Vita*. School officials initially prohibited photographs showing nude students in front of identifiable university buildings and photographs displaying erections or sexual intercourse. In addition, all student models are still required to be eighteen years old and sign two consent forms allowing their images to appear in the magazine, one prior to their modeling and one after reviewing the photographs set to be used. The administration also reviewed magazine content in early issues three times prior to publication and was instrumental in stopping past editors' efforts to start a related website. But the restrictions do come with support. While Trevick's parents helped pay for the first *Vita*, the magazine received approximately six thousand dollars from the university during the 2007–2008 academic year as a registered student organization. "We try very hard to not make a judgment one way or another in terms of the value or something our students want to do," said a University of Chicago assistant vice president for student life. "I think the University of Chicago is very committed to the free and open exchange of ideas."[17]

In the end, for some student editors it has been their school's lack of a public stand either way that has served as the greatest show of support. As top editors of *! Mag* (pronounced "Bang Mag") at Swarthmore College said in 2004, "As we see it, silence is complicity."[18]

Do You Think John Edwards Is a Dreamboat?

The cover of the first *H Bomb* in May 2004 contained an image of biblical proportions. It features a full rear view of a nude man and woman, both seemingly student age. Their bodies are visible in shadowy gray and black against a stark white backdrop. The woman is tightly grasping the man's right butt cheek with one hand and holding a red apple before his eyes with the other, in an obvious Adam-and-Eve-style enticement. "Was it a bit unoriginal? Maybe. Was it just plain titillating and blasphemous and sinful? According to some people, sure," said Camilla Hrdy with a laugh. "But there's more to it. This was our introduction, our seduction, our money shot. You know, follow the apple. It was a lead-in. We wanted to get beneath the surface of sex, you know, beyond the shame and sinfulness associated with it all. We wanted to start a conversation, a conversation about what is on everyone's minds but never really talked about."

Behind their covers, the conversations being carried out in student sex magazines are a clutter of highbrow and indisputably lowbrow content. More serious sentiments appear in the form of poetry, first-person confessionals, and academic-style essays. They explore issues such as the fluidity of sexual identity; the positives and evils of online pornography; the dangers of date rape, sexual assault, and sexually transmitted infections; the difficulties in defining the allusive generational term "hooking up"; the failures of sexual education in U.S. schools; and a debunking of popular sexual myths such as "big penises are the sexiest" and "if you are in a relationship your partner should never have to masturbate."

For example, in the first issue of *X-Magazine* at Washington University in St. Louis, a male alumnus in a wheelchair wrote about the intermixing of sexuality and disability. By comparison, a past issue of *Open* at Rice featured "a Buddhist monk's experience with celibacy, reactions to abstinence-only sexual education, the AIDS prevalence in Botswana, the *Kama Sutra* as a historical text, as well as a personal essay about the way sex is treated in the United States and India." And an issue of *H Bomb* published around the same time included a feature on Harvard's transgender housing policies, an extended profile of a nineteen-year-old pornographic film star, and a report on women who undergo mastectomies and subsequently get tattoos over the spots on their bodies where their breasts used to be. Magazines also feature interviews with sex industry professionals or individuals known for the sexuality of their work, including Alison Bechdel, creator of the popular syndicated comic "Dykes to Watch Out For"; a noted manufacturer of handcrafted glass dildos; a representative of New York City's Museum of Sex; and Annie Sprinkle, a former porn star and current performance artist and photographer who created the first prominent pornographic movie filmed from a female perspective.[19]

The most conceptual portions of the publications are the poetry and fiction stories that account for a sizable chunk of many issues' editorial slates. Often composed in free verse and featuring explicit sexual themes, the poems frequently center on two main sentiments: sexual desires and insecurities. For example, in "Rag Doll," a short poem published in *X-Magazine*, a student recounted the physical pleasure and emotional emptiness of a one-night stand:

I did not know when you kissed me.
I knew when I kissed you back.
We were going to sleep together.
I knew when you slipped your hand in my jeans we were going
    to fuck.
. . .
When you flipped me on top of you like a rag doll, I knew I'd leave in
    the morning bruised and shaken.
When you closed your eyes, I knew it was only because you didn't
    want to look into mine.
. . .
I knew when I cried out in my pleasure you wouldn't perceive the
    insincerity.
And I knew when you said "goodnight" that fucking is what we do
    when we're in love with someone else.[20]

Meanwhile, less seriously, a short story published in the opening issue of *Penitalia* focused on a heterosexual couple on a road trip who turn to sex to kill time while stuck in Montana. As one portion of the piece mentioned, "The last night we had the room, she said she would try anything but that I had to choose it. I had trouble looking at her after that, so my eyes searched for something to put inside her." The female soon thereafter begins masturbating with a Coors beer bottle. Later, the couple is described eating fried chicken and coleslaw, with the male narrator admitting, "I did feel a bit like a pig, eating so much in front of her but was glad that she ate lightly—I wanted to fuck her in the ass that afternoon."[21]

Such blasé graphicness is a patented part of the publications' other regular features. The magazines run frequent ribald reviews of sex toys and pornographic films. They publish numerous essays caked in satire, epitomized by an article in *Outlet* at Columbia University on "vaginal personality" that carried the subheading "How Snarky Is Your Punani?"

Playful lists also run rampant, such as a two-page glossary of words for masturbation published in *Boink* that included phrases like "Answer the Bone-A-Phone," "Beat the Beaver," "Rubbin' the Nubbin," and "Pulling the Piss Pump." Meanwhile, recurring advice columns tend to be aimed more at humor than insight, such as the *Vita* feature "Ask Syd Anything" that once informed a male student wondering if he should trim his pubic hair, "Sweetheart, if it were up to me, no one would ever have to suffer the wrath of a wild bush."[22]

The best example of the silly-serious content mix emerged online in January 2008, in a series of YouTube-style videos created by *H Bomb* staff. In short video reports, student Jenna Mellor traipsed across New Hampshire prior to the state's presidential primary election, asking voters, campaign staffers, and even presidential candidate Dennis Kucinich an array of questions about their sex lives and the connection between politics and sex. Queries included: "Do you think John Edwards is a dreamboat?"; "What do you think is the most important sexual issue facing this country?"; "What's sexier—freedom, liberty, or democracy?; "Has being a politician affected your sex life?"; and, to a supporter of candidate Ron Paul, "Do you think he [Paul] is a tits or ass man?" One of the more engaging exchanges occurred with a Kucinich staffer in front of the candidate's campaign bus, after Mellor revealed her *H Bomb* affiliation:

Staffer: "What is a sexuality magazine doing covering the New Hampshire primary?"
Mellor: "Well, what do you think?"
Staffer: "I think sex and politics are connected in a very immediate way. People see people on TV. They make a snap decision about who's sexy. Yeah, people might be voting for who they want to fuck."[23]

Amid this jumble of earnestness and jocularity, photographic spreads pop up like red-light districts. They serve as the centerpieces and most common features of many publications. The spreads are run in both black and white and color, featuring topless and fully nude male and female students. The students at times simply vamp for the camera. In other shots, they are shown simulating sexual activity with one or more partners of the same or opposite sex. And occasionally they are pictured engaging in their own sexual pleasure, through staged or what appear to be actual acts of masturbation that periodically include the use of sex toys such as vibrators and dildos. The settings for students' posed coitus or self-gratification are normally nondescript dormitory rooms or apartment bedrooms; identifiable on-campus and off-campus locations (frequently the university library); and other more anonymous milieus, such as a grassy park or deserted beach.

For an issue of *Vita*, staffers selected an empty indoor pool, featuring members of the university's Frisbee team posing, dry and in the buff, at the bottom in the style of old-world Greek statues. In an issue of *Boink*, by comparison, young models included: Kaz, a blue-haired white female wearing a dog collar and posing naked on a motorcycle and in front of a lake; Douglas, a brown-haired white male posing nude except for a pair of sunglasses in a bachelor pad; and Anna, an Asian female posing in a studio against a soft-gray backdrop and at various times sporting only a faux shirt, bra, and pants spray-painted onto her.[24]

Overall, the photographs are a mix of the intense, the inane, and the eccentric, with an emphasis on the latter. The model for such eccentricity: a tattooed, heavily pierced female student with shoulder-length black hair and the word "ardeo" (Latin for "I burn") scarred into her chest, who is featured naked in *Boink*'s debut issue with a large live snake coiled around her. *H Bomb* has similarly displayed alternative and just-plain-weird sexual spreads, including a nude male student in a soapy bath surrounded by bits of Froot Loops cereal; a shadowy nude female sitting cross-legged on an opened toilet; scantily clad women with seashells and starfish-shaped tape covering their nipples taking part in Coney Island's annual Mermaid Parade; and a single shot of a topless female cuddling in bed with a naked male wearing a horse head. The latter photo's title: "Stranger Than Life."[25]

Some spreads do paint clearer editorial pictures. For example, a prominent feature containing six photographs in a past *Sex Week at Yale* captured the sequence of a typical collegiate sexual encounter. The photographs show the progression of alcohol use, flirting, physical intimacy, and disrobing between a male and female student, noting the time at which each action occurred. In the concluding shot, labeled "2:02 A.M.," the couple is in bed, the woman sitting up and scratching her head, with a look of contented bewilderment on her face. The title of the spread: "Step-by-Step: A College Hook Up."[26]

Pornless Porn

"You can call it whatever you want." Seven words. Camilla Hrdy was distressed by those seven words more than almost anything else in her college career. Hrdy's *H Bomb* co-founder Katharina Cieplak-von Baldegg spoke the words nonchalantly in response to a question from the *Harvard Crimson* about how to define *H Bomb* to the public: "You can call it whatever you want."

In an interview two years after they were first spoken, Hrdy said the seven words still haunted her mainly because of the immense controversy and media attention they caused during the lead-up to *H Bomb*'s launch. In the end though, it was not Baldegg's comment that opened the floodgates of debate and almost caused the magazine to lose university approval. Instead, it was how the comment allowed critics and media outlets to define the magazine for themselves. And their definition, the real source of the controversy and identity crisis surrounding *H Bomb* and sex magazines in general, is not seven words long. It is one word: porn.

Pornography has long existed at a crossroads in American life. It is enjoyed obsessively and turns astounding profits. According to Ben Shapiro in *Porn Generation*, it rakes in "more than all the combined revenues of pro football, basketball, and baseball franchises, as well as the combined revenues of ABC, CBS, and NBC." At the same time, it is relentlessly attacked as degrading, immoral, and downright villainous. For example, after World War II, according to historian David Allyn, pornography in the form of stag films and underground bondage magazines was so widespread "some people felt it posed a greater problem to society than either Communism or narcotics."[27]

In the 1960s and 1970s, pornography in magazines and alternative newspapers became a form of countercultural protest. The pornographic film industry also skyrocketed, in part through the advent of the VCR and the popularity of sexually explicit VHS films. Porn feature films such as

Deep Throat and *The Devil in Miss Jones* became unparalleled crossover successes and cultural reference points. The films were symbolic of a larger societal mainstreaming of pornography, dubbed alternately "Porno Chic" and "The Porno Plague." In 1970, the report of the first Presidential Commission on Obscenity and Pornography shocked many in government by declaring the relative harmlessness of pornography and its potential benefits in increasing education and communication about sexual issues. The ultimate irony, according to Allyn: While denounced by President Nixon, "Americans rushed to buy copies of the controversial report."[28]

In the 1980s, the sexual revolution segued into the "Age of Guilt." The Moral Majority and entities such as the federal Meese Commission swept in a conservative stance toward sexual content deemed pornographic. The feminist movement continued to pour gasoline on their own flaming protests about pornography they perceived as misogynistic. AIDS spread quickly, and the hysteria surrounding it even quicker, coupling with a dramatic increase in cases of herpes, "the new Scarlet Letter." Sex was abruptly mixed with fear, uncertainty, and medical jargon out of place with once carefree foreplay and free love. Interestingly, as the decade came to a close, amid the sexual malaise cemented into the American psyche, the media's carnality increased. Icons such as Madonna, hit films such as *American Gigolo* and *Risky Business*, and a pornography industry booming through "premium networks" and VHS rentals presented sexual fantasies as breaths of fresh air, enabling the public to enjoy sex without the suddenly dangerous consequences.[29]

Beginning in the 1990s, porn became the norm. According to *Boston Magazine*, "American culture differs from Sodom's only by the fact that we have air conditioning. From low-rise jeans to MTV to the very existence of Jessica Simpson, it seems as if there's porn in our very groundwater." The principal medium connecting the mainstream public frequently, graphically, and wirelessly to soft and hardcore porn: the Internet. As a pair of characters in the 2004 Tony-award-winning musical *Avenue Q* converse in song: "The Internet is really really great / For porn / I've got a fast connection so I don't have to wait / For porn . . . / There's always some new site / For porn! / I browse all day and night / For porn! / It's like I'm surfing at the speed of light / For porn!"[30]

Pornographic sites lurk like pop-up ads, waiting to entice purposeful or accidental visitors. Gossip sites such as TMZ and PerezHilton.com post "news" involving celebrity sex tapes, nipple slips, and nude photos. Online erotica groups, fetishistic dating services, and even social networking sites enable everyday Americans to submit user-generated pornographic photos, videos, and stories featuring themselves or people they know. "Porn used to be relegated to a video hidden in the bottom drawer, or a magazine under the mattress," an Associated Press report noted. "Today, it's part of everyday life. Hugh Hefner's girlfriends have become TV's 'girls next door.' Porn stars have MySpace pages and do voiceovers for video games." Seminars and full college courses also now focus on pornography, its groundings, incarnations, and cultural influence. Pornography filming has even taken place on campuses in recent years, including at the University of California, Chico; Arizona State University; and Indiana University. In this respect, according to Pamela Paul, author of *Pornified: How Pornography Is Transforming Our Lives, Our Relationships, and Our Families*, "Porn is cool, porn is hip, porn is not something to get upset about on college campuses today."[31]

Yet, explaining that to the public, the press, and university administrators has been incredibly tough for student magazine editors. The main quarrels about the magazines' identities have long been pornographic in nature. From the publications' beginnings, the media and various critics have called many porn, a label or connotation that ironically rests at the heart of what most student editors are fighting to eradicate or, at the very least, to alter.

At Harvard, the initial proposal for *H Bomb* met with little resistance from the university's Committee on College Life (CCL), the governing body of Harvard student groups. The joint faculty-student board approved the publication by a twelve-to-zero vote, with two abstentions. Then came what the *Washington Post* called "the tsunami," what *Boston Magazine* referred to as a "media tornado," and what Hrdy said "was a wicked and wild time."[32]

For a February 2004 story on *H Bomb*'s CCL approval, Baldegg told a *Harvard Crimson* reporter she did not object to the magazine being labeled pornography and, according to Hrdy, said, "You can call it whatever you want." The ensuing *Crimson* article did just that, stating in the headline, "Committee Approves Porn Magazine." Stories in the local, national, and international print, online, and broadcast media soon followed. All played off the porn reference in the *Crimson* story, running pieces with headlines such as "Nudie Mag," "Naked Ambition," and "Mag Will Turn 'Em Crimson." The curiosity and criticisms surrounding *H Bomb* quickly spread across campus, triggering especially angry reactions from the university's conservative and religious groups. "No matter how you cut it, crop it, light it, or shade it, whether you publish it, print it, or just pick it up and read it, exploitation is still a denial of anyone's, and everyone's, dignity," said Reverend Mark D. W. Edington, a Harvard College chaplain, during a sermon prior to the magazine's premiere. "And it will still be true whether the *H Bomb* manages to, umm, go off, or simply turns out to be more dud than stud."[33]

Amid such critical sermonizing and sensational media spreads, Harvard administrators waffled, hinting in public statements that the magazine might not be approved after all. CCL called the editors to a follow-up meeting and told them approval was contingent on their avoidance of any "pornographic material" in the magazine. The committee also required a CD containing images that editors were considering for publication to be submitted for prior review. But no subsequent censorship occurred, the approval was ultimately upheld, and *H Bomb* received two thousand dollars in funding through university-approved grants. Student staffers and school officials also reached an agreement stating that no administrative oversight of editorial content would occur in the future and that editors had the right to deliver the magazine free to students.[34]

Even with the approval crisis averted, however, the media's application of the pornography label in preview pieces made the magazine "notorious before it ever existed." As Hrdy said, "It was frustrating because people rushed to these judgments and simply declared it pornography, calling it things like '*Hustler* at Harvard,' but didn't really look to see what we were trying to do with it. We didn't think about the pornography connection at all, and that was our biggest weakness. . . . In hindsight, we could have explained it more delicately, but we were just so excited about the idea we had." According to Hrdy and Baldegg, the planned nude photographs depicting Harvard students were a small part of the larger picture that they hoped the magazine would encompass. "We had one line about nude photo-graphs [in the proposal submitted to the CCL], and everyone assumed that would be the sole goal and purpose of the magazine—to parade Harvard's sexuality around," Baldegg said. "The real purpose was to have a verbal discussion of sex, because basically any intelligent discussion about it is really lacking from campus."[35]

A majority of founders and top editors similarly contend that student sex magazines are not meant to be ogled or viewed as "mere masturbatory material." The problem: Many student readers and pockets of the media do not see past the masturbatory angle, complaining that editors are fighting against the very identity of such publications by trying to make them something more. After the first set of prominent magazines debuted, critics pounced, reporting that the poetry, glossy photographs, complex headlines, and spirited editorials did not mask the infantile or titillating nature of the productions overall. They called the endeavors pornography-light, "art porn," "Ivy League pornography," "thinking smut," "smut rag[s] with extensive footnotes," "pornless porn," and "intellectualized soft-core porn, if there is such a thing." As the popular IvyGate blog noted about Columbia's *Outlet*, "Let's be honest here: the magazine's primary purpose is boobies. But it stumbles when trying to enhance them . . . with smug, belabored prose." The *National Review* was harsher, stating about student sex magazines in general, "It's one thing to engage in a bit of naughty publishing . . . on the university dime . . . but quite another to do so and pretend that it's something high-brow."[36]

The reality that critics miss: The students are not pretending. Editors describe their publications as more akin to art—art that is not just meant to arouse but to explore sex and sexuality, and present that exploration in a manner unique to their individual campuses. Student staffers and their supporters call their efforts "literature and arts magazine[s]," an "erotica review," "intelligent art," "literary erotica," "sex and sexuality journals," and magazines of "smut and sensibility."[37]

As former *Squirm* editor Sasha Albert said, "I think it's to make people think about sex. It's to stimulate them to ask the question, 'What do I think about sex? How do I think about it? What about it do I think about? What aspects of it are valuable or frightening to me?' . . . We try to feature content that makes people think. It's such a huge topic and we want to honor that and not just be like, 'Oooh, naked people!'" Kimi Traube, a former *Outlet* editor, put it more bluntly in an editor's note, writing, "This magazine is about discussion and exploration, not spreads of co-ed college buttporn. We're here to talk about buttporn, not to make it. So stop asking for it, and ask yourself instead: why is it acceptable to show sex, but not to talk about it?"[38]

To this end, the editors' principal goal is jump-starting conversations—about sex, sexuality, gender, love, intimacy, relationships, and the human body—regardless of the ultimate form they might take. As *Vita* founder Stephen Trevick said, employing two animal analogies, "Look, it's a great time in this country. I mean, everybody's screwing like rabbits. But at the same time . . . I think people have a huge fear of sex. You can do it, but you can't talk about it publicly right now without somebody either giggling or clamming up like a turtle in its shell. It has this crazy barrier around it. We wanted to break that barrier down. We wanted to start a real conversation. If we gave somebody a hard-on, we were happy for them, but that wasn't our primary purpose."

From its start, *Boink* remained the exception. In Oleyourryk's words, the magazine was founded to be "user-friendly porn." Co-founder Christopher Anderson similarly said, "We're not afraid to call it porn. If we turn people on, get people off, get them excited, that's okay. That doesn't make it bad. Trying to pretend it isn't pornography we feel is just intellectually dishonest."[39]

Art or porn? The competing classifications, criticisms, and calls to arms surrounding the question ultimately sum up magazines' most defining collective identity: the lack of a single, coherent one. As former *Vita* editor Stephanie Mielcarek asked, "Are we artistic or pornographic? It's obviously a fine line to draw. You know, what's the difference between publishing this magazine and going out and performing lewd acts in the street?" *X-Magazine* editor Alana Burman said that identity should not even be an issue under discussion. "A debate over being either porn or art misses the main point," she said. "It's too this-or-that. I mean, why can't we be a little bit of both or something else entirely?" Or in the words of *H Bomb*'s Katharina Cieplak-von Baldegg, *"You can call it whatever you want."*

Contribution, Not Quality

Beyond the pornography-versus-art question, the most enduring debate among readers, editors, and the media centers on the magazines' larger purpose within the campus press and student social scene. After their premieres, the criticisms came first, and sounded the loudest, with media reports dismissing early publications as superficial, trite, crude, and irrelevant. Various sources called the content overall nothing more than "repurposed term papers," "dense treatises," "vaguely intellectual under-graduate musings," and "predictable collegiate stuff: erotic poetry, some saucy doodles and ponderous essays." The magazines' layouts also have been appraised as amateurish—a valid assessment. Many publications are beset with awkward formatting, extra or missing periods at the ends of sentences, missing words, improper verb tenses, and superfluous white space.

As a letter to the editor in *Boink*, written by a young Boston University alumnus, noted, "Freedom of speech, sexual liberation, I'm all for it. But a magazine with bad photography, laid out in a way that makes readers more nauseous than horny? Absolutely not." Even *H Bomb*'s faculty adviser, Harvard psychology and evolutionary biology professor Marc Hauser, sounded a note of dissatisfaction with the magazine's initial efforts. "It hit the ground with all this big fanfare, but it didn't really do its thing," he said. "Stylistically it succeeded, but everyone felt it didn't really succeed in terms of content, that's where it fell flat."[40]

The editors, in many cases, own up to the critiques. "In the end, we're not going to be perfect," said Alana Burman. "I mean, we're students, we're trying, we're learning as we go. If we can get people talking or thinking about sex and sexuality in a new light then we've accomplished our goal. It's about the contribution, not quality." In this respect, even amid their scattered flaws, spots of amateurishness, and regular tumbles into territory all too clichéd, the magazines do impart a lasting contribution to student readers and advance sexualized media messages in a number of significant ways.

First, along with college newspaper sex columns, the magazines exist as the most personal, comprehensive records of modern students' sexual thoughts and experiences. Former *H Bomb* editor Martabel Wasserman described the magazines as "sexual scrapbooks," each one chronicling a specific sexual environment at specific moments in time. "The magazine is really nothing more than an arbiter of what's on students' minds, sexu-ally speaking," said *X-Magazine* founder Kristi Nigh. "The content since the beginning has not really been seen as groundbreaking to students, because, well, we're living it." *Squirm* co-founder Barnett Cohen similarly said that the key component of the magazine's creation was its location at the epicenter of Vassar's sexual scene. "A lot of students come to a place like Vassar and are free more than at other schools, from what I've heard from friends, to explore—explore your sexuality, drinking, drugs, your identity, a whole host of things," he said. "I think *Squirm* was in line with that exploration. . . . At the time *Squirm* really stood as the apotheosis of what students at Vassar were talking about and living and aching for day by day."

Magazines are also significant for their portrayal of *real* students, away from what one editor called "the all-too-perfect, airbrushed fantasy worlds of *Playboy* and *Maxim*." More specifically, along with the expected slew of tanned, thin, and physically attractive models, many students featured in magazine photographs possess imperfections—visible body hair every-where, excess weight, pimples, scars, piercings, tattoos, sweat stains, throbbing veins, glasses, birth control patches, a general paleness, ratty clothes, and a vulnerability in certain poses that make it appear as if they are almost afraid of being so exposed. "We really wanted to show a lot of body diversity," said *Squirm* co-founder Deva Kyle. "We had a spread with this woman who was over two hundred pounds. We wanted to be inten-tional about diversity . . . with real students, all shapes, all sizes." As a whole, the slate of models appearing in the magazines would not be judged unattractive as much as simply ordinary. The *New York Times Magazine* offered the keenest observation, noting that students featured in *Boink* specifically were "fit and fresh-faced but hardly all homecoming kings and queens." As *Boink* co-founder Alecia Oleyourryk similarly said, "You might see the model on page seven in biology lab tomorrow, or the guys in photo spread number two at the bar."[41]

Playboy first adopted the "girls next door" approach not long after its launch in the 1950s, purporting to show "fresh, wholesome [women] from the byways of ordinary American life." To this end, unknown amateurs often mixed with professional models as Playmates in early issues, including an airline stewardess, a telephone operator, and *Play-boy*'s own subscription manager—who agreed to pose in exchange for an Addressograph machine to lessen her workload. Yet, the supposed genu-ineness of their images was still closer to "an erotic vision," one that was put together through painstakingly posed shots meant to look natural, inflated or outright fictitious accompanying biographical information, and women whose "ordinary" beauty was still beyond most men's reach. "After all, a vast majority of young American women were not *that* pretty, *that* healthy, *that* well-endowed, or, to be honest, quite *that* enthusiastic about sex," historian Steven Watts confirmed. "The Playmate as represented . . . was the fantasy of the girl next door." In the age of Photoshop, this fantasy has continued. Women's and men's magazines regularly sport cover models slimmed, dimpled, tanned, coiffed, and outfitted to a level of perfection that is almost as laughable as the exclamatory headlines laid out beside them.[42]

By comparison, students appearing in campus sex magazines are the reality. A majority even pose without a stylist's touch-up, with little or no makeup, and, prior to publication, without the application of Photoshop tools to erase or blur out flaws. In this sense, their images represent a visual protest against the airbrushed-pornography era, enabling students to flip through pages filled not just with fantasy beauties but also reflections of themselves. "The last frontier may well be what *Boink* is peddling: naked pictures of people you know," the *Boston Globe* declared. "If not literally the girl next door, then at least the one you've spotted across the lecture hall in Psychology 101." *Boink*'s Christopher Anderson said, "We are proud of the fact that we feature average people and that they are not perfect. You know, real people. So, students can pick it up and literally wonder if they'll see someone they know. The allure is in their attainability."[43]

Magazines also highlight the sexuality of smarter students or what Mielcarek called "the geek squad." Photo spreads attempt to portray a marriage between sexuality and intellect and to satirize the perceptions that separate the two in the public mind. This interlocking of sexiness and intelligence is most epitomized by a photo shoot for *Vita* that resulted in a spread called "Classroom Fantasies." Editors said that student models posed provocatively in academic settings and then actually completed their homework during breaks in the shoot. In past issues, *Vita* has also run a regular feature on its inside cover called "Hot Girls Reading Books," which displays photographs of scantily clad female students engrossed in highbrow literature. For example, in the spring 2005 issue, an amply endowed, corset-wearing young woman is pictured in bed seemingly enraptured by Adam Smith's *The Wealth of Nations*. Meanwhile, a photo spread in *H Bomb*, "Labcoats and Lingerie," worked to show the sexy side of female scientists, while simultaneously alluding to the controversy surrounding the comments of then university president Lawrence Summers about the genetic incapacity of women to achieve at the highest levels in the sciences.[44]

The magazines' other pronounced realism push has come in the form of intimate revelations, or a concerted effort to reveal students' true sexual philosophies, insecurities, and quirks. As Oleyourryk said, "Sadly, there are few formal forums for people our age to share their sexual experiences and to learn from others who are on the same journey." Most magazines are submissions-based, publishing content created mainly by students, alumni, and staffers at their host schools. Issues represent what editors call "a safe space," allowing students to divulge their most lighthearted or heartrending sexual memories and to ask private questions about their sexualities, sexual activities, and the sexual issues most pertinent to the modern college crowd.[45]

Squirm editor Sasha Albert recalled one humorous example. "A guy a couple of years ago wrote instructions on auto-fellatio [the act of performing oral sex on yourself]," she said. "Clearly, this was something he valued and wanted to share. And where else would he have to talk about it? A lot of people wouldn't go around to their friends, saying, 'Hey, I figured this out. Want to try it?' He wrote about why he decided to try doing it, how he figured out how to make it work, why it's important to him, and, well, why he made all that effort to bend himself into strange shapes." Separately, in a confessional published in *Quake*, a student revealed her conflicted feelings about wanting to engage in sadomasochistic sexual behavior. As she described her thoughts while on a date with a male student, "Honestly, what self-respecting woman would want to be bent over a man's knee, have the clothing removed from the tenderest part of her body, exposed, vulnerable, and submit herself to the sting of his slap, over and over until the pain washed over her and made her beg. . . . Oh god. I would. All in a moment I realize I wouldn't mind if he grabbed me by the hair and forced me over his knee, or led me to my desk and bent me over. I'm thrilled at this idea, and ashamed that I'm thrilled, and ashamed that I'm thinking on it for so long."[46]

X-Magazine's most prominent revelation since its debut has come in poster form. As part of a past issue's theme, "Reveal Yourself," seventeen anonymous students appeared naked on the cover. Their nude bodies were partially obscured by poster boards that divulged a specific sexual secret each had never before shared with the world. One male student wrote on his poster that he secretly was attracted to both women and men. A female student pictured nearby wrote in red marker, "I like the way my vulva looks." Another female wrote she was no longer afraid to admit that she masturbated. "It was a horrible rainy day, like right before midterms," Burman said, recalling the related photo shoot. "We were in this sort of off-distance building . . . stopping people outside and begging them to come inside and take their clothes off and write their sexual secret on a poster board. You know, the usual. Well, we ended up getting people to come in, and we had a little party and snacks and music and people drawing their stories and getting naked. . . . I think it was really freeing for people and got a lot of people talking around campus."[47]

Apart from a reliance on such personal revelations and a larger push toward "gritty realism," the magazines are praised for their adoption of a more comprehensive sexual perspective than mainstream predecessors such as *Playboy*, *Cosmopolitan*, *Penthouse*, *Hustler*, and *Maxim*. Simply put, hetero is not normative in student sex magazines. Instead, there is an all-comers approach to the presentation of sexual activity. Many editors describe the publications' perspective as pan-sexual, omni-sexual, and sex-positive. For example, in a past *Sex Week at Yale*, a report headlined "Wo/Man's Room" focused on the difficulty transgender students faced in selecting appropriate restrooms on campus. "It's tough to find a bath-room that's right for you when your image falls somewhere between the triangle-skirted woman and the square-shouldered man that hang on restroom doors," the piece's writer noted, adding that wrong choices by students in the past led to arrests, assaults, and "shifty stares or abrupt exits from other students who don't understand what it means to be trans."[48]

Similarly, nude and erotic photographs of both women and men, some engaged in homosexual activity, repeatedly appear in the magazines' pages. It is an editorial decision that many readers and news media describe as the most visible, dramatic shift toward equal-opportunity sexual empow-erment. As *Boston Magazine* noted about *Boink*, "Next to the expected images—blondes twisted in lingerie, blooming breasts . . . are pictures of pantless men, some of them enjoying one another. The effect is disorienting, like walking through an orchidarium and into a butcher's shop." For example, on the much-debated cover of the second issue of *H Bomb*, two males and one female student are shown sexually entangled in a bed wearing only their undergarments. The males are engaged in a passionate kiss, while the forgotten female in the middle gazes into the camera, lips puckered, hair askew, and eyebrows arched. "I just *loved* that cover," Hrdy said. "It's literally an in-your-face stare-down and kind of a call to arms, you know, that the rules of sex are changing."[49]

In early issues of *Boink*, about half the photographs depict fully nude men. Some are simply posing and others are engaged in pantomimed foreplay or sexual activity with members of the same or opposite sex. A student in the second issue is even shown in a series of photographs masturbating to orgasm with what appears to be his seminal discharge visible on his chest in the final shot. Anderson said the decision to feature male models cost *Boink* financially, but fit with the magazine's deeper purpose. "We [co-founders Anderson and Oleyourryk] just both thought sex was for everyone," he said. "Obviously, it's a controversial decision because a lot of people, especially some straight males, don't appreciate turning the page and seeing it [a picture of a nude man] and are turned off by it. Commercially it probably wasn't the smartest thing we could have done. We just really didn't want to put out yet another men's magazine."[50]

The decision has earned respect in unexpected circles for its political correctness. The past president of the Boston University Women's Center, an on-campus feminist organization, told the *New York Times Magazine*, "What really stood out is that there were male students in it. . . . Because there were men in it, and gay men, under the same cover, it was sort of alternative. It kind of equalized it: gay men could look at it, women could look at it, and that was great."[51]

In the end, the magazines' most prominent sex-positive stances are embodied by their titles. Swarthmore's short-lived *! Mag* was exclamatory in its promotion of sex in all forms. *Redlight* at Canada's McGill University is named after Montreal's famed red-light district, symbolizing a sentiment summed up by magazine founder Nessie Giovanna in three words: "Yay for fucking!" *Open* at Rice and *Unlocked* at Wesleyan University are overtly calling for greater sexual freedom and expression.

Meanwhile, *Squirm* co-founder Barnett Cohen said his father originally suggested the magazine's name, in part as a play on his reaction when Cohen first told him about it. According to co-founder Deva Kyle, "We wanted people to ask themselves why something like this would make them squirm. We wanted this to just be normal. This is not something to squirm about. This is human sexuality." A note to readers in the preview issue of *Quake* at Penn similarly shared, "To us, *Quake* is more than a pun of our school mascot [the Quaker, a pacifist religious figure]—the verb represents a feeling about intelligent sexual discourse that we feel needs to be engaged. To 'quake' means to tremble before strong emotions—and most of us never quite get over our insecurities, complexes, and fears about sex. By providing a forum . . . to discuss sex, we hope to . . . provoke honest self-exploration that will strengthen the Penn community as a whole."[52]

The X in *X-Magazine*, by comparison, is meant to exist as a blank slate, a general classification that can be filled by whatever form of sex or sexuality a student wants to adopt. "It was a play on the idea of X-rated, to sort of entice people," said Nigh, "but it was also just sort of like, 'Place anything here,' instead of the X. It was a way to encompass everything." And, according to editors, the title *H Bomb* is not an allusion to the infamous weapon, but a riff on a well-known, discomfiting Harvard rite of passage. In Hrdy's words, "When you drop the 'H Bomb,' it's the moment where you have to say you go to Harvard." As she explained:

When someone asks a Harvard student, "Where do you go to school?" for some people there's always an awkward pause before you have to be like, "I go to Harvard." It's complicated because usually the person then hates you or they'll be intimidated or start asking tons of questions. Whatever their reaction, it inevitably changes everything about how a person perceives you, so dropping the H Bomb is, like, this legendary stage of awkwardness for people. So, the title choice is meant to connect this awkward moment that all Harvard people experience with the only thing that seems even more awkward and something people *really* don't want to talk about or can imagine happening, which is the idea of Harvard people actually being interested in sex.

Similar to *H Bomb*, most magazines are still in their infancy, beholden more to a small, impassioned set of individuals than a long-term outpouring of support or staff infrastructure. At some universities, there is skepticism that the publications will survive far beyond the graduation of their founding editors. And the total number of issues put out by the magazines combined is still small, leading a few student editors to joke that the number of column inches focused on them in news reports far exceeds the amount they have actually created with the publications themselves.

The small number of issues and the irregular publication schedules of certain magazines prompted *Playboy* in October 2007 to already present the story of the phenomenon in the past tense in a short feature headlined "The Rise and Fizzle of the College Sex Mag." The concerns cited by the piece at the time were accurate, but the fizzle forecast is shortsighted. Many magazines continue to publish or have plans in place to start again soon. And additional magazines are regularly joining the initial set, at the rate of about one or two per year, confirming students' desire to take greater ownership of their sexual messages. "Just the fact that we exist is this huge victory," said *H Bomb*'s Hrdy, now a Harvard alumnus. "We're young, but that doesn't mean we don't have intelligent thoughts about sex and obviously important decisions to make related to it. For years, everything's been dumped in our face by the media. They tell us what it means to be young and sexual and wanting to explore. Well, it's our bodies, our sexualities, you know, our sex lives. So, with the magazine, we're just taking back what's ours."[53]

My College Paper Was Not Like That!
The Journalistic Legacy
of the Student Sex Column

> That some of this information . . . makes some of our readers uneasy is absolutely no justification for censoring or limiting it. Quite the contrary, if the language and subject matter are causing a stir among readers, it may mean that we are stretching beyond the bounds of the mundane and truly reaching an unexplored but powerful issue.
>
> STAFF EDITORIAL
> *"Free Speech . . . And Sex,"* Flat Hat, *February 24, 2006*

McLean Robbins wanted student readers to know one thing during the two years she wrote the "She Said" sex column for the *Old Gold & Black* at Wake Forest University: She had no interest in their genital warts, venereal diseases (VD), or erectile dysfunction (ED). "There was this whole vibe out there that I was supposed to be an expert, a sexpert of some sort," she said. "You know, that I could identify on sight every type of VD in the book and spout out cures for ED from memory or, like, be able to tell students what's up with their genital warts." Her reaction: "I don't know what's up with your genital warts! My father's a physician, so if I wanted to know what was up with genital warts, I'd ask him, or I'd call an ob-gyn. . . . I'm not an expert. I don't want to be one. It was like, 'Sorry, I'm just a college student.'" The start of Erin Kaplan's first *Michigan Daily* sex column began with a similar apology. "I regret to inform you," the piece stated. "I must preface this first column by saying that you should not, under any circumstance, listen to me. I know nothing. I have had one short-lived and not very fulfilling relationship and a few not-so-romantic one-night stands. I know little about sex and even less about love or relationships. I have no idea what the hell I'm doing."[1]

A small number of columnists do back up their sexpert status with a traditional set of qualifications. For example, Kathy Greaves began writing "Ask Dr. Sex" for the *Daily Barometer* while a doctoral student and instructor in human sexuality at Oregon State University, continuing after she earned her degree. On the East Coast, Yvonne Fulbright wrote "Sexpert Tells All" for New York University's *Washington Square News* while a doctoral candidate in international community health education. It built on her master's degree in human sexuality education and special recognition she received from the U.S. surgeon general. Meanwhile, in her first "Sex and Balances" column for the *Cavalier Daily* at the University of Virginia, Lisa Hermann joked that as a fourth-year medical student she had become used to serving as a source of "free medical advice" to family, friends, and hospital patients. Other columnists tout relevant experience as peer health educators and through academic concentrations in human sexuality, sexual health, medicine, and gender studies.[2]

In general, however, according to the Associated Collegiate Press, "most of the sex columns are written by student journalists or columnists who don't have, other than their own dating experience, any clinical training in sex education." This admittedly deficient knowledge base is at the crux of everything columnists champion as right and critics decry as wrong with sex column content. In the latter camp, the disapproval focuses on the potentially harmful ramifications of inexpert students providing misinformation, relying on outdated stereotypes, and, as a press report noted, "playing loose with the facts and not doing their homework." Critics call columnists "non-professional novices," "baby pundits," and "undergraduate imitators" of sex and health experts such as Dr. Ruth and established social advice mavens like Dan Savage and Candace Bushnell. "An important difference, though, separates Dr. Ruth and Bushnell," the *Atlantic Monthly* reported. "The writer of a college column usually has little experience and no special knowledge. . . . And that's where the columnists come in—putting up a brave front, pretending to knowledge and experience that they don't necessarily have."[3]

Students' main counter to the criticism: There is no fronting of any kind. As embodied by Kaplan's column confession and Robbins's anti-genital declaration, most student writers passionately flee from the sexpert label like Carrie Bradshaw from fake Fendi purses. "I'm no sexpert," announced *Columbia Spectator* columnist Miriam Datskovsky. "Dr. Drew [Pinsky] is a sexpert. The women who wrote *Our Bodies, Ourselves* are sexperts. I write a sex column for a college newspaper. Despite the research I do— and by research I mean procrastinating at Starbucks while reading *The Idiot's Guide to Amazing Sex* for the entire world to see—there is a lot I still don't know, and might never know, about sex." *Temple News* columnist Nadia Stadnycki wrote in similarly sarcastic fashion, "As much as I enjoy drawing dirty pictures on bar napkins and intimidating people with crude gestures, you won't get any anatomical sex ed from me here. I'm just not qualified."[4]

Interestingly, throughout history, a majority of professional advice columnists, even those most famous and synonymous with sage wisdom, have similarly disclosed their lack of formal qualifications. For example, according to David Gudelunas in *Confidential to America*, Esther Lederer, the writer of "Ann Landers," "has always been very straightforward about the fact that she is not trained in psychology or any other science." Dan Savage once similarly wrote, "I can't claim to have any 'real' qualifications." Carolyn Hax, the writer of the popular *Washington Post* syndicated advice column "Tell Me About It," also admitted, "I am not a doctor or psychologist or trained observer/opiner of any sort. I write a newspaper column regardless . . . and I am aware this is a semi-weekly act of gall on my part. I've maintained since the beginning that I have no more experience than your next-door neighbor." In general, Gudelunas writes, "Although the advice column genre may have shifted in tone, the self-perceived role of the columnist has remained unchanged. Columnists are not professionals, just someone who can listen like a friend and give advice like a third-party observer."[5]

While similarly amateurish or average, student columnists' main advantage over older, wiser, and perhaps more sexually experienced adult advice givers: They are regularly invited to the parties—and the beer pong tournaments, barhops, frat rushes, football pregame mixers, spring break weeks, and summer road trips. They are not simply outside observers, but active participants with a firsthand presence in the same sexual and social universe that their student readers inhabit. Instead of medical degrees, therapy licenses, or formal sexual health backgrounds, the students' entrenchment in what one columnist called the "sex, love and rock 'n' roll world" of their generation is what most qualifies them to discuss the accompanying social scene and students' concerns within it. "Absolutely, it's location, location, location," said former *Red and Black* sex columnist Lauren Morgan. "We're in the trenches with other students. We see the world they see, you know, more than any outsider could. When we write, students can identify with us, with what we're saying. They can say, 'This is someone like me, writing about me.'"[6]

A majority of columnists constantly mine story ideas from social gatherings, dorm root chats, classes, phone calls, e-mails, instant messaging sessions, and acquaintances, including family members, friends, roommates, teammates, co-workers, sorority sisters, and significant others. Several keep journals with them at all times or have open files on their computers to type notes from sex-centric conversations that play out nearby and seem worth a mention in print. As former *Emory Wheel* sex columnist Haley Yarosh recalled, "That was always the big thing, things being 'column worthy.'"

For former *Daily Californian* "Sex on Tuesday" columnist Mindy Friedman, the column-worthy ideas flowed late at night from the drunken mouths of residents who stumbled into the dorm in which she worked as a security assistant. Former *Rebel Yell* columnist Lindsay Johnson solved her "idea droughts" by phoning friends and saying simply, "Oh my God, give me an idea. What's going on in your sex life?" As former *Arizona Daily Wildcat* columnist Caitlin Hall shared, in a sentiment echoed by many, "When I was a political columnist, nobody ever had story ideas for me, but when you're a sex columnist even the most casual acquaintances always have ten different ideas for you and they become really eager to talk about their own sex lives."

Extending from others' eagerness, columnists also turn to their own sex, relationship, and life experiences for substance. For example, former *Tartan* sex columnist Jenna Hall at Radford University once wrote that she was happy with her boyfriend's penis size. Jessica Ramsey Golden, a former sex columnist at the University of Alaska, Anchorage, wrote about her pregnancy. Onetime *Bottom Line* columnist Amanda Baldwin at Frostburg State University wrote about the embarrassment of being caught by her boyfriend's parents while having sex, sans clothes. In the *Heights*, Boston College's Anna Schleelein openly recounted an embarrassing run-in with airport security, who mistook an electric toothbrush in her suitcase for a vibrator or other pulsating sex toy. And *Temple News* columnist Nadia Stadnycki once even wrote about a breakup with a fiancé. "I recently was left with an engagement ring I'd gotten that, to make a long story short, isn't being used anymore," said Stadnycki in spring 2005. "So I wrote a column literally asking people what to do because I couldn't seem to make a decision." More generally, *Michigan Daily*'s Erin Kaplan called her columns "a catalogue of my experiences and the experiences of my friends."[7]

The columnists' peer status enables them to present their social and sexual catalogues to students in an accessible manner that cannot be matched by a parent sex talk or health center pamphlet, and is not being delivered enough in schools during most students' formative years. In respect to the latter, health experts and columnists describe a sexual education system stunted by a lack of funding; sterilized by conservative politicians, parents, and schools; and undercut by antiseptic teaching resources, ineffective educators, and required "'non-discussions' of sexuality" focused only on abstinence. "The reality . . . [as to] why more of these columns are springing up is that students know that they were left out, misinformed in high schools, where you have so little good sex education," said Sandra Caron, a professor of family relations and human sexuality at the University of Maine. Jennifer Bass, communications director for the Kinsey Institute, similarly noted, "In the past five years, we've seen an explosion on campus of this [sex columns]. Despite the barrage of sex images, there is very little information for students out there, and they are confused. They want help."[8]

Columnists agree with these assessments. "There was a lot of misinformation floating around in high school and a lack of information presented to students about things we should be learning about," said Lane Taylor, a former sex scribe for the *Grizzly* at Ursinus College. "Like, I only first learned that STDs could be transmitted through oral sex thanks to an 'ER' episode." Erin Riedel, a former sex columnist for the *Daily Cardinal* at the

University of Louisville, likewise noted, "I do feel like the way sex education plays out in the public schools, you're *not* learning anything in high school and you come to college completely clueless about this stuff. You know, I remember, my first UTI [urinary tract infection]. I had no idea what it was and it really goddammed hurt. And it's important for people to know about that stuff."

Along with providing knowledge missing from the classroom, the columns are also much more effective at connecting with students than the many adult-speak attempts in outside media. Among the high-profile efforts columnists cite as inauthentic or inadequate: Tom Wolfe's collegiate-behind-the-scenes opus *I Am Charlotte Simmons*; occasional student sex and socialization reports in newspapers and magazines that base their findings on statistics, a small sampling of student interviews, and a few nights of observation; middle-of-the-road sex and relationship advice smeared onto the pages of mainstream newspapers and within television talk shows helmed by figures such as Dr. Phil and Sue Johanson; and faux-hipster media personalities such as Dr. Drew Pinsky.

By comparison, Tufts University Health Service medical director Margaret Higham said, "Students are often able to say things in a way that gets other students' attention." According to Abi Medvin, a former sex columnist for the *Dartmouth*:

I think it's definitely different when you have one of your peers writing about what you're going through every day versus an older figure who, like, went through it back in the day but doesn't truly know what's going on now and how things work and what's acceptable and what's not and what the issues are that we're facing. You know, some things never change, but the nuances are very different. To have the voice of one of your own talking about sex and love and life nowadays is a vastly superior product than what an outside adult could muster.[9]

This sense of peer superiority extends to the main issues addressed in the columns: student concerns that are social, not simply medical, in nature. Sarah Brown, CEO of the National Campaign to Prevent Teen and Unplanned Pregnancy, said:

The reason I think these columns are valuable is that young people's questions and concerns about sex and love and relationships often go so far beyond the medical. This is not just a conversation about body parts. . . . The questions are more sort of attitudinal and behavioral. Things like, 'How should I feel about hooking up with three different guys in one weekend?' or 'I'm a girl and I accidentally had sex with a girl last night and now I'm just like out of my mind.' And I think with some legitimacy students are saying that the notion you're going to get this figured out with somebody who's forty-seven [years old] is off the mark.

In this respect, the opinions about sex and socializing that columnists form through their own experiences, however limited or baffling, resonate with students in a manner that experts outside college are unable to grasp. "I think one of the central things to being a successful sex and relationships columnist in college is that you actually have to be in a state of confusion," said former *Hoya* sex columnist Julia Baugher. "As crazy as it sounds, that way it's more real. It's an actual person dealing with an actual subject."

To this end, columnists represent a new breed of sexperts—individuals who do not just admit their ordinariness but literally tout it as the epitome of their expertise. "What I brought to the table was a *lack* of experience," former *Harvard Independent* columnist Katie Giblin said. "Just that every-thing was new, I was seeing things through new eyes, so I thought that would be relatable to students." Caitlin Hall agreed, noting, "With my columns, I'm not sure you would want somebody who had dated or had sex with a million different people already, because part of the focus was on the awkwardness of sexual relationships and you can't really be an expert and still comment knowledgably on that awkwardness."

• • •

Dave Franzese's penis penned his first sex column. Introducing himself as "Little Joe Namath," the genital appendage explained that he was asked to fill in for Franzese to offer a unique perspective. "I've been Dave's penis for all of his life . . . peeing, growing, shrinking, making girls laugh and generally enjoying my existence as a tiny wiener flapping around in the breeze. . . . [And now] here I am, the first penis to ever write a sex column. And there you are, the first group of people to ever read an article written by someone's genitals. What a historic Wednesday this turned out to be, right?"

Franzese, the former "Wednesday Hump" columnist for the *Daily Nexus* at the University of California, Santa Barbara, turned to his "zipper muse" for inspiration after a prolonged bout of writer's block left him stumped about how to begin his debut column. His brainstorm: Instead of directly introducing himself to readers, he would have his background provided by what he called "the man behind the fly." Within the column, "Dave's ding-dong" explained that Franzese preferred legs over breasts, the Rolling Stones over the Beatles, the froggy-style position for sexual intercourse, and, in celebration of completing his first column, "masturbated into a sock." In Franzese's words, "It was meant to be entertaining and make a small point about the lack of men writing and hopefully connect with people and make them laugh from the get-go. Was it actual journalism?" He paused for a moment, laughing. "That I don't know."[10]

Now in their second decade of mass popularity, sex columns have remained mainstays of many of the student newspapers in which they first appeared, under various titles and through different student writers. Their continuation is no small feat, considering they appear in a student media universe whose life-force has long been spurred by change—from new cultural trends to ever-shifting editorial staffs. "It's become an institution, a regular feature, you know, even if it's not always being run, it's definitely being talked about in editorial meetings and considered at the start of every year," said Franzese. "A few years ago, a column focused on sex just wasn't part of the discussion at all. Now, it's here to stay."

The columns have also spawned an increasing number of spin-offs, most prominently campus sex magazines, full-blown student newspaper "sex issues," and campus sex blogs such as Harvard student Lena Chen's high-profile effort, Sex and the Ivy. They have ascended to a stratosphere of popularity unmatched by much else in the history of the student press, and simultaneously have triggered some of the most significant, ferocious criticisms and free press fights within modern college media. Amid all the successes and furors, the question spurring Franzese's laughter remains the columns' chief legacy: Are they journalism? Debates abound in newsrooms, media reports, and letters to the editor about the relative journalistic value of the columns'"editorial intercourse." In the words of Caitlin Hall, "Yeah, it's sex, but is it news?"[11]

Critics call the columns "useless fluff," "a waste of ink and space," blatant pornography masquerading as reputable journalism, and a needless publicizing of matters best kept private. "I DON'T WANT TO HEAR ABOUT YOUR SEXUAL ENCOUNTERS. Period," a student reader wrote to one columnist. "What you do with your personal life should be completely separated from your professional life." A Boston College philosophy professor similarly wrote in a letter to the editor against a sex column in the *Heights*: "A college newspaper is not the proper place for a personal testimonial on the virtues, vagaries, and boundaries of oral sex. Some matters are intensely private; they are not 'dirty' or 'taboo' but, rather, too important and intimate to be paraded before strangers . . . A college newspaper is not the proper forum for a young person to wrestle with her sexuality." Or as a student wrote in response to a sex column in the *Oracle* at the University of South Florida, "It's really unnecessary and a bit uncomfortable. It's like going to your grandmother and asking her to tell you about her first sexual experience: You just don't do it."[12]

Detractors frequently go so far as to assert that the presence of a sex column in a student newspaper devalues all other content around it. In an op-ed, a Boston University student made a broader claim, arguing that a sex column "undermines all of college print journalism." A member of the student senate at Louisiana State University even formally asked his fellow senators to discontinue funding for the *Daily Reveille* due to the newspaper's printing of a sex column that he said offended the tenets of good journalism. According to the student objector, "The sex column does not have a place in a school newspaper, and readers do not see 'that junk' in the *New York Times* or *Washington Post*."[13]

It is most likely a symbolic assertion, but incorrect nonetheless. For more than one hundred years, sex and social advice columns have appeared in professional newspapers large and small. As Gudelunas shared in *Confidential to America*:

> For most of the twentieth century, advice columns collected and organized the thoughts, ideas, and words that weren't considered relevant to the other pages of the newspaper. Quite literally, the

modern question-and-answer "lovelorn" advice column began as the place where "non-news" went. Marie Manning [the writer behind the first U.S. newspaper social advice column, "Beatrice Fairfax"] was handed a stack of letters in 1898 that didn't seem to belong in the *New York Evening Journal* because they didn't contain substantive discourse. However, publishers and editors realized that people still wanted to talk about these topics, no matter how insipid they might have seemed. Crushes and kisses may not rank with assassinations and elections in terms of news value, yet for readers and writers these issues were more immediate and pressing to their everyday lives.[14]

College newspaper sex columns are the boldest, most pervasive caretakers of this tradition. The difference between the columns and the lovelorn pieces of old: What used to be considered non-news is now journalism. The columns embody the best of the student press's idealism and Journalism 2.0's accessibility, while simultaneously altering the boundaries of journalism as we know it. As the Poynter Institute's Al Tompkins wrote in an entry on his popular Al's Morning Meeting blog about the sex column phenomenon, "Something has changed in college newspapers." The entry's headline put it even more simply: "My College Paper Was Not Like That!" In the words of former *Post* sex columnist Brynn Burton at Ohio University, "My whole goal going in as a journalist was not to be the next Woodward and Bernstein and that's what they teach you to be. You know, 'This is news and this is serious.' . . . The column was kind of my way of saying journalism isn't just what they're teaching you, that you have to be the reporter at the typewriter with the pen behind your ear. You know, it's what you want it to be. It's personal, even sexual."[15]

In this spirit, columnists round up the most personal issues, acts, and thoughts and hurl them into the public domain with eye-opening abandon. They dare to proclaim that the most offensive and hushed words are now fit for mainstream teen and twentysomething consumption. They treat love and sex lightly, drenching columns in a sarcasm rarely seen in professional newspapers, even when tackling supposedly serious or taboo topics such as anal sex and STIs. They expose their innermost sexual selves to a depth that shocks old-school journalists and new media mavens alike. They dismiss the notion that age or inexperience should be a barrier to writing about activities in the bedroom and beyond, proving that young people can have passionate, intelligent discussions about sex and socialization.

Most significantly, they are the preeminent individuals helping to fill a deplorable gap in the news media's treatment of sex and relationships. In a 2003 review of mainstream news media sex coverage—one of the only appraisals of its kind—the Poynter Institute's Kelly McBride discovered that a majority of reports focused solely on sex crimes and sexual depictions within the entertainment media, which crop up mostly in features and reviews of fictional films, television shows, and books. "The mainstream secular media is mostly concerned with the sex lives of criminals and made-up people!" she wrote in a summary of her findings. "Is this how sex should be represented by mainstream newsrooms? Are we missing something in our coverage? . . . The state of sex coverage in America today: narrow and limited."[16]

Narrow and limited, except from students, in column form. The pieces set a wide sexual and social berth, transforming the everyday moments of student love and lust into newsworthy components of campus papers' overall content mix. "In no way is the News Record encouraging promiscuous sex," an editorial in the News Record at the University of Cincinnati noted. "We simply advocate the right for UC students to be informed about issues relevant to their lives, whether it be tuition issues, Clifton-area construction, Black History Month, Student Government initiatives, on- and off-campus events, the latest student band, or even sex." The pieces at times respect their place, providing a source of relief from the presentation of traditional news. "Our country is about to go to war," a Pitt News columnist wrote in October 2002. "There's a mad sniper shooting men, women and children in Maryland. Anthrax is a household word. To quote from the opening song of the sitcom 'Family Matters': 'You don't read any good news on the newspaper page.' So, why not a brief comment on the technique of oral sex, just for fun. Readers need more heated diversions than Beatle Bailey and crossword puzzles. Something to get the blood pumping. Remind them of the good things in life."[17]

Couched in between such fun is the columns' more serious side, a sexed-up version of public service journalism. Columnists cite many instances of meaningful outcomes precipitated by their pieces that go far beyond mere laughter or eight hundred words of entertainment. "For several years now,

The Flat Hat has published a weekly column that has, from time to time, angered and upset a portion of our readers," a staff editorial about Kate Prengaman's "Behind Closed Doors" column shared. It continued:

> Some have felt the column's inclusion in a weekly student newspaper is inappropriate, given its subject matter. . . . Some have asked us to remove the column, some have asked us to tone down its content and some have even suggested that the column is pornographic and thus is in criminal violation of decency standards. . . . In actuality, the Sex Column . . . performs a valuable service for the sexual health of our campus. Not only does it allow students and other readers to face and examine contemporary sexual taboos, but it also fosters informed activity over ignorance. In a time of peculiar need for widespread understanding and openness on matters of sexual health and safety, Ms. Prengaman's column is an invaluable resource.[18]

Former *Daily Campus* columnist Aly Murphy at the University of Connecticut recalled a particularly significant response to a piece she penned on herpes awareness, testing, and prevention. In the column, she shared the story of a friend who unexpectedly caught the STI the previous summer. In her words:

> The entire front page of the Focus section was covered with this huge spread, "Surviving with Herpes," and it caused a huge reaction on campus. . . . I remember we had a little café on campus, and everyone had the front page open to this story. They did the background in black, and the writing was actually white so it really, really stood out. And I was like, "Oh my God," looking at everyone reading it and talking about it. I mean, there it was in black and white. . . . A staffer at the student health center told me at one point, "Yes, let me tell you, we had students coming in that whole week, that whole month, asking about that column and asking if it was really true and wanting to get tested." She said it was such a huge eye-opener.

The most memorable response for Lauren Morgan came in the form of praise from an area rape prevention education coordinator about a column

Morgan wrote on rape awareness after a spate of on-campus sexual assaults. As Morgan recalled, "She wrote me a really heartfelt letter just basically saying, 'Thanks for doing this. This is the message that we're trying to get out every day of the week, and you did it in six hundred words with your column and we can't express how much we want to thank you for this.' And she told me she clipped it out and put it on her blackboard. I didn't realize I was impacting people that much. You know, I was thrilled. . . . That's really what journalism should be all about."

The columns also represent what the student press has long been about. College journalists, a researcher noted in 1971, "possess with their idealism . . . an opportunity which they will probably never again have in their lives—to be forthright, to be courageous, to be agitators in the best democratic tradition." Student sex columns are the modern agitators, enabling the campus press to continue challenging the status quo, defining new limits of good taste, and delving into an array of controversial issues that in the sexualized America of today cannot and should not be ignored. Collectively, the columns advocate a sexual utopia—one that is safe, consensual, nonjudgmental, impassioned, enlightened, empowering, and orgasmic, many times over. The pieces are tolerant of almost all sexual and social positions, posturing, and proclivities. The only stance with which they find fault: close-mindedness, in bed and in life.[19]

Ironically, since the columns' ascendance, many critics have contended that it will not be their divisiveness, but their popularity that will lead to their ultimate disappearance from campus newspapers nationwide. A growing amount of press coverage has characterized the columns as crazes whose media overexposure and rapid expansion is transforming sex from something private and mysterious into a topic that one report called as "titillating and fresh as microwaved lasagna." A *Boston Herald* columnist wrote, "I'm fearful that dissecting sex in the newspaper . . . is an excellent way of doing for sex what we have already done for globalization, Third World debt, Bosnia-Herzegovina and good cholesterol: make it boring. So let the college kids have their fun. Look, Ma! We're writing about sex in the newspaper! You'll just have to excuse Ma if her reaction is not righteous outrage but merely . . . Zzzzzzzzzzzzzzzzzz."[20]

The aside is witty, but shortsighted on two counts. First, students are not writing for Ma, but their peers—an ever fresh audience with no knowledge of what was written before they enrolled and an aching for sex, sex, sex. Second, sex sells, period. The universality of sex creates a buffer from overexposure and the subsequent reader indifference that accompanies media mania surrounding almost everything else. "Media critics . . . have talked about 'Katrina fatigue,' and 'Iraq fatigue,' and 'midterm election fatigue,' and so many other kinds of topics that the general population has simply lost interest in hearing about 24/7 for so long," wrote one former columnist who asked to remain anonymous. "But have any of them ever used the words 'sex fatigue'? I don't think so. . . . I think the very subject matter of these columns gives them a practically infinite shelf life, and I don't see the trend ending anytime soon—make that ever."

Similarly, in a statement echoed by many, former *Driftwood* sex columnist Wes Muller at the University of New Orleans said, "I think people just don't want to believe it. They want to go back to the old days . . . the clichéd 1950s sitcom, which is completely past. It's never going to be like that again. I think people just don't want to accept this outburst of sexual expression for what it is. . . . The sex column phenomenon is a revolutionary thing. It's the rebellion of the moment, and it's going to continue taking off and be huge for generations to come."

A Student Sexicon
Sexual Slang
in College Newspaper Sex Columns

Word fabrication is exactly the kind of power unique to a sex columnist.
NADIA STADNYCKI
"Come and Get It While the Gettin's Good,"
Temple News, *January 19, 2006*

The media have long held a prominent position in not only defining and normalizing different facets of sex and courtship, but also in creating and challenging the words used to identify them. Since the start of the sexual reform press in the 1870s, the media have been the principal catalysts behind the expansion of the country's sexual lexicon, or what *Harvard Independent* sex columnist Katie Giblin once called the "sexicon" ("The Harvard Sexicon," *Harvard Independent*, Apr. 29, 2004).

Over the past decade, college newspaper sex columns have coined or publicly solidified the largest amount and most varied set of words, acronyms, and euphemisms relevant to the modern student "sexicon." This sampling of terms has been culled from more than two thousand columns published since the trend's start in the late 1990s in more than one hundred student newspapers in the United States and Canada. It is the first known inventory of modern student slang focused on sex and social interaction that cites verified student sources, and builds on book-length collections of general student jargon published in the 1990s and 2000s, including Connie Eble's *College Slang 101* and Pamela Munro's *Slang U.: The Official Dictionary of College Slang*.

After-bad-sex moment (n.): an uncomfortable period between sexual partners following an unpleasant bout of sexual activity. Aka: the mourning after. (Bonnie Sultan, "The Mourning After: Surviving a Lame Shag," *GW Hatchet*, Oct. 18, 2004.)

After-sex smell (n.): a strong bodily scent accrued through intense sexual activity, comprising what *Lumberjack* columnist Claire Fuller called "perspiration, semen and vaginal fluids." (Claire Fuller, "Something to Think About," *Lumberjack*, Jan. 29, 2004.)

Air Jordan (n.): more commonly known as a queef. As *Post* columnist Brynn Burton wrote, it is a noise emitted from the vagina during sexual intercourse that is "odorless, spontaneous, virtually undetectable and unpreventable, but it produces a sound so vile, it has the ability to kill a night of serious lovin.'" Aka: coital cacophony, coochie fart, cunt trumpet, hiccup down below, little poonany "pffffffffffff," vaginal virtuoso, and vart. (Brynn Burton, "Vaginal, Um, Noises Worth Celebrating," *Post*, Oct. 17, 2002.)

All-American head push (n.): an aggressive downward shove on the head of an individual performing oral sex on a male. Example: "It's the worst of them all, the devil of bad manners. . . . We [women] know the act, you first rub our neck, next you massage our head, and then all of a sudden you push us down like a plunger in a toilet bowl. As much as you like it, we don't. As much as you think it will make the experience better, all it will get you is an abrupt stop." (Brynn Burton, "Maintain Bedroom Manners for Successful Sex," *Post*, Feb. 27, 2003.)

Angel of the morning (n.): a female completing what was traditionally known as "the walk of the shame." Aka: that girl. (Bonnie Sultan, "Who's That Girl?" *GW Hatchet*, Apr. 4, 2005.)

Anti-anals (n.): individuals against engaging in anal sex. As *Daily Californian* columnist Sari Eitches wrote, "Anti-anals have three objections: it's dirty, it'll hurt and it's gay." (Sari Eitches, "Entering the Exit Door," *Daily Californian*, Sept. 21, 2004.)

Anti-Vagina Day (n.): a reformation of Valentine's Day created by male students angry at women who broke their hearts. As *Hoya* columnist Julia Baugher quoted undergraduate men exclaiming, "'Everything that Valentine's Day stands for, Anti-V Day is against.' . . . 'No romantic dinners, no wine, no expensive jewelry!'" (Julia Baugher, "Don't Diss on Valentine's Day," *Hoya*, Feb. 7, 2003.)

Approach and avoid (n.): a complicated relationship game in which one partner alternates being extremely intimate and subsequently very standoffish, leaving the other partner confused about where the relationship stands. Aka: mixed-message romance. (See Elspeth Keller, "Saying Goodbye to Chutes and Ladders," *Daily Trojan*, Mar. 24, 2006; and Rose Afriyie, "Avoiding Mixed Message Sex," *Pitt News*, Sept. 6, 2005.)

ARF (n.): alcohol-related flaccidity of the penis during sexual activity. Example: "Boys, consider ARF nature's way of telling you that your penis, like heavy machinery, should not be operated when you're completely wasted." (Anna Schleelein, "A Lot to Be Thankful For," *Heights*, Nov. 26, 2002.)

Bangability vs. personality scale (n.): a comparison of an individual's physical attractiveness with his or her mental capacity and social traits. (Abi Medvin, "The Friday Quickie: Reaching Outside the Toolbox," *Dartmouth*, May 4, 2007.)

Basement hounds (n.): individuals socializing at darkened house parties who, according to *Dartmouth* columnist Abi Medvin, are "just looking to get laid." (Abi Medvin, "The All or Nothing Dilemma," *Dartmouth*, Feb. 16, 2007.)

Bathroom body cavity search (n.): a female's post-sex examination of her genitalia to find a used condom or other contraceptive possibly stuck along her vaginal wall. (Beth Van Dyke, "The Wednesday Hump: Race to the Bathroom," *Daily Nexus*, May 14, 2003.)

Beef jerky (n.): men's genitalia. Aka: Captain Happy, Denny Chimes, fluid friends, four-inch beast, George Gonads and his little Chicken McNugget, kalamata olives and feta cheese, penis pillow, Rocky Mountain oysters, and wolverine. (Nadia Stadnycki, "Talking Dirty for Dummies," *Temple News*, Oct. 4, 2005.)

Betty-Veronica syndrome (BVS) (n.): a simultaneous attraction to two separate types of women, alluding to the main female characters in the *Archie* comic. As *California Aggie* columnist Archie Garcia explained, "So many of us are guilty of the BVS that Archie suffered from. At parties, I can't help but sympathize for the intelligent, witty girl who spends half the night talking to a guy only to see him leave her as soon as a girl with large breasts walks by, wearing a shirt with an imaginary big flashing sign pointing to her overly exposed cleavage and giving him an alcohol-induced seductive smile." (Archie Garcia, "Betty-Veronica Syndrome," *California Aggie*, Nov. 18, 2003.)

Big hurrahs (n.): periods of excessive sex and celebration during an academic year, such as spring break and Halloween. As *Emory Wheel* columnist Haley Yarosh explained, "Big hurrahs may look like any other day on the calendar, but they are actually hours of temporary insanity that allow college students to run free." (Haley Yarosh, "Mouth to Mouth: Parties and Visitors Yield Similar Results," *Emory Wheel*, Nov. 16, 2004.)

Booty call types:

Accidental booty call: an unplanned sexual solicitation via a phone call, text message, or in-person chat, typically caused by drunkenness. Example: "Last week, my friend Rebekah came across an accidental booty call. After a couple reunions with Captain Morgan's Spiced Rum, Rebekah ran into the lips of an ex-boyfriend. He, too, felt the bite of the bottle and was led up the stairs to his apartment by the feisty Rebekah only to be tossed like a rag doll and rummaged, much to his own pleasure." (Erin Thomas, "Relationships: The Booty Call," *Daily Evergreen*, Sept. 7, 2005.)

Desperation booty call: a call or text soliciting sex made frantically to the first applicable person whose name shows up on an individual's mobile phone contacts list. (Archie Garcia, "Booty Calls," *California Aggie*, Feb. 17, 2004.)

Fantasy booty call: As *California Aggie* columnist Archie Garcia explained, "This is the girl who you would love to answer your drunken phone call. She never does. No matter how intoxicated you are, you would find a way to get there even if you have to run, bike or ride a shopping cart. If she only picked up. Which she never does." (Garcia, "Booty Calls.")

In-advance booty call: a call or text soliciting sex made prior to the start of an evening in which an individual plans to drink and be seeking late-night sexual activity. As *Heights* columnist Anna Schleelein explained, "This is when you call up a girl who you're reasonably attracted to, sober, at a relatively decent hour, and invite her over to 'watch a movie' later. (Yes, we do know that the translation of that statement tends to be, 'Hey I'd like to get in your pants.')" (Anna Schleelein, "'Booty Call' Blunders," *Heights*, Feb. 25, 2003.)

Mandatory booty call: a call or text supposedly soliciting sex to an individual to whom the caller is not actually attracted. This call is typically made as a favor to a friend or as a result of a relationship set up by mutual companions. (Beth Van Dyke, "You Get One Phone Call," *Daily Nexus*, Apr. 23, 2003.)

"My-balls-are-blue-just-thinking-of-you" call: a call or text soliciting sex that occurs the day after a pair's first bout of sexual activity, spurred by extreme sexual desire. (Van Dyke, "You Get One Phone Call.")

Old reliable booty call: a call or text soliciting sex to an individual who can be counted on to answer and who has been a guaranteed sexual conquest in the past. (Garcia, "Booty Calls.")

Week-after booty call: a call or text soliciting sex made after an extended period has elapsed since the initial bout of sexual activity. (Van Dyke, "You Get One Phone Call.")

Booty IM (n.): an online version of the traditional booty call made via an instant messenger program or through a social networking site such as Facebook. (Julia Baugher, "To Booty Call or Not to Booty Call—Is There Really a Question?" *Hoya*, Jan. 31, 2003.)

Born-again virgin (n.): an individual previously sexually active who decides to begin refraining from sex starting at a specific point in time, occasionally due to a religious conversion or a bad relationship breakup. Example: "You might be an involuntary born-again virgin if . . . 1. You walk past a construction site full of shirtless workers and wonder what they're building. 2. You see a used condom on the ground and mistake it for a balloon animal that's seen better days. 3. You eat a chocolate-covered banana without smirking. . . . 6. Your ideal date involves Scrabble, Monopoly or any game of cards that doesn't entail someone ending up naked. 7. You go more than three days without changing your underwear and it's not a cause for alarm. . . . 13. You really do read *Playboy* for the articles." (Nadia Stadnycki, "Determining Your Born-Again Virginity," *Temple News*, Nov. 1, 2005.)

Boyfriend season (n.): a time of year in which colder weather, homesickness, or stress forces students "under the covers, lights out, listening to sad music and longing to be spooned by a member of the opposite sex," according to *California Aggie* columnist Anna Ritner. (Anna Ritner, "All the Kids Are Doing It," *California Aggie*, Dec. 7, 2004.)

BT (ball torture) (n.): a range of activities that employ weights, leather straps, or chrome clips focused on causing pleasurable pain to the male testicular area. (Beth Van Dyke, "Guys Go Nuts When Ladies Go Balls Out," *Daily Nexus*, Feb. 19, 2003.)

Calientelingus (n.): a burning sensation in one's genital region caused by an individual's mouth being too hot while performing oral sex. Example: "A couple of my friends who are dating once told me about their trip to Mexico. One night . . . the guy . . . enjoyed a few shots of tequila; these were chased by a flavoring of peppers. . . . Horny, the boy marched home and greeted his girlfriend with a kiss on the lips—under the covers. While the girl appreciated the gesture, she did not appreciate that 'bad' burning sensation from the peppers exploding through her body. Screams escaped her mouth and within two minutes security was in her room trying to understand why her boyfriend gave such bad head. She gestured 'down there' and pointed to his tongue." (Daniel Crowder, "Laughing It Off," *Daily Northwestern*, Apr. 7, 2005.)

Carpe datem (n.): a variation on the traditional phrase "carpe diem" (Latin for "seize the day"). In this case, to "seize the date" means to more actively attempt dating instead of hooking up, and to engage in personal interactions with friends and relationship partners instead of relying on electronic means of communication. As explained by *Old Gold & Black* columnist McLean Robbins, "If you care to continue a friendship or instigate a relationship beyond the safe bounds of a computer or cell phone, carpe datem. Pick up the phone. Get off IM. Take your cell number off of Facebook. Make actual plans—ones that don't require electrical outlets." (McLean Robbins, "Electronic Communication Ruins Our Sex Lives," *Old Gold & Black*, Mar. 22, 2007.)

Cell phone trick (n.): a ruse to remember the name of a hookup partner the morning after sexual activity occurs. As *Review* columnist Laura Dlugatch explained, "When your hook-up wakes up, act so concerned you have their number correct [in your cell phone], even ask the spelling of their name. But you're SOL [shit out of luck] if she responds 'M-E-G.'" (Laura Dlugatch, "Post-Hook-Up Etiquette: How to Save Face," *Review*, Nov. 14, 2006.)

Cock block (n.): an individual or situation unintentionally or purposefully interfering with a student's attempt to engage in sexual activity. According to *Yale Daily News* columnist Natalie Krinsky, the four most common types of cock blocks:

Friends-don't-let-friends-drive-drunk cock block: "In this situation, a best friend swoops in to save one of the inebriated parties from Sunday morning mortification. According to my research, this is the most common type of cock-block."

Hard-knock cock block: "In this sort, a close friend approaches YOU and spills that he really likes the girl you're talking to. Your friendship is put to the test and you are forced to let your lady-killer skills slide."

Highway-robbery cock block: "After all those rounds of drinks, a Rico Suave, more intelligent (and more attractive) than yourself, has come over and slung his arm around YOUR girl. They are chatting like two old friends and you are left behind in the dust."

Inadvertent cock block: "This is the school of thought that takes advantage of the 'take one for the team' philosophy. The girl agrees to go home with you, on the condition that you find a buddy for her friend. One look at this 'friend' and you realize your chances are shot. The girl looks like the love child of Sideshow Bob and Missy Elliot." (Natalie Krinsky, "Friends: Don't Let Friends Cock-Block!" *Yale Daily News*, Nov. 15, 2002.)

Coffee shop and café scenario (n.): a traditional romantic date, described as basically nonexistent in the modern student social scene. Aka: "so Bogey and Bacall, so *An Affair to Remember*." (See Scott Gentry, "Ask the Wise Guy: The Red Damn Line," *Broadside*, Oct. 26, 2007; and Eve, "The Do's and Don'ts of Getting Some This Year," *GW Hatchet*, Feb. 12, 2007.)

College marriage (n.): a long-term relationship. Aka: Boyfriendland, cult of the boyfriend, declaration of codependence, land of monogamy, relationship town, and status of twoness. (Miriam Datskovsky, "No Dating: The Extremes Make More Sense Than You Think," *Columbia Spectator*, Apr. 11, 2005.)

Confirming the relationship talk (n.): As *Mustang Daily* columnist James Whitaker explained, "It is the inevitable conversation between hook-up buddies that ends in either the termination of the nightly booty calls or the beginning of an actual relationship." Aka: define the relationship (DTR) talk, relationship clarifying talk (RCT), "the talk," and the "where is this going" conversation. (James Whitaker, "The Relationship Clarifying Talk," *Mustang Daily*, Oct. 23, 2004.)

Dance floor erection (DFE) (n.): an erection experienced while dancing in public. Example: "Let me just introduce a situation in which the DFE might, shall we say, pop up. Lights are turned low. Add a little bass. Maybe a little strobe. Perhaps a booty cam for good measure. Feelin' it? Yeah you are. And you REALLY love this song. You're backing that ass up like it's your job. OOOH! And there's cute Bobby. . . . You start dancing with cute Bobby. . . . Bobby seems to love it: Whoa! What's that? Yup, that's right, it seems you have backed into, well, Bobby's bobby. Bobby appears to be pitching his tent on your campsite. To put it bluntly, Bobby has a Dance Floor Erection. He's been struck with a DFE. Poor kid can't even control it." (Natalie Krinsky, "Is That a Bud in Your Pocket? Or Are You Just Happy to See Me?" *Yale Daily News*, Nov. 9, 2001.)

Dash to the quickie mart (n.): a rapidly executed sexual experience, traditionally known as a "quickie." (Amber Madison, "Condom Sense," *Tufts Daily*, Nov. 6, 2002.)

Dating with a lowercase "d" (n.): the more casual one-on-one activities historically known as "courting" that, according to *Hoya* columnist Julia Baugher, "on the relationship spectrum . . . falls after hooking up but before monogamous commitment." (Julia Baugher, "Dating with a Lower Case 'D,'" *Hoya*, Oct. 4, 2002.)

Death stare (n.): a flirting faux pas, according to *California Aggie* columnist Anna Ritner, which "involves noticeably staring at someone so long that he would rather die than ever have to see you again. This can be likened to when you try to cheat off of someone's test and even though she's looking away, they somehow know you're staring. . . . People are highly aware of staring and they hate it. So stop staring, weirdo." (Anna Ritner, "Stalking 101," *California Aggie*, May 17, 2005.)

Defensive screwing (n.): engaging in protected sexual intercourse to avoid STIs. (Amber Madison, "Genital Warts: Another Reason to Have Sex with the Lights On," *Tufts Daily*, Oct. 16, 2002.)

Delightful interior Chinese finger trap (n.): the vagina. Aka: bubble gum, and snickerdoodle. (Kristina Hines and Katrina Rogachevsky, "Vulvagraphy," *Daily Princetonian*, Apr. 21, 2005.)

Derriere diving (n.): anal sex. Aka: dirtiest of dirties, entering the exit door, flying over the Black Sea, and poop-chute sliding. (Eitches, "Entering the Exit Door.")

De-virginizer (n.): an individual who actively attempts to engage in sexual activity with virgins. (Miriam Datskovsky, "Insertion Is Nine Tenths of the Law," *Columbia Spectator*, Nov. 15, 2004.)

DIADD ("**Do it**" **attention deficit disorder**) (n.): As explained by *Diamondback* columnist Emily Apatov, "While most normal people experience thoughts of sex as a constant, light buzzing noise in the background of their daily routines, I believe there are some young people for whom the first thought of 'doing it' sends them into a black hole from which their mind cannot return." (Emily Apatov, "Classroom Distraction," *Diamondback,* Aug. 31, 2005.)

Dick dipping (n.): sexual intercourse. Aka: do the hibbity dibbity, G-spot two-step, give her the magic stick, let one slip past the goalie, park the beef bus in tuna town, and put away wet. (Dave Franzese, "You Can Do It Anywhere," *Daily Nexus*, Apr. 13, 2005.)

Dickus nervosa (n.): the loss of an erection during sexual activity, more traditionally known as "limp dick" or "whiskey disk." (Jessica Lee, "Are You Done Yet?" *Sophian*, Feb. 28, 2008.)

Dild-ego (v. or n.): masturbation of the ego or general conceitedness. As *Cavalier Daily* columnist Kate Carlisle explained, "The blatant focus on outward appearances is a certain way to make all those precious hours at the gym completely worthless; a perfectly proportioned body all too often leads to an enormously-sized head." (Kate Carlisle, "Your Dild-ego," *Cavalier Daily*, Sept. 19, 2005.)

Ditch the magic (v.): moving away from the romantic idealization one often holds about his or her first planned sexual experience. Example: "All of those high school sex-ed classes and very 'special' episodes of *Saved-by-the-Bell-Blossom-Step-by-Step-Boy-Meets-World* type shows you grew up with were lying to you. The first time you have sex isn't going to be earth-shattering no matter who you're with. There are no fireworks, and the only loud bangs are likely to be your head cracking against the very un-sexy post of your twin dorm bed." (Roxy Sass, "Roxy Says: First Is the Worst," *Stanford Daily*, Mar. 10, 2006.)

Dude X (n.): an anonymous student with whom an individual is hooking up, without worrying about the student's name. (Medvin, "All or Nothing Dilemma.")

DUI (v.): dialing under the influence of alcohol, typically to solicit sex. (Garcia, "Booty Calls.")

Easier to get into than a community college (adj.): a female known for being sexually promiscuous. Aka: wet more times than a Slip 'n Slide. (See Wes Muller, "Sometimes Means Gay," *Driftwood*, Feb. 20, 2007; and Rebecca Bode, "Good Morning, Sunshine?" *Maine Campus*, Sept. 11, 2003.)

ED (n.): emotional dysfunction. (Robin Cooper, "ED: Emotional Dysfunction," *New Paltz Oracle*, Dec. 8, 2005.)

Engagementringophobia (n.): an intense fear of becoming engaged or dealing with the obligations of a more serious relationship. (Nadia Stadnycki, "Straight Up Sex," *Temple News*, Oct. 26, 2004.)

Erecto-mania (n.): a temporary, uncontrollable erection that typically occurs in public. Example: "Erecto-mania only lasts several minutes, which for the stricken seems like an eternity. . . . He is certain that EVERYONE in the room KNOWS what just occurred, that everyone in the room is zeroing in on his pants, wondering why they look like THAT. Erecto-mania may lead to sweaty palms, severe anxiety, jumpiness and perhaps even a slight tic. These symptoms last only a few minutes and may be easily rid by several more drinks." (Krinsky, "Is That a Bud in Your Pocket?")

Ex (v.): As explained by *Johns Hopkins News-Letter* columnist Jess Beaton, "It has become a phenomenon. 'Ex' used to just be a former lover. Recently, a combination of slang and relationship behavior has caused it to become a verb, 'to ex': to hook-up or, in some cases, get back together with an old boyfriend or girlfriend." Aka: return of the ex. (Jess Beaton, "Sex with Your Ex," *Johns Hopkins News-Letter*, Feb. 27, 2004.)

Ex File (n.): As *Daily Trojan* columnist Elspeth Keller explained, "The Ex File has also been called 'The Little Black Book,' and it can contain exes of all kinds: boyfriends, hookups or just dates." A few of the most common types, according to columnists:

> **Funk-master-sketch ex:** a former relationship partner who sincerely hurt an individual by acting shady or "sketchy." After a breakup, a student

always regrets running into this person. (Natalie Krinsky, "Vacation Strategy: How to Keep Score Against the Ex," *Yale Daily News*, Nov. 30, 2001.)

I-will-always-love-you ex: a former relationship partner who still holds a place in a student's heart. In Keller's words, "Seeing this kind of ex is like riding a bike, every time you go back to it, it's the same feeling. The I-Will-Always-Love-You Ex is a tattoo: dark, under the skin and very permanent." (Elspeth Keller, "Spring Cleaning Means Glance at the Ex-Files," *Daily Trojan*, Apr. 14, 2006.)

I-will-always-lust-for-you ex: a former relationship partner who inspires continued feelings of sexual arousal even after the breakup. (Ibid.)

Peter Pan ex: a former relationship partner who has not changed at all since the breakup. (Julia Baugher, "The Dos and Don'ts of Ex Sex," *Hoya*, Jan. 17, 2003.)

We-should-have-just-been-friends ex: a former relationship partner who easily segues into a platonic acquaintance because there is no sustained sexual chemistry. (Keller, "Spring Cleaning Means Glance at the Ex-Files.")

What-the-hell-was-that? ex: a relationship partner who demands or causes a very abrupt breakup, leading to avoidance and no desire for reconciliation. Aka: I-will-never-talk-to-you-again ex. (Ibid.)

What's-the-point ex: a former relationship partner who offers an individual no reason to want to keep in touch. (Ibid.)

Examine-every-crevice-in-my-body-and-fuck-me-with-the-lights-on nudity (n.): an intimate exploration of a sexual partner's body away from a darkened bedroom. (Miriam Datskovsky, "Absolut Nude," *Columbia Spectator*, Oct. 16, 2006.)

Extra-mattressal intercourse (n.): sexual activity outside the bedroom, possibly in public. (Melissa Meinzer, "Suggestions for Boinking Beyond Boundaries of Bed," *Pitt News*, Jan. 26, 2004.)

Faking Females Anonymous (FFA) (n.): a group of female students who admittedly fake orgasms during sexual intercourse. (Anthony Ciarrochi, "Don't Worry About Faking It, Just Do It," *Pitt News*, Sept. 21, 2004.)

Farewell sex season (n.): the period just before the end of an academic term or graduation in which students engage in a considerable amount of sexual activity and sexual promiscuousness. (James Whitaker, "Say Goodbye with Sex," *Mustang Daily*, June 3, 2004.)

Fart-compatible (adj.): a stage of intimacy in a serious relationship in which partners feel entirely uninhibited in front of each other, even to pass gas. (Aly Murphy and Elena Gaudino, "Having a Gas," *Daily Campus*, Nov. 30, 2005.)

Faux boyfriend (n.): an individual who serves as a stand-in relationship partner as needed. According to *Phoenix* columnist Kaiko Shimura, "These are the boys—and girls—that spend a majority of their time with attached individuals and do 'couple-y' things together when the real boy/girlfriend just isn't around. It's not sneaky in any way; just one lonely attached individual who finds himself with another person who happens to be single and available." (Kaiko Shimura, "If You Can't Be with the One You Love," *Phoenix*, Mar. 24, 2005.)

Fellationship (n.): a combination of the words fellatio and relationship, connoting a relationship built solely on sexual activity. Aka: bed-buddy-ships, fuck buddy, and luvah. (See interview, Haley Yarosh, July 18, 2006; Lindsay Johnson, "Squash That Evil Label Bug," *Rebel Yell*, Apr. 13, 2006; Giblin, "Harvard Sexicon"; and Sari Eitches, "Who Do You Screw?" *Daily Californian*, Nov. 23, 2004.)

Females taste icky department (n.): individuals against performing cunnilingus because they dislike the taste of a woman's genital region. (Timaree Schmit, "Sexpert Covers Female Flavors, Male Piercings," *Daily Nebraskan*, Dec. 3, 2003.)

Filibuster of fellatio (n.): an oral sex session focused on a man that takes an especially long time to reach its conclusion. (Eve, "Is That a Flask in Your Pocket or Are You Just Flaccid to See Me?" *GW Hatchet*, Oct. 2, 2006.)

First month bliss period (n.): the start of a relationship in which a couple is excited about every new activity and talk. (Nadia Stadnycki, "Finding the True Meaning of 'Do You,'" *Temple News*, Feb. 7, 2006.)

Five days, no boom boom for soul sister (n.): the time during a woman's period in which some females refrain from engaging in sexual intercourse. (Amber Madison, "A Mixed Blessing," *Tufts Daily*, Apr. 23, 2003.)

Fornitalent (n.): a play off the word "fornication," referring to an individual's pornographic talent or sexual aptitude. Aka: sack skills. (Denise Brundson, "Is That a Gold Medal Nestled Between Your Tits?" *McGill Daily*, Sept. 23, 2004.)

Franken-mate (n.): a Frankenstein-type creation of the ideal man or woman. As *Daily Californian* columnist Duni Heimpel recalled a student telling her, "'You know you would just take chunks of whatever girl you thought was attractive and throw them together to make the perfect girl.' . . . [He] pointed to a girl not more than ten feet from us. All we could see was her rump covered by jeans that had an intentional rip just where buttocks meet leg. 'See, I would take her rump.'" (Duni Heimpel, "Franken-mate: Saturday Night's Perfect Date," *Daily Californian*, Nov. 30, 2004.)

Gamer widow (n.): a female who is forgotten in a relationship in favor of video games. (Anna Tauzin, "Hedonism 101: Gamers and the Widows Who Love Them," *University Star*, Oct. 30, 2007.)

Getting jiggy alone (n.): masturbation. Aka: auditioning the finger puppets, big M, coming into your own, do-it-yourself technique, getting down and deliciously dirty with your own bad self, rocking your own world, rock-paper-scissors, and she-bop. (Maghan McDowell, "Frisky Bedroom Resolutions," *Independent Florida Alligator*, Jan. 12, 2006.)

Girl types: According to *California Aggie* columnist Archie Garcia:

Bad fashion girl: "This girl completely stands out because of the outrageous ensemble she has on. She is seen with a group of Trendy Girls, and no one knows how they let her out of the house looking like she came out of a John Hughes movie."

Bitter girl: "She is bitter because she doesn't receive half the attention her more attractive friend does."

Bottle blond girl: "She is not comfortable with her natural hair color and feels being blond is the best way to get attention, even if it is negative attention."

Buy me a drink girl: "Always seen near the bar, looking for some schmuck to buy her a drink."

Cell phone girl: "She talks on her cell phone all night, almost ignoring her surroundings."

Clown girl: "This girl wears far too much makeup."

Collapsing girl: "This girl is often seen being propped up by her friends because she cannot handle her alcohol intake. Stay away from her unless you want to look like someone who takes advantage of drunken women."

Exhibitionist girl: "Put a couple drinks into this girl, and she wants nothing but attention. She can be seen making out with both men and women. In addition, she wants everyone to take body shots off her."

FUPA (fat upper pubic area) girl: "This girl wears tight shirts and low-rise jeans showing off her impressive beer gut she has been working on all of college. She isn't exactly fat, but FUPA girl needs to learn she can't dress like Britney Spears and expect to get away with it."

Man-hater girl: "This hardcore feminist is not gay, but hates men with a passion. She doesn't look at men when they try to dance with her or she ignores them at the bar as they try to buy her a drink."

Six-headed girl: "She is seen with five of her sorority sisters. This girl cannot function without all of her parts. This multi-headed girl does not separate all night, fearing the one with the mental capacity to order drinks may get lost without the one who has the sense of direction to get them home."

Slut-slipper girl: "She wears flip-flops that make her five inches taller. She thinks they are cool, but they actually make her walk like a retarded . . . duck." (Archie Garcia, "Time to Classify Bar Flies," *California Aggie*, Feb. 3, 2004.)

Girlie-kiss virginity (n.): a female's first same-sex kiss. (Jessica Saunders, "Kissing Jessica Saunders," *Cornell Daily Sun*, Feb. 20, 2003.)

Good-bye sex (n.): engaging in sexual activity one last time with a relationship partner before or immediately after a breakup. (Paul Shugar, "It's Over . . . Except the Sex," *Post*, May 15, 2003.)

Go-to conversation (n.): According to *Yale Daily News* columnist Natalie Krinsky, "The Go-To is that part of you that is reserved for kick-off situations with a soon-to-be-significant-or-insignificant other." Among the most popular go-to anecdotes employed on a first date, in Krinsky's words:

Go-to drunk story: "This is used to indicate to the other person that you are a fun and cool kid to be around. It starts with something exotic, like, 'One time I was so WASTED in Guadelajara [*sic*] when—' and it goes on to talk about how you met peasants in the jungle and you all hung out and played the travel version of Yahtzee."

Go-to ex story: "This is quite possibly the most important Go-To story. It is also one that needs to be handled with [the] most care. You cannot have the other person think that either you or your ex is particularly crazy (which you both are). You discuss your ex rationally and make it seem as if you had a healthy relationship that just 'somehow' went wrong."

Go-to high school story: "This story encompasses who you were in high school—jock, drama queen, artsy-fartsy—while describing your battle with teenage angst." (Natalie Krinsky, "First Date 101: It's All About Assets," *Yale Daily News*, Sept. 28, 2002.)

Guy types: According to several columnists:

Attractive dumb-as-a-box-of-rocks guy: "At first glance, he appears to have the most potential. He's tall, muscular, and he smells so good that it makes you want to do obscene things in public. But don't be fooled. This guy will bore the living hell out of you. That glimmer in his eye that caught your attention from across the room in Public Speaking class will glaze over with confusion the minute you start wanting to have a conversation about something with more depth than [the Fox animated show] 'Family Guy.'" (Kimberly Maier, "Dr. Kim," *Clackamas Print*, May 14, 2007.)

Dorm guy: "He will spot you and try to enter your drinking group by reminding you that he lived on your dorm floor. Seems innocent until, in front of a girl, he recollects that farting contest you guys had." (Archie Garcia, "What to Do About Girls' Night Out," *California Aggie*, Nov. 25, 2003.)

Groping guy: "His mother never taught him how to treat a lady or behave in public. He is constantly grabbing a female's posterior or trying to fondle other portions of her body." (Ibid.)

Hat-cocked-to-the-side guy: "This fellow wears his hat tilted at a 45-degree angle to the left or right. Notice this guy is always out with guys and rarely has a girlfriend. Women do not take him seriously; they have trouble maintaining eye contact because they keep staring at his crooked hat." (Ibid.)

Know-everybody guy: "This is the guy who says 'Hi' to everyone he has ever met in college. It does not matter whether it is an old classmate, old dorm neighbor, or someone who urinated next to him in the restroom." (Ibid.)

Nerdy, awkward guy: "This particular dude probably won't hit on you. More likely, he'll have one of his friends that you know tell you that he's sweet on you. . . . This guy isn't right for you because he spends too much time playing video games and talking about 'Star Wars.'" (Maier, "Dr. Kim.")

Obnoxious guy: "This individual tends to be really loud with or without alcohol. He tells long, boring stories that seem to never end, or even bad jokes he just memorized from *Maxim*." (Garcia, "What to Do About Girls' Night Out.")

Penis guy: "Wants to show everyone his penis, claiming it's bigger than Ron Jeremy's tool. He threatens to whip it out when people doubt his manhood." (Ibid.)

Really nice guy with emotional issues: "This is the guy who puts a little too much effort into getting to know you. He calls too much. He leaves notes. And letters. And messages. Everywhere you turn—there he is, waiting in anticipation like a dog trying to be good for a piece of scrap meat from the dinner table." (Maier, "Dr. Kim.")

Really smart, nice guy who's not so attractive: "We call these guys our friends." (Ibid.)

Rich, older guy who wants to control you: "This guy wants to wine and dine you, but don't let him do it! The next thing you know, you'll be barefoot and pregnant, playing trophy wife to a dude with a muffin top hanging over his pants, almost busting out of a shirt two sizes too small." (Ibid.)

Smoker guy: "This guy needs to leave the group often for a smoke break, and comes back smelling like girl repellent. He never knows what you are talking about because he misses half the night smoking outside." (Garcia, "What to Do About Girls' Night Out.")

Tag-along guy: "This guy somehow tags along with you guys everywhere. He offers nothing to the conversation and usually just laughs at what others are saying or stares at girls' chests hoping they don't notice." (Ibid.)

Half-night stand (n.): a shortened version of the one-night stand; leaving a sexual partner's bedside before morning, typically before the partner wakes.

(See Dlugatch, "Post-Hook-Up Etiquette"; and Sari Eitches, "Morning-After Manners," *Daily Californian*, Sept. 7, 2004.)

Hand-job slut (n.): a student known for "jerking off" a large number of male students, while not engaging in any other type of sexual activity. (Kate McDowell, "The Down-Low on Third Base," *Cornell Daily Sun*, Oct. 17, 2002.)

Hand-me-ups (n.): clothing a student borrows from a younger friend or family member. (Carlisle, "Your Dild-ego.")

High Holy Day of dating (n.): Valentine's Day. In the words of *Hoya* columnist Julia Baugher, it is "a fabulous flirtation fiesta . . . a crush courting celebration, a pulchritudinous passion party, a licentious love liaison." (Baugher, "Don't Diss on Valentine's Day.")

Hookup bell (n.): an unofficial time period, normally late at night, when students simultaneously begin seeking sexual partners. Example: "It's 3:30 A.M. The hook-up bell just went off, and everyone who will be 'getting to know each other better' that night is marching to a bedroom." (Brynn Burton, "If You Can't Take It Lightly, Don't Ring the Hook-Up Bell," *Post*, Oct. 30, 2002.)

Hookup hair (n.): a disheveled head of hair caused by a passionate bout of sexual activity. Aka: just-escaped-murder-by-a-moving-vehicle look, and sex hair. (See ibid.; and Van Dyke, "You Get One Phone Call.")

Hookup with fries on the side (n.): a twist on traditional dating, equating a majority of college relationships with a trip to a fast-food restaurant: quick, cheap, and enjoyed for its convenience. (Kate Carlisle, "A Hook Up with Fries on the Side," *Cavalier Daily*, Apr. 18, 2005.)

Horizontal rule (n.): a standard for defining whether sexual activity constitutes a full "hookup," in respect to the relative positioning of students' bodies. Example: "Were your bodies horizontal for more than a minute? Definitely a hook-up. Passionate making out on the steps . . . in the rain? Not a hook-up." (Heather Strack, "To Hook-Up, or Not to Hook-Up: The Horizontal Rule," *Dartmouth Free Press*, Feb. 10, 2006.)

Hot number (n.): the amount of sexual partners a woman must refrain from accruing to avoid being labeled sexually promiscuous. Aka: X-equals-slut debate. (Miriam Datskovsky, "Finding the Solution: The Hot Number," *Columbia Spectator*, Oct. 4, 2004.)

House booty (n.): engaging in sexual activity with an individual in a student's immediate geographic proximity or inner circle, including in the same dormitory, student organization, or academic major. Aka: dormcest, floorcest, and hallcest. (Jess Beaton, "Getting Some T&A from Your Own TA," *Johns Hopkins News-Letter*, Mar. 12, 2004.)

Hungry mungry (n.): an individual obsessed with performing cunnilingus. (Natalie Krinsky, "Heading Down There? Don't Waste Your Time," *Yale Daily News*, Feb. 15, 2002.)

I-know-all-these-chicks-but-they-never-seem-to-want-to-do-me-itis (n.): an affliction among men in which their female companions and potential sexual partners do not return their level of interest. (Rachel Axelbank, "What Women Want: Sex, a Defense of the Female Libido," *Daily Princetonian*, Apr. 29, 2004.)

Imports (n.): potential sexual partners from outside a college who visit friends or significant others on campus during "big hurrah" weekends such as homecoming. (Yarosh, "Parties and Visitors Yield Similar Results.")

I've gotta go's (n.): improvised excuses employed by an individual to make a quick exit from a relationship partner's residence. (Lindsay Johnson, "Getting Comfortable Is Anything But," *Rebel Yell*, Oct. 6, 2005.)

Jackrabbit sex (n.): bad sex stemming from a male's overaggressive, repetitive thumping. (Miriam Datskovsky, "Six Degrees of Sexual Frustration," *Columbia Spectator*, Nov. 29, 2004.)

Jekyll and Hyde erection (n.): unexplained bursts of penile arousal and flaccidity. (Beth Van Dyke, "Men Dangle Between Rock Hard and a Soft Place," *Daily Nexus*, May 28, 2003.)

Jizz gut (n.): a fictitious stomach bulge supposedly caused by swallowing the male secretion upon orgasm while performing oral sex. (Caley Meals, "The Age-Old Question: Spit or Swallow?" *Badger Herald*, Apr. 9, 2003.)

Kiss her south (v.): performing oral sex on a woman. (Sari Eitches, "Heading South," *Daily Californian*, Oct. 5, 2004.)

Kisser classifications: According to *University News* columnist Liz Townsend:
> **Blower:** "I have no idea why some people think that blowing into your partner's mouth is sexy."

Crowbar: "The Crowbar is a kisser that forces your mouth open as wide as it will go. This can be quite uncomfortable and can result in split lips at the corners of the mouth."

Deep throat: "This refers to a kisser who thrusts their tongue aggressively into your mouth (and sometimes on into your throat)."

Duct tape kisser: "The Duct Tape Kisser has extremely sticky spit. When this gets spread around one's face, it takes not only a towel but a wet nap to remove."

Flutterer: "This, in my opinion, is one of the highest-ranking kinds of kissers. Using the tongue to lightly caress your partner's mouth and tongue, it brings to mind a butterfly, hence the name."

Pecker: "The Pecker enjoys leaving sweet little kisses all over the face. While nice on occasion, the pecks can get quite annoying if over-used."

Slobberer: "A slobberer has a tendency to leave a lot of extraneous spit on one's face. While not the worst thing in the world . . . the last thing I want to do after kissing someone is to find a towel to wipe down my face."

Sucker: "While light sucking on a lip or tongue can get the juices flowing, intense sucking can cause not only pain but actual physical injury. . . . I've known of cases that actually ended up in an emergency room visit."

Teeth knocker: "The Teeth Knocker gets its name from the tendency to bump front teeth with whomever they are kissing. This kiss has no redeeming qualities. Just take it easy, 'kay? Most people don't want a forced dentist visit due to chipped front teeth." (Liz Townsend, "Sexploration," *University News*, Oct. 6, 2003.)

Lesbionic (adj.): a characteristic indicating a female student's sexual attraction toward other females. (Brook Taylor, "Straight Girl Goes Gay," *Carolinian*, Oct. 4, 2005.)

Little girl (n.): clitoris. (Meghan Bainum, "Female Genitalia: More Than Just a Vagina," *Daily Kansan*, Oct. 3, 2002.)

Look at posters (v.): going home with an individual under the pretense of looking at the posters on his or her wall while truly expecting to engage in sexual activity. (Kate McDowell, "Wisdom of the Ages," *Cornell Daily Sun*, Apr. 17, 2003.)

Love at first spook (n.): the phenomenon of love at first sight occurring between two people in costume on Halloween. (Eve, "The One Night You Can Have Sex with Superman," *GW Hatchet*, Oct. 30, 2006.)

Man muff maintenance (n.): male pubic hair care. (Sari Eitches, "Pimp Your Ride," *Daily Californian*, Feb. 22, 2005.)

McThreesomes (n.): quick, spontaneous, convenient group sex encounters. (Interview, McLean Robbins, June 12, 2007.)

Mid-coitus giggle (n.): a laugh emitted during sexual activity. Example: "A mid-coitus giggle is anything but a slutty flirtation. It can be as simple as a way to relax the moment, a way to keep things lustful or a sign that it's okay to be a bit kinky." (Kate Carlisle, "Laugh About It: It's Just Sex," *Cavalier Daily*, Oct. 17, 2005.)

Mid-semester walking-in-on-your-roommate-bent-over-like-a-Gumby-doll incident (n.): an accidental interruption of a roommate engaged in sexual activity. (Caley Meals, "So, We've Been Living Together for Over a Month Now," *Badger Herald*, Oct. 2, 2002.)

Mind the stepchildren (v.): remembering to stimulate the testicles of a male while engaging in sexual activity. (Kate Prengaman, "Students Offer Tips for Keeping Sex Life Exciting," *Flat Hat*, Sept. 10, 2004.)

Mojo-depleting interruption (n.): a disruption during sexual activity leading to a loss of arousal. (Caley Meals, "Pick Up the Phone, It's Your Libido Calling . . . ," *Badger Herald*, Oct. 30, 2002.)

Momentary celibacy (n.): a temporary dry spell during which an individual engages in no sexual activity, more traditionally known as virginity of circumstance. Aka: no-penetrance penitence, nun phase, and sexual famine. (Brook Taylor, "Beginning a New Sexual Era," *Carolinian*, Oct. 25, 2004.)

Mo' money, mo' maturity, less mama (adj.): a slogan citing the positives of entering into a relationship or engaging in sexual activity with older individuals. (Julia Baugher, "It's My Birthday and I'll Date Who I Want To," *Hoya*, Feb. 28, 2003.)

Mount Baldy (n.): a woman's shaved genital area. (Caley Meals, "Bushy v. Barren," *Badger Herald*, Apr. 26, 2003.)

My sex (n.): a label for a partner, symbolizing the ambiguity involved in student relationships. Example: "'So I was at my Sex's place,' my friend began. Your what? 'My Sex. I don't know what to call him. The guy I'm having sex with.' Apparently neither of them had popped the question yet. You know, the one that goes, 'What, like, are we?'" (Eitches, "Who Do You Screw?")

The night (n.): a never-ending evening between relationship partners that solidifies their mutual interest and attraction. Example: "Leslie and Daniel were hanging out the other night and he kissed her. Not just that, the rest of the evening quickly turned into 'the night.' You know, 'the night' where you and a guy have a wonderful conversation for hours and make out until the sun comes up." (Nicole Wroten, "Get Out of My Dreams and Into My Column: Girl Code," Ask E. Jean, n.d.: http://www.askejean.com/campus-columnists/columns.php?column_id=105.)

No-kiss blow job (n.): a type of oral sex performed on a male in which no kisses on the lips are exchanged after the activity is concluded. Antonym: "Sucking off, then sucking face." (Jess Beaton,˙ "One-Way Hookups: Down for the Count," *Johns Hopkins News-Letter*, Sept. 10, 2004.)

Non-genital aspects of life (n.): parts of students' daily routines that do not involve sexual activity or the pursuit of such activity. (Eitches, "Who Do You Screw?")

No-privacy libido-killing death chamber (n.): a dorm room shared with a roommate in which it becomes difficult to be alone with a sexual partner. (Roxy Sass, "Holiday Hook-Up, Fo Sheezy," *Stanford Daily*, Nov. 17, 2006.)

NO SIR (National Organization of Sisters Inspired by Repression) (n.): a fictitious group fighting for the rights of female students. (Kourtney Jason, "No Sir!" *Orion*, Jan. 24, 2007.)

O-less (adj.): an inability to achieve an orgasm during sexual activity. (Timaree Schmit, "The Pioneering Episode of 'Sex with Timaree,'" *Daily Nebraskan*, Oct. 15, 2003.)

Operation GLWC2 (Get Laid with Commitment and Conversation) (n.): a determined effort to secure a relationship partner who provides stability and intellectual stimulation along with sex. (Natalie Krinsky, "Phase TWO: Get Myself a Man," *Yale Daily News*, Jan. 18, 2002.)

OTPHJ (Over-the-pants hand job) (n.): physical stimulation of a man's genital region while the man is still wearing pants. (Natalie Krinsky, "Manual Manipulation: A Dying Art," *Yale Daily News*, Oct. 26, 2001.)

Out-slut (v.): to engage in more sexually promiscuous behavior than another individual. (Robin Cooper, "'Slut' Is in the Eye of the Beholder," *New Paltz Oracle*, Oct. 27, 2005.)

Oval Office hours (n.): a sexualization of professors' traditional office hours, referring to the Bill Clinton-Monica Lewinsky scandal. (Kate Carlisle, "This is Not 'Good Will Humping,'" *Cavalier Daily*, Mar. 21, 2005.)

Overly organized orgasamers (OOOers) (n.): individuals who multitask during sexual activity, including making mental to-do lists. Example: "Some women make very efficient use of this time [sexual intercourse]. . . . Between a moan and an oh! Oh! OH! she can map out her day. She's thinking, 'If this ends by 9, I'll have time to write the tail end of that paper, pluck my eyebrows, and maybe alphabetize my DVD collection.'" (Natalie Krinsky, "More Than You Ever Wanted to Know About Fake Orgasms," *Yale Daily News*, Nov. 16, 2001.)

PDA-idue (n.): residue left behind on an individual's face after engaging in a public display of affection, such as spit, lipstick, or hair. (Natalie Krinsky, "You Might Be Swapping Spit in Front of Me . . . ," *Yale Daily News*, Oct. 11, 2002.)

PDA p's and q's (n.): the proper etiquette for public displays of affection. (Aly Murphy and Elena Gaudino, "PDA P's and Q's," *Daily Campus*, Mar. 22, 2006.)

Pictures on your wall of fame (n.): a count of all past sexual partners, more traditionally known as "notches on one's bedpost." Aka: sex tallies. (Laura Dlugatch, "Playing the Numbers Game: It Just Doesn't Add Up," *Review*, Sept. 19, 2006.)

Piece of overly cologned meat (n.): a male. Aka: living on the corner of Easy and Penis streets, male genome project, and Mr. Lust Object. (Kate Carlisle, "Curiosity Killed the Kate," *Cavalier Daily*, Sept. 5, 2005.)

Porn star moan and wiggle (n.): a sensual body movement and simultaneous groan of pleasure to heighten a partner's excitement during sexual activity. (McLean Robbins, "Porn Keeps Girls Curious and Guys Busy," *Old Gold & Black*, Mar. 23, 2005.)

Postcoital bite (n.): a meal shared by a couple after engaging in sexual activity. (Abi Medvin, "The Friday Quickie," *Dartmouth*, Feb. 23, 2007.)

Postcoital Game Boy session (n.): the playing of a video game after engaging in sexual activity. Example: "With a recently cleared mind, thanks to the recently cleared load, I found myself breezing through three levels of Metroid while the little lady snoozed happily next to me." (Dave Franzese, "Forget the Pillow Talk," *Daily Nexus*, Jan. 19, 2005.)

Post-drunk-dial hangover (n.): a groggy, sick feeling the morning after engaging in a booty call, spurred by the foggy memories of who was called and one's drunken behavior while on the phone. (Elspeth Keller, "Going Out? Then My Cell Phone Stays at Home," *Daily Trojan*, Jan. 13, 2006.)

Post-hookup phone call (n.): As explained by *Yale Daily News* columnist Natalie Krinsky, "The one that comes three days after you hooked up. Or at least, it's supposed to come three days afterward. Not one, that's too desperate, and not a week after, because that's far too late, but is two days OK? How about four?" The most popular types:

> **I'm-a-little-too-happy-to-call call**: "This one comes a little early. Why? Because that guy hasn't gotten ass in 6 months, and he's really excited that you came through in the clutch. Then again, he really could like you. We all know what beautiful, lifelong relationships develop from a romantic encounter at Zeta Psi."
>
> **Maybe-if-I-call-right-now-you'll-come-over-and-get-naked-with-me-again call**: "This person is really optimistic. It's 11:30 on a Wednesday, he or she doesn't have any work, and you need to write a 12-page paper about the pottery of ancient southwest Eritrea. No one is coming over. No one is getting naked. Thanks for playing." Aka: MIICRNYCOAGNWMA.
>
> **Obligatory phone call**: "You don't really like the other person. You regret that you've seen his or her body after three months of not going to the gym and two rounds of the freshman fifteen. Really, you just want to get it over with. You'd rather be on the phone with your grandmother. With the flower lady. Anyone. There's chitchat, it's uncomfortable, and when you hang up, you both realize there's no hope." (Natalie Krinsky, "Afraid I'll Miss Your Third-Day Call? Don't Worry, I'll Dial Star Sixty-nine," *Yale Daily News*, Nov. 2, 2001.)

Practice monogamy (n.): committed relationships entered into by students while in college, without the immediate prospects of marriage, children, mortgage payments, and other trappings of post-graduation relationships.

(Miriam Datskovsky, "Thoughts for Another Day," *Columbia Spectator*, Jan. 23, 2006.)

Pre-cherry-poppin' state (n.): virginity. (Stadnycki, "Determining Your Born-Again Virginity.")

Pre-ex-sex agreement (n.): a fictitious contract outlining the limitations of sexual activity with an ex, normally to make it clear that a recommencement of a full relationship is not permissible. Example: "When deciding to undertake 'Ex-Sex,' it's smart to have your attorney draw up a little 200–300 page 'pre Ex-Sex agreement,' like a pre-nuptial agreement, only more important. You see, for lots of people, the resumption of sexual activity automatically signals the resumption of dating activity. Nothing could be further from the truth. There is nothing worse than waking up in the morning only to find your ex curled on your couch, in your boxers, eating your cereal. If this is the case you will have to break up with them all over again. . . . The 'pre Ex-Sex agreement' will take care of all this and other problems ahead of time." (James Whitaker, "X Marks the Spot," *Mustang Daily*, Oct. 9, 2004.)

Pre-relationship (n.): a period of romantic or sexual interaction between two potential partners prior to officially becoming a couple. Example: "Forget the honeymoon, or even the wedding night. For men, the greatest, most carefree, innocent time of any relationship is actually the brief span of bliss before the relationship actually starts. . . . Thus, the pre-relationship is the answer to all the things men need to survive, like hot action, yet contains none of the things we don't need, like holding hands, watching 'Friends,' or listening about the new pair of shoes down at Reign." (Whitaker, "The Relationship Clarifying Talk.")

Pseudo-O savvy (n.): ability to superbly fake an orgasm. Aka: fake-O MO. (Caitlin Hall, "Faking It," *Arizona Daily Wildcat*, Jan. 28, 2004.)

QGPs (Questions to get into an individual's pants) (n.): As *Daily Reveille* columnist Jessica Pivik wrote, "First dates follow a sequence, they may be with different people but the topics of conversation are often the same. . . . We all have our own form of QGP's [*sic*]." The three most popular types, according to Pivik:

    QGP of favorites: "You ask the person their favorite food, color, sexual position, etc. You can analyze a lot about a person by their favorite things."

QGP of extracurricular activities: "This is where we discuss what kind of things the person does outside of school. Asking someone their extracurricular activities is a polite way of asking them to categorize themselves: jock, brain, criminal, princess, and a basket case."

QGP of past relationships: "This is the most sensitive and important QGP's. It's like buying a car. You need to know its history before you buy it." (Jessica Pivik, "On Top," *Daily Reveille*, Jan. 22, 2004.)

Quick-to-blow Romeo (n.): a male who ejaculates prematurely or right after beginning to engage in sexual intercourse. Aka: two-hump chump. (Anna Schleelein, "The Great O Debate," *Heights*, Apr. 8, 2003.)

Rainbow sprinkles (n.): orgasms. (Stadnycki, "Talking Dirty for Dummies.")

Rapid relationships (n.): interactions between students that go from hooking up to full-scale monogamous commitment within days, skipping the courting period. (Nicole Wroten, "Getting Off the Hook: 'Hooking Up' Is Leaving Old-Fashioned Dating Rituals in the Dust," *Maroon*, Nov. 17, 2006.)

Relationship ADD (n.): a faux disorder in which a relationship partner fails to exert adequate romantic effort or pay ample attention to his or her significant other. (Amber Madison, "V-Day Blues," *Tufts Daily*, Feb. 18, 2004.)

Sacrificing the XOXO for the XXX (n.): foregoing love and romance for pure sexual satisfaction, while in a relationship or while searching for a potential partner. (Hall, "Faking It.")

Sex furniture (n.): furniture designed or creatively employed for sex. (Claire Fuller, "Something to Think About," *Lumberjack*, Apr. 1, 2004.)

Sexpel (v.): expelling a roommate from a shared dorm room or residence because of an individual's engagement in sexual activity, more traditionally known as "sexiling." Aka: sexpatriate. (Valerie Arvidson, "Sex and Sensibility: How Are You Spending Valentine's Day," *Dartmouth Free Press*, Feb. 10, 2005.)

Sextra credit (n.): extra credit earned by a student for engaging in sexual activity with a professor or teaching assistant. As *Stanford Daily*'s Roxy Sass explained, "Nothing screams 'A plus!' like a good student-teacher relationship. Give your TA some T and A, and you'll have a 4.0 [grade point average] in no time. If not, hey, at least you got another sort of 'OH' out of it." (Roxy Sass, "Get More Out of Your Experience Here," *Stanford Daily*, Oct. 13, 2006.)

Sexually transmitted nasties (n.): sexually transmitted infections or STIs. (Denise Brundson, "What You Should Know . . . ," *McGill Daily*, Jan. 6, 2005.)

Sexvine (n.): the sexual grapevine or circle of gossip about individuals' sexual activities or reputations. (Jenna Hall, "Aphrodisiacs Come in All Shapes and Sizes," *Tartan*, Feb. 7, 2007.)

She that knocks the socks off (n.): a woman whom an individual loves deeply and declares "The One." (Seth Lake, "Relationships Can Suffer When Flaws Become Glaring," *Daily Evergreen*, Mar. 29, 2006.)

Shoe fall (n.): a test of one's level of intoxication, centered on whether an individual falls over while bending down to put on his or her shoes. A fall indicates too much drinking and an inability to rationally decide whether to engage in sexual activity with a potential partner whom one has just met. (Denise Brundson, "Attack of the 50 Ft Cock," *McGill Daily*, Oct. 21, 2007.)

Sig. fig. (n.): significant figure, or significant other in a serious relationship. (Haley Yarosh, "If It Ain't Broke, Don't Fix It: Relationships Need No Update," *Emory Wheel*, Apr. 5, 2005.)

Slut pride (n.): a feeling of immense self-satisfaction about one's sexual prowess, possibly labeled by others as promiscuity. (Jenna B., "Slut Pride," *Cornell Daily Sun*, Aug. 23, 2007.)

Slut stage (n.): As *Badger Herald* columnist Jenny Kalaidis explained, this stage "is characterized by promiscuous behavior, rowdy weekends and multiple playmates. People in this stage exhibit uncontrollable urges to get it on with whomever they please, and they will not be content until it happens." (Jenny Kalaidis, "Sexual Stages Come Full Circle," *Badger Herald*, Apr. 12, 2007.)

Slut wannabe (n.): a fairly innocent individual who aspires to be more sexually active and is in awe of sexually promiscuous friends. (Sarah Walsh, "One Time—A Sexual Charm?" *Phoenix*, Oct. 21, 2004.)

SMFs (n.): serial monogamy fiends. As *Phoenix* columnist William Tran explained, "They're the people who just always have to be dating someone. For them, life . . . would be utterly meaningless if they weren't in a relationship." (William Tran, "Beware the Serial Monogamist," *Phoenix*, Apr. 3, 2003.)

So-good-that-I-start-believing-it's-real fake (n.): a type of fake orgasm in which individuals' committed efforts to pretend they are achieving orgasm trigger an actual orgasm. Aka: fake it until you make it. (Krinsky, "More Than You Ever Wanted to Know About Fake Orgasms.")

Stride of pride (n.): the trip home from a hookup's residence, typically the morning after engaging in sexual activity, traditionally referred to as the "walk of shame." Aka: post-sex swagger, strut of infamy, victory lap, and walk of fame. (Miriam Datskovsky, "Otherwise Known As Walking," *Columbia Spectator*, Oct. 24, 2005; and Dlugatch, "Post-Hook-Up Etiquette.")

Students for Sensible Dick Policy (SSDP) (n.): a fictitious female student group advocating an increase in male sexual activity solely for the purpose of pleasing female students. As *Diamondback* columnist Emily Apatov wrote, "The motto of SSDP is 'I demand, you supply—on demand.'" (Emily Apatov, "Sex Ed Meets Econ," *Diamondback*, Sept. 14, 2005.)

Tag-team boobs (n.): a female's strategic flaunting of her cleavage to exert influence over men. Aka: Secret weapons. (Anna Schleelein, "The Secret Weapons," *Heights*, Apr. 1, 2003.)

Team-date (n.): the common practice of students socializing with potential relationship partners in groups, even while engaged in courtship rituals traditionally conducted one-on-one. (Haley Yarosh, "Mom's Always Right: Say No to Team Dates," *Emory Wheel*, Feb. 8, 2005.)

Thinking off (v.): the act of arousing or even stimulating oneself fully to climax through sexual fantasizing. (Sari Eitches, "It's All in Your Head," *Daily Californian*, Apr. 5, 2005.)

Toothpaste (n.): an oral sex technique that involves the squeezing of a man's penis or testicles. (Miriam Datskovsky, "Spitting, Swallowing, and Some Other Secrets," *Columbia Spectator*, Sept. 26, 2005.)

University-induced separation (n.): the physical disjoining of hometown couples due to their enrollments at separate schools or one's enrollment at a school in a location far from the couple's hometown. (Seth Lake, "Leave the Long Distance Relationship at Home," *Daily Evergreen*, Aug. 21, 2006.)

U-TAG (Up-the-ass girl) (n.): a female known for engaging in anal sex. (Natalie Krinsky, "Take Dead Aim at Your Favorite Clique and Do 'Em—No, Not There!" *Yale Daily News*, Feb. 8, 2002.)

Vagina owners (n.): females. (See Eitches, "Heading South"; and Lara Loewenstein, "Bone Up on Stimulating Masturbation Techniques," *Daily Bruin*, Feb. 28, 2005.)

Vagina revolution (n.): a growing cultural openness about the genital region of the female body. As *Badger Herald* columnist Aubre Andrus wrote, "It's everywhere—sort of a positive public-relations campaign. This semester, *The Vagina Monologues* was here, and the authors of *Vaginas: An Owner's Manual* were here last night. . . . It's in the magazines we read . . . and the shows we watch (I can think of multiple *Sex and the City* episodes focusing on the vagina)." (Aubre Andrus, "Female Anatomy Subject for Debate," *Badger Herald*, Apr. 7, 2006.)

Vampire (n.): a sucking technique for performing oral sex on a male in which no teeth are used. (Datskovsky, "Spitting, Swallowing, and Some Other Secrets.")

Virgin vault (n.): a dormitory or campus residence known for housing students of either sex who do not seek or engage in much sexual activity. Example: "First semester, Brumby Hall is known as the 'virgin vault.' However, after fall semester, it becomes the 'Nine Floors of Whores.'" (Lauren Morgan, "Abstinence Worth Wait If for Love," *Red and Black*, Mar. 31, 2006.)

Voterginity (n.): the status of a person who has not yet voted in an election. (Sari Eitches, "Election Night Erections," *Daily Californian*, Nov. 2, 2004.)

Wet mix (n.): a combination of songs typically burnt onto a CD or arranged on an iPod playlist used as a soundtrack for foreplay or sexual activity. Example: "Ciara, 20, recalls with fondness one of the first times Shad seduced her. Ciara was really into pictures, so Shad, 21, invited her up to his room to take a peek into his photo album. While she paged through, Shad proceeded to play his 'wet mix,' a mix CD full of baby-making, R&B hits." (Rose Afriyie, "One Pitt Couple's Sex Life: Seduction, Fetishes, Lessons," *Pitt News*, Sept. 27, 2005.)

Wet spot (n.): the awkward point in a relationship between casual sex and monogamy in which confusion reigns over a couple's status. Aka: "we need to talk" territory. (See Bonnie Sultan, "Who's That Girl?" *GW Hatchet*, Apr. 4, 2005; and Jess Beaton, "How to Keep a Hook-Up As Just a Hook-Up," *Johns Hopkins News-Letter*, Feb. 4, 2005.)

Winter break breakups (n.): relationship splits prior to a university's winter break, in part due to the temporary separation faced by couples who live far apart. (Christina Liciaga, "Winter Break: Break-Ups and Lie-Downs," *Muhlenberg Weekly*, Jan. 27, 2005.)

WWGS (What would Grandma say?) (n.): a reference point for dating etiquette, imploring students to consider their grandmother's reaction to their behavior while out with a relationship partner. Example: "Let's talk manners. While your date and your grandmother may not have much in common, both can—and will—immediately identify even your smallest faux pas. You didn't open the car door? BAD! You didn't let her walk first to the table? She'll make a mental note, you can be sure. You looked at her expectantly when the check came? You're done." (Julia Baugher, "Guys: Learn Your Set of 'Rules,'" *Hoya*, Nov. 22, 2002.)

NOTES

Chapter 1. Sex, Sex, SEX!: The Explosion of Sexual Expression in the Student Press

1. Glory Fink, "S-E-X: Early Lesson in Word Power Lasts a Lifetime," *Student Printz*, August 31, 2006.
2. Glory Fink, "Pillow Talk: Find a Group You Can Flirt In," *Student Printz*, November 30, 2006.
3. See "Sex Columnist Sacked at USM," Inkblots, September 21, 2007: http://www. mspress.org/inkblots/2007/09/21/sex-columnist-sacked-at-usm/; "Audio: USM Honors Forum on Pillow Talk," *Student Printz*, March 8, 2007: http://www. askglory.com/HonorsForum.html; Nancy Kaffer, "Thames Opposes Sex Column in Campus Paper," *Hattiesburg American*, October 3, 2006; "Sex Column May Offend, but Silencing Is Worse," *Hattiesburg American*, October 5, 2006; and Jim Brown, "Sex Column at So. Miss. Raising Some Hackles," *AgapePress*, September 13, 2006: http://headlines.agapepress.org/archive/9/afa/132006d. asp.
4. Kim Palmer, "Sex 101: College Scribes Add Sizzle to Student Newspapers," *Minneapolis Star Tribune*, March 22, 2003.
5. See Emily Steel, "Big Media on Campus: College Papers Around the U.S. Are Drawing Young Readers," *Wall Street Journal*, August 9, 2006; Tim Johnson, "Campus Newspapers Thrive," *Burlington Free Press*, October 21, 2008; Josh Keller, "Student Newspapers Escape Most Financial Problems of Larger Dailies," *Chronicle of Higher Education*, September 11, 2008; Bryan Murley, "College Media Has Come a Long Way Online," *MediaShift*, Public Broadcasting Service, November 19, 2008: http://www.pbs.org/mediashift/2008/11/college-media-has-come-a-long-way-online324.html; Nick Summers, "College Papers Grow Up: They Have the Ads, the Readers—and Budgets to Match," *Newsweek*, December 5, 2005, 48; Nick Madigan, "College Papers Deliver," *Baltimore Sun*, November 20, 2006; and Derrick Harris, "No Harm Done in Saying 'Penis,'" *Spectator*, September 19, 2002.
6. See Mary Beth Marklein, "Sex Is Casual at College Papers," *USA Today*, November 14, 2002; and Marah Eakin, "Sex and the Single College Grad," *WireTap*, May 4, 2005: http://www.alternet.org/story/21932.
7. See Tom Ashbrook, "Hooking Up on Campus," *On Point*, National Pubic Radio, September 29, 2006: http://www.onpointradio.org/shows/2006/09/20060929_ b_main.asp; Kathleen Deveny and Raina Kelley, "Girls Gone Bad," *Newsweek*, February 12, 2007, 40; "Students on Students: Eight College Girls (and One Obnoxious Guy) on the State of Sex on College Campuses Today," *Playboy*,

October 2007, 56; and Amy Cameron, "Campus Kama Sutra," *Maclean's*, April 4, 2005, 40–41.

8. See Sara Franklin, "Challenging the Taboos of Pleasure," *Tufts Daily*, February 14, 2006; and Ethan Jacobs, "Sex 101: BU Students Publish Porn," *Bay Windows*, February 10, 2005.

9. Rebecca Schwartz, "Sex and the University," *Outloud*, March 2003: http://www.outloud.com/2003/March%202003/sex_university.htm.

10. Rachael Parker, "Sex Smarts: Sex Column Can't Promise to Please All," *Penn*, April 27, 2007.

11. Jessie Gardner, "Confessions of a Sex Columnist," in Rachele Kanigel, *The Student Newspaper Survival Guide* (Ames, Iowa: Blackwell, 2006), 51.

12. Rodger Streitmatter, *Sex Sells!: The Media's Journey from Repression to Obsession* (New York: Westview Press, 2004), x.

13. See Archie Garcia, "The Lost Art of Dating," *California Aggie*, October 28, 2003; Caley Meals, "Let's Get It On," *Badger Herald*, September 25, 2002; Elizabeth Stortroen, "Dating and Doing It: Anything Goes in Modern Dating Game," *Campus Press*, April 25, 2007 (*Campus Press* is now *CU Independent*); Mindy Friedman, "Hook Up for Communism," *Daily Californian*, November 15, 2005; and Anna Scheelein, "The One That Got Away," *Heights*, October 8, 2002.

Chapter 2. Sexual, Revolutionary: The Pioneering College Newspaper Sex Column

1. See "23,000 Newspapers Stolen," *Student Press Law Center Report* 18.1 (Winter 1996–1997): 27; "California Thievin': Six Thefts of the University of California, Berkeley's Daily Californian Head a Long List of Disappearing Publications This Year," *Student Press Law Center Report* 18.3 (Fall 1997): 26; Jim Herron Zamora, "Daily Cal's 23,000 Copies Disappear After Angry Call," *San Francisco Examiner*, November 6, 1996; Hannah Miller and Jennifer Mukai, "Students Protest Against Daily Californian," *Daily Bruin*, November 11, 1996; and Brooke Olson, "Cal's Freedom of Press Thrown into Wind," *Daily Bruin*, November 11, 1996.

2. See Antonia Simigis, "Coed Sex Advice: The Best New Trend in College Newspapers," *Playboy*, February 2003, 80–82, 136; Brendan Cavalier, "My View from the Soapbox: Sex Columns Damage Integrity," *Daily Free Press*, February 11, 2003; and Rachele Kanigel, *The Student Newspaper Survival Guide* (Ames, Iowa: Blackwell, 2006), 50.

3. See Rory Laverty, "College Sex Columnists Shift Gears," *Alameda Times Star*, October 29, 2002; and Amelia Heagerty, "Sex on Tuesday Exposes Six Years of Sexcapades," *Daily Californian*, December 3, 2002.

4. See Max Shulman, ed., *Max Shulman's Guided Tour of Campus Humor* (Garden City, N.Y.: Doubleday, 1955), xxxi; Beth Bailey, *Sex in the Heartland* (Cambridge, Mass.: Harvard University Press, 1999), 159; untitled aside, *Pennsylvania Punch Bowl*, September 1928, 22; and Harvey Richter, ed., *Best College Humor: The First Collection from the American College Humorous Magazines* (Reading, Pa.: Handy Book Corporation, 1920), 27.

5. See "Yes, We Are Collegiate," *Time*, November 11, 1946, 68; and Richter, *Best College Humor*, 21, 45, 66.
6. See Richter, *Best College Humor*, 18; "Wake Up, Little Girl," *Pennsylvania Punch Bowl*, September 1928, 27; and Dan Carlinsky, ed., *A Century of College Humor* (New York: Random House, 1971), 82.
7. Beth Bailey, *From Front Porch to Back Seat: Courtship in Twentieth-Century America* (Baltimore: Johns Hopkins University Press, 1989), 159.
8. See untitled aside, *Buccaneer*, November 1939, 23; Bill Seeman, untitled cartoon, *Buccaneer*, November 1939, 11; and Sanford Stein, "Buccaneer Monthly Survey: Question This Month; Is Sex Here to Stay?" *Buccaneer*, November 1939, 10.
9. See "Bradshaw Lists Events That Led to Action of Council," *Daily Tar Heel*, November 12, 1939; "Buc Editor Goes Home Unaware of All Happenings," *Daily Tar Heel*, November 12, 1939; "No Action Is Taken on November Issue," *Daily Tar Heel*, November 12, 1939; and "The Buccaneer Issue," *Alumni Review* 28.3 (December 1939): 87 (*Alumni Review* is a magazine published by the General Alumni Association at the University of North Carolina).
10. See Julius Duscha and Thomas Fischer, *The Campus Press: Freedom and Responsibility* (Washington, D.C.: American Association of State Colleges and Universities, 1973), 21–22; Errol Zimmerman, "Rights vs. Rules," *College Press Review* 17.3 (Spring 1978): 12; and Sherri Taylor, "The College Press: An Outlet for Expression of Changing Social Values in the Fifties as Shown in the Daily Texan and Other College Papers," *College Media Review* 31.1 (Winter–Spring 1992): 46.
11. See "Virgin for Short," *Exponent*, May 14, 1969; and "Yes, No Virgin Came to UAH," *Exponent*, June 18, 1969.
12. See David Allyn, *Make Love, Not War: The Sexual Revolution: An Unfettered History* (New York: Routledge, 2001), 38–39; Duscha and Fischer, *Campus Press*, 1, 32–34; David Nelson, "Give Me Liberty and Give Me Debts," *College Media Review* 28.1 (Spring 1989): 8–9; Dario Politella, "The Changing Role of the Student Press in America," *College Press Review* 8.1 (Fall 1968): 5; David Rubin, "The Campus Press Slouching Toward Respectability," *Change*, April 1976, 34–36; and Robert F. Stevenson, "A Comparative Study of Assessment and Change Practices at Collegiate Newspapers in the United States," *College Media Review* 43.1–2 (Winter–Spring 2005): 38.
13. See "Campus Survey: Underground Press a Major Campus Influence," *Renaissance*, June 1969, 29; Kenneth S. Devol, "Obscenity: Boon or Bust?" *College Press Review* 14.2 (Winter 1974): 4; Robert J. Glessing, *The Underground Press in America* (Bloomington: Indiana University Press, 1970), 115; Esther Kitzes, "Before the Revolution Come the Words," *College Press Review* 8.3 (Spring 1968): 3; Abe Peck, *Uncovering the Sixties: The Life and Times of the Underground Press* (New York: Pantheon Books, 1985), xiii; Thomas Pepper, "Underground Press: Growing Rich on the Hippie," *The Nation*, April 29, 1968, 570; Peggy Scott, "The Underground Press," *College Press Review* 9.2–3 (Winter–Spring 1969): 7; and Rodger Streitmatter, *Sex Sells!: The Media's Journey from Repression to Obsession* (New York: Westview Press, 2004), 201.

14. Phil Angelo, "News Comes Alive: Campus News Need Not Be Dull or Irrelevant," *College Media Review* 24.3 (Spring 1985): 19.

15. See Louis Chunovic, *One Foot on the Floor: The Curious Evolution of Sex on Television from I Love Lucy to South Park* (New York: TV Books, 2000), 125–126, 143–144; Mary Beth Marklein, "Sex Is Casual at College Papers," *USA Today*, November 14, 2002; and Streitmatter, *Sex Sells!*, 115–116, 183, 187–189, 212–213.

16. See Bailey, *From Front Porch to Back Seat*; Streitmatter, *Sex Sells!*, xviii; and Steven Watts, *Mr. Playboy: Hugh Hefner and the American Dream* (Hoboken, N.J.: Wiley, 2008).

17. Leland Elliott and Cynthia Brantley, *Sex on Campus: The Naked Truth About the Real Sex Lives of College Students* (New York: Random House, 1997), 5–35.

18. See Eric Gibson, "Go to College, Learn the Skin Trade," *Wall Street Journal*, February 13, 2004, 15; Joe Jablonski, "Porn Studies Latest Academic Fad," *Accuracy in Academia Campus Reports*, October 2001; Jack Mabley, "More and More College Newspapers Relying on Sure-Fire Sales Technique," *Chicago Daily Herald*, October, 9, 2002; Marklein, "Sex Is Casual at College Papers"; Jillian Straus, *Unhooked Generation: The Truth About Why We're Still Single* (New York: Hyperion Books, 2007), 7, 80; and Streitmatter, *Sex Sells!*.

19. Laura Lambert, "Out for Sushi," *Daily Californian*, January 21, 1997.

20. See ibid.; Laura Lambert, "Ragtime," *Daily Californian*, March 18, 1997; Laura Lambert, "Knuckle Sandwich," *Daily Californian*, April 1, 1997; Laura Lambert, "How's Your Appetite?" *Daily Californian*, March 4, 1997; Laura Lambert, "Condom Day Is Coming," *Daily Californian*, February 11, 1997; and Laura Lambert, "Love Lines," *Daily Californian*, April 29, 1997.

21. See Laura Lambert, "An O by Any Name," *Daily Californian*, February 18, 1997; and Laura Lambert, "Exploring a Man's Sensitive Areas," *Daily Californian*, February 25, 1997.

22. Laura Lambert, "Desperately Seeking Skilled Bottoms," *Daily Californian*, February 4, 1997.

23. See Lambert, "An O by Any Name"; Lambert, "Ragtime"; Laura Lambert, "Don't Give Me No Lip," *Daily Californian*, January 28, 1997; and Lambert, "Knuckle Sandwich."

24. See Lambert, "Ragtime"; and Laura Lambert, "Talking Taboos," *Daily Californian*, April 15, 1997.

25. See Lambert, "How's Your Appetite?"; Lambert, "Knuckle Sandwich"; and Laura Lambert, "Breaking the Tie," *Daily Californian*, April 22, 1997.

26. Josh Coates, "Letter to the Editor," *Daily Californian*, February 27, 1997.

27. Laura Lambert, "One Last Ride," *Daily Californian*, May 13, 1997.

Chapter 3. Carrie Bradshaw of the Ivy League:
The Celebrity of Sex Columnist Natalie Krinsky

Epigraph: Natalie Krinsky quoted in Erica Dietsche, "Sex Columnist Has High Standards," *Hackensack Record*, April 21, 2006.

1. See Bruce Fellman, "Details: The Natalie Show," *Yale Alumni Magazine*,

Summer 2002: http://www.yalealumnimagazine.com/issues/02_07/details. html; Maggie Kim, "Q&A with . . . Natalie Krinsky," *Happen Magazine*, March 2005: http://www.match.com/magazine/article1.aspx?articleid=3644; "Natalie Krinsky," *Entertainment Weekly*, January 21, 2005: http://www.ew.com/ew/article/0,,1017492,00.html; Natalie Krinsky, "Spit or Swallow? It's All About the Sauce," *Yale Daily News*, December 7, 2001; and Sara Rimer, "Sex and the College Newspaper: Student Columnists Explore a Familiar Campus Topic," *New York Times*, October 4, 2002.

2. See David Gudelunas, *Confidential to America: Newspaper Advice Columns and Sexual Education* (Edison, N.J.: Transaction Publishers, 2007), 37–38, 42, 47–51, 206–207; Marie Manning, *Ladies Now and Then* (New York: E. P. Dutton, 1944), 123; and Robert Staughton Lynd and Helen Merrell Lynd, *Middletown: A Study in Contemporary American Culture* (New York: Harcourt, Brace, 1929), 116.

3. See Gudelunas, *Confidential to America*, 63; and Harnett Kane and Ella Bentley Arthur, "Dorothy Dix, Common Sense Philosopher," *Quill*, January 1953, 6.

4. See Gudelunas, *Confidential to America*, 79, 84–89, 93–97; Rick Kogan, *America's Mom: The Life, Lessons, and Legacy of Ann Landers* (New York: William Morrow, 2003), 56–58; Rory Laverty, "College Sex Columnists Shift Gears," *Alameda Times Star*, October 29, 2002; Jack Mabley, "More and More College Newspapers Relying on Sure-Fire Sales Technique," *Chicago Daily Herald*, October, 9, 2002; Sonya Moore, "Student Sex Columns Provide Service, Raise Eyebrows," *Editor and Publisher*, March 25, 2004: http://www. allbusiness.com/services/business-services-miscellaneous-business/4700750-1.html; and Kim Palmer, "Sex 101: College Scribes Add Sizzle to Student Newspapers," *Minneapolis Star Tribune*, March 22, 2003.

5. Gudelunas, *Confidential to America*, 94, 131–132, 138–139.

6. See Robert J. Glessing, *The Underground Press in America* (Bloomington: Indiana University Press, 1970), 104–105; and Rodger Streitmatter, *Sex Sells!: The Media's Journey from Repression to Obsession* (New York: Westview Press, 2004), 208–209. As Streitmatter wrote, "Many young people across the country, in fact, bought the *Barb* solely to hear what Dr. HIPpocrates had to say, his information being equally relevant to people living in Berkeley, Boston, Baton Rouge, or, for that matter, Bangkok." See Streitmatter, *Sex Sells!*, 209.

7. See Gudelunas, *Confidential to America*, 146, 161–162, 166; Sheelah Kolhatkar, "You Are Not Alone: College Newspapers Discover the Sex Column," *Atlantic Monthly*, November 2005, 144–147; Moore, "Student Sex Columns Provide Service"; Palmer, "Sex 101"; and Deborah Rivers, "Candace Bushnell: 'New York Is a City of Energy Vampires,'" CNN, June 4, 2009: http://edition.cnn. com/2009/TRAVEL/06/01/bushnell.interview/index.html.

8. See Christopher Beam and Nick Summers, "College Sex: Going Home Alone," *Washington Post*, September 23, 2007; and "Sex Column Report Card," IvyGate, October 10, 2006: http://www.ivygateblog.com/2006/10/sex-column-report-card/.

9. See Anna Dolinsky, "Sex and the Talmud," *New Voices*, February 14, 2008:

http://one-village.spaces.live.com/blog/cns!BC643D0EE3B38628!10590.entry;
Marah Eakin, "Sex and the Single College Grad," *WireTap*, May 4, 2005: http://
www.alternet.org/story/21932; Fellman, "Details"; and Julie Wiener, "Hooking
Up with Natalie Krinsky," *Jewish Week*, August 5, 2005.

10. See Kim, "Q&A with . . . Natalie Krinsky"; and Wiener, "Hooking Up with
Natalie Krinsky."

11. See Wiener, "Hooking Up with Natalie Krinsky"; and Maureen Miller, "Ways to
Screw Yale Without Making Love," *Yale Herald*, March 3, 2005.

12. Natalie Krinsky, "What's Love Got to Do, Got to Do with It?" *Yale Daily News*,
April 26, 2002.

13. Natalie Krinsky, "First Time for Everything: Losing the V-Card," The
Frisky, April 14, 2008: http://www.thefrisky.com/post/246-first_time_for_
everything_losing_the_v_card/.

14. Tara Weiss, "Yale Grad Parlays Sex Column into a 'Chick-Lit' Page-Turner,"
Hartford Courant, March 9, 2005.

15. See ibid.; and "Natalie Krinsky and Yvonne Fulbright, Who Write Sex Columns
for Their Student Newspapers, Discuss the Growing Popularity of Sex Columns
in College Newspapers Across the Nation," *Today*, NBC, October 7, 2002.

16. Natalie Krinsky, "Is That a Bud in Your Pocket? Or Are You Just Happy to See
Me?" *Yale Daily News*, November 9, 2001.

17. See Catherine Elsworth, "Naked Parties . . . Very Odd, Unnatural," *Daily
Telegraph*, February 3, 2006; Eakin, "Sex and the Single College Grad"; and
Dietsche, "Sex Columnist Has High Standards."

18. Moore, "Student Sex Columns Provide Service."

19. See Peter L. Hopkins, "Hopkins on Krinsky: Fm's Peter L. Hopkins Heads to
Yale for Some 'Sex' Ed.," *Harvard Crimson*, April 18, 2002; and Natalie Krinsky,
"Manual Manipulation: A Dying Art," *Yale Daily News*, October 26, 2001.

20. See Kolhatkar, "You Are Not Alone," 144; Natalie Krinsky, "Phase TWO: Get
Myself a Man," *Yale Daily News*, January 18, 2002; Krinsky, "Is That a Bud
in Your Pocket?"; Krinsky, "Manual Manipulation"; and Rimer, "Sex and the
College Newspaper."

21. See Weiss, "Yale Grad Parlays Sex Column into a 'Chick-Lit' Page-Turner"; Greg
Yolen, "I Dated Natalie, and You Didn't," *Yale Daily News*, September 28, 2002;
Kim, "Q&A with . . . Natalie Krinsky"; and Fellman, "Details."

22. See Krinsky, "Spit or Swallow?"; Eric Hoover, "The New Sex Scribes," *Chronicle
of Higher Education*, June 14, 2002; Amy Cameron, "Campus Kama Sutra,"
Maclean's, April 4, 2005, 40; Molly Fischer, "Yale in Pop Culture, from Gatsby
to Gossip Girl," *Yale Daily News*, February 6, 2009; Nahal Toosi, "UW-Madison
Columnist and Her Colleagues Have Little Shame Exploring What Used to Be
Pillow Talk," *Milwaukee Journal Sentinel*, November 17, 2002; and Fellman,
"Details."

23. Rimer, "Sex and the College Newspaper."

24. See ibid.; and Cameron, "Campus Kama Sutra," 40.

25. See Cameron, "Campus Kama Sutra," 40; Eakin, "Sex and the Single College

Grad"; Rimer, "Sex and the College Newspaper"; and Hopkins, "Hopkins on Krinsky."

26. See Jessica Marsden, "Krinsky '04 'Does Yale' in New Novel," *Yale Daily News*, February 21, 2005; Eakin, "Sex and the Single College Grad"; and Hoover, "New Sex Scribes."

27. See "Natalie Krinsky and Yvonne Fulbright," *Today*; Olivia Barker, "Novel 'Chloe' Flirts with Sexy Tales from Yale," *USA Today*, March 3, 2005; Cameron, "Campus Kama Sutra"; Fellman, "Details"; Hopkins, "Hopkins on Krinsky"; "Natalie Krinsky," *Entertainment Weekly*; Abigail Tucker, "Sex Writers Graduate to Real Jobs: Experience Adds Too Much Spice to Some Resumes," *Chicago Tribune*, May 1, 2005; and Elsworth, "Naked Parties." Krinsky said her parents' initial anger slowly turned to support, especially once she started writing *Chloe Does Yale*, which she dedicated to them. "I told them that people thought it was funny," she said. "It wasn't about me, it was about sex and yes, parents, that happens at college. Then they really got behind me. Mind you, if you tell your parents you have a book deal, they soon come around." See Elsworth, "Naked Parties."

28. See Wiener, "Hooking Up with Natalie Krinsky"; and Fellman, "Details."

29. Natalie Krinsky, "Food Is Messy, but It Still Gives Great Metaphor," *Yale Daily News*, November 22, 2002.

30. Dietsche, "Sex Columnist Has High Standards."

31. Natalie Krinsky, "A Trip to the Toy Store: Good Vibrations, Sweet Sensations," *Yale Daily News*, September 13, 2002.

32. Natalie Krinsky, "Take Dead Aim at Your Favorite Clique and Do 'Em—No, Not There!" *Yale Daily News*, February 8, 2002.

33. See Natalie Krinsky, "The Touching Diary of a Recovering Shop-aholic," *Yale Daily News*, September 6, 2002; Natalie Krinsky, "More Than You Ever Wanted to Know About Fake Orgasms," *Yale Daily News*, November 16, 2001; Natalie Krinsky, "Boys Will Be Boys—With or Without Their Cotton Boxers," *Yale Daily News*, March 1, 2002; and Natalie Krinsky, "Heading Down There? Don't Waste Your Time," *Yale Daily News*, February 15, 2002.

34. See Krinsky, "Is That a Bud in Your Pocket?"; Krinsky, "Manual Manipulation"; Krinsky, "More Than You Ever Wanted to Know About Fake Orgasms"; Natalie Krinsky, "Afraid I'll Miss Your Third-Day Call? Don't Worry, I'll Dial Star Sixty-nine," *Yale Daily News*, November 2, 2001; Rachel Avi, "When Chloe Met Charlotte: MIICRNYCOAGNWMA? The Attack of the Female Sex Columnist!" *Village Voice*, April 12, 2005; and Krinsky, "What's Love Got to Do, Got to Do with It?"

35. See Krinsky, "A Trip to the Toy Store"; Natalie Krinsky, "First Date 101: It's All About Assets," *Yale Daily News*, September 28, 2002; Natalie Krinsky, "No Matter What It Costs—Keep It Neat, Keep It Clean, Keep It Real," *Yale Daily News*, April 12, 2002; and Krinsky, "Heading Down There?"

36. See Rimer, "Sex and the College Newspaper"; Natalie Krinsky, "Vacation Strategy: How to Keep Score Against the Ex," *Yale Daily News*, November 30,

2001; Krinsky, "Heading Down There?"; Krinsky, "No Matter What It Costs"; Krinsky, "Phase TWO"; and Krinsky, "Afraid I'll Miss Your Third-Day Call?"

37. See Krinsky, "Manual Manipulation"; Natalie Krinsky, "The Top 10 Rules of Hook Ups, Bible Style," *Yale Daily News*, April 5, 2002; and Krinsky, "Is That a Bud in Your Pocket?"

38. See Weiss, "Yale Grad Parlays Sex Column into a 'Chick-Lit' Page-Turner"; and Rimer, "Sex and the College Newspaper."

39. See Eakin, "Sex and the Single College Grad"; Tucker, "Sex Writers Graduate to Real Jobs"; and Weiss, "Yale Grad Parlays Sex Column into a 'Chick-Lit' Page-Turner."

40. Marsden, "Krinsky '04 'Does Yale' in New Novel."

41. See Paul Harris, "Columnists Lay Bare Sex and Single Student," *Observer*, October 16, 2005; Matt Apuzzo, "Sex and the Ivy League: Book Describes Another Side of Life at Yale," Associated Press, March 29, 2005; and Eakin, "Sex and the Single College Grad."

42. See Colleen Long, "Chick-Lit Author Needs Some Advice: Sex and the Coed Tale Lacks Originality," *Houston Chronicle*, March 25, 2005; Charlotte Abbott, "Fiction Heats Up," *Publishers Weekly*, January 24, 2005, 120-123; Sarah M. Seltzer, "Yalie Chloe Pens Screed About Sex and the Safety School," *Harvard Crimson*, April 22, 2005; and Marsden, "Krinsky '04 'Does Yale' in New Novel."

43. Apuzzo, "Sex and the Ivy League."

44. See Elsworth, "Naked Parties"; Natalie Krinsky, "Bio," The Frisky: http://www.thefrisky.com/profile/15/; and Dietsche, "Sex Columnist Has High Standards."

45. See Yolen, "I Dated Natalie"; and Elsworth, "Naked Parties."

Chapter 4. Kate Has Become Sex:
The Impact of Sex Columns on Students' Personal Lives

Epigraph: Jessie Gardner, "Confessions of a Sex Columnist," in Rachele Kanigel, *The Student Newspaper Survival Guide* (Ames, Iowa: Blackwell, 2006), 51.

1. Leonora LaPeter, "Sexual Curiosity Is College Columnist's Muse," *St. Petersburg Times*, April 19, 2004.

2. Kate Carlisle, "Growing Up to Be 'Kelly Kapowski,'" *Cavalier Daily*, February 28, 2005.

3. See Mark Shanahan, "Hooking Up with Amber," *Boston Globe*, September 12, 2006; Amber Madison, "Breasts, Sex, and Power," *Tufts Daily*, April 9, 2003; and Amber Madison, "Angel in the Centerfold," *Tufts Daily*, October 9, 2002.

4. See Janet McCabe with Kim Akass, "Welcome to the Age of Un-Innocence," in *Reading Sex and the City*, ed. Kim Akass and Janet McCabe (London: I. B. Tauris, 2004), 2; Louis Chunovic, *One Foot on the Floor: The Curious Evolution of Sex on Television from I Love Lucy to South Park* (New York: TV Books, 2000), 155-157; and Lisa Schwarzbaum, "'Sex' and the Single Girl," *Entertainment Weekly*, August 23, 1996, 116.

5. See Margo Jefferson, "Finding Refuge in Pop Culture's Version of Friendship,"

New York Times, July 23, 2002; McCabe with Akass, "Welcome to the Age of Un-Innocence," in Akass and McCabe, *Reading Sex and the City*, 2; Deborah Jermyn, "In Love with Sarah Jessica Parker: Celebrating Female Fandom and Friendship in Sex and the City," in Akass and McCabe, *Reading Sex and the City*, 202; and Ashley Nelson, "Outsiders in the City," in Akass and McCabe, *Reading Sex and the City*, 232.

6. See Stephen Holden, "Tickets to Fantasies of Urban Desire," *New York Times*, July 20, 1999; Diana Werts, "She's Late to the Party," *Newsday*, June 4, 2000; and Chunovic, *One Foot on the Floor*, 155.

7. Leslie Kaufman, "Channeling Carrie," *New York Times*, March 30, 2008.

8. See Michelle Hainer, "Sexpert," *Washington Post*, September 14, 2003; LaPeter, "Sexual Curiosity Is College Columnist's Muse"; Ashley Konrad, "Letter to the Editor," *Oracle*, April 13, 2004; Allison Buchan-Terrell, "You Are Not the Next Carrie Bradshaw," *Gazette*, December 8, 2005; Julia Allison, "Carrie Bradshaw 101: The Rise of the College Sex Columnist," *COED Magazine*, November 2006, 18–20; Nicoletta Sabella, "College Sex Column Causes Controversy," *Loquitur*, February 2, 2006; and Elspeth Keller, "In Dating, Beware of the Next 'Mr. Huge,'" *Daily Trojan*, January 27, 2006.

9. Kelly Height, "Sex in the South Side," *Brown and White*, February 3, 2000.

10. Eric Hoover, "The New Sex Scribes," *Chronicle of Higher Education*, June 14, 2002.

11. Kate McDowell, "Time Flies When You're Getting Laid," *Cornell Daily Sun*, May 2, 2003.

12. Elizabeth Stierwalt, "I Could Have Called It Something Worse," *Crimson White*, April 27, 2006.

13. Rachel Kramer Bussel, "Miriam Datskovsky, Sex Columnist, *The Columbia Spectator*," *Gothamist*, November 7, 2005: http://gothamist.com/2005/11/07/miriam_datskovsky_sex_columnist_the_columbia_spectator.php.

14. Anna Ritner, "The Campus Lust List," *California Aggie*, February 8, 2005.

15. Erin Kaplan, "Where Has All the Dating Gone?" *Michigan Daily*, September 11, 2003.

16. James Whitaker, "A Day in the Life of the J-Spot," *Mustang Daily*, April 21, 2004.

17. See Brook Taylor, "Celibacy—It's Not Just for Priests," *Carolinian*, September 20, 2005; and Whitaker, "A Day in the Life."

18. Nadia Stadnycki, "Talking Dirty for Dummies," *Temple News*, October 4, 2005.

19. See Cristina Rouvalis, "Pitt News Columnist Dispenses Advice About Social Encounters in a Frankly Funny Manner," *Pittsburgh Post-Gazette*, April 8, 2004; and Sarah Walsh, "Departing Shots: A Potpourri of Sex Tips," *Phoenix*, December 4, 2003.

20. Brynn Burton, "Women: Take Control of Your Sexuality," *Post*, November 7, 2002.

21. Eve, "Revealing Yourself: Eve's Identity Crisis," *GW Hatchet*, April 30, 2007.

22. See Miriam Datskovsky, "Sexual Stereotypes in the Sack," *Columbia Spectator*, September 20, 2004; Miriam Datskovsky, "What Your Mother Didn't Tell You When You Had 'The Talk,'" *Columbia Spectator*, April 25, 2005; and Miriam Datskovsky, "Insertion is Nine Tenths of the Law," *Columbia Spectator*, November 15, 2004.

23. Bussel, "Miriam Datskovsky."

24. Jessica Saunders, "Time Flies When You're Getting Laid," *Cornell Daily Sun*, May 2, 2003.

25. Bussel, "Miriam Datskovsky."

26. Kim Palmer, "Sex 101: College Scribes Add Sizzle to Student Newspapers," *Minneapolis Star Tribune*, March 22, 2003.

27. Rouvalis, "Pitt News Columnist Dispenses Advice."

28. Stierwalt, "I Could Have Called It Something Worse."

29. See Amanda Baldwin, "A Lesson from Mom," *Bottom Line*, April 12, 2006; and Haley Yarosh, "Waxing Poetic on Hair-Raising Trends for Daters," *Emory Wheel*, December 6, 2005.

30. Beth Van Dyke, "For Some, There Is Beauty in the Beast," *Daily Nexus*, January 8, 2003.

31. Kaufman, "Channeling Carrie."

32. Caitlin Hall, "Sex, Lies, and Broadband," *Arizona Daily Wildcat*, April 2, 2007.

33. See "Reviews," Amber Madison Online: http://www.ambermadisononline.com/HookingUp; and "Hooking Up: A Girl's All-Out Guide to Sex and Sexuality," *Publishers Weekly*, July 24, 2006, 55.

34. Martha Irvine, "Not Just Sex, but Advice, Too, Popular on Campus," *Miami Herald*, September 15, 2002.

35. Amy Cameron, "Campus Kama Sutra," *Maclean's*, April 4, 2005, 40–41.

36. See Maria Sudekum Fisher, "Dr. Ruth She Isn't, but KU Journalism Student Says Her Beat Is Sex," *Wichita Eagle*, March 4, 2002; Aaron Passman, "Sex Column Creating Career?" *Daily Kansan*, October 10, 2002; Caitlin Kirley, "Columnist Became National Phenom," *Daily Kansan*, September 15, 2003; and Hoover, "New Sex Scribes."

37. See Fisher, "Dr. Ruth She Isn't"; Hoover, "New Sex Scribes"; and Kirley, "Columnist Became National Phenom."

38. Meghan Bainum, "Columnist Hops into Hef's World," *Daily Kansan*, October 24, 2002.

39. Ian Stanford, "Not a Typical School Girl," *Daily Kansan*, September 14, 2006.

40. Meghan Bainum, "Writer Says Goodbye in Final Sex Column," *Daily Kansan*, December 12, 2002.

Chapter 5. Love, Lust, and Every Kink In Between:
The Columns Tackle Modern Students' Social and Sexual Lives

1. See Rob Antle, "Pleasure and Payne: Memorial University Student Newspaper's Sex Columnist Aims to Inform, Not Titillate, but a Debate Is Raging Within the Paper About the Column," *St. John's Telegram*, February 7, 2004; Kaya Payne,

"Mind-Blowing Cunnilingus," *McGill Daily*, November 11, 2004; and Kaya Anderson Payne, "My Experiences as a Sex Columnist," *Spokeswoman*, Spring 2004, 8–9.

2. See Lindsay Harding, "Lay Off the Sex Columnists," *Muse*, April 5, 2006; and Kaya Anderson Payne, "Mind-Blowing Cunnilingus: A How-To Guide," *Muse*, February 10, 2004.

3. Antle, "Pleasure and Payne."

4. See ibid.; and Payne, "My Experiences as a Sex Columnist," 10.

5. See Antle, "Pleasure and Payne"; and Payne, "My Experiences as a Sex Columnist," 10.

6. Payne, "Mind-Blowing Cunnilingus." In comments made to Payne and *St. John's Telegram*, Wells said that a number of factors led him to not run the column's second half, including space concerns and eventually the elapsing of time, which made him question "whether it would still be valuable, because it's kind of gone stale." After the controversy, the *Muse* did publish separate articles by Payne on sex toys and masturbation. See Antle, "Pleasure and Payne."

7. See Christina Liciaga, "Make Some Noise, in Bed," *Muhlenberg Weekly*, April 7, 2005; Meghan Bainum, "Lawrence's Sex Spark Already Heating Up," *Daily Kansan*, August 22, 2002; and Chris Keegan, "Sex and the Cigar: One Man's Prophecy," *Good 5 Cent Cigar*, January 14, 2004.

8. Brynn Burton, "Vaginal, Um, Noises Worth Celebrating," *Post*, October 17, 2002.

9. See Emily Sparr, "Sex Column Fitting for a College Newspaper," *Tiger*, October 6, 2006; and Alexis McCabe, "Sexually Speaking," *Oracle*, March 6, 2006.

10. Sheelah Kolhatkar, "You Are Not Alone: College Newspapers Discover the Sex Column," *Atlantic Monthly*, November 2005, 144–147.

11. See Aly Murphy and Elena Gaudino, "PDA P's and Q's," *Daily Campus*, March 22, 2006; Jessica Pivik, "On Top," *Daily Reveille*, January 22, 2004; William Tran, "Beware the Serial Monogamist," *Phoenix*, April 3, 2003; Eve, "Is That a Flask in Your Pocket or Are You Just Flaccid to See Me?" *GW Hatchet*, October 2, 2006; Caitlin Hall, "Under Covers: Faking It," *Arizona Daily Wildcat*, January 28, 2004; Nadia Stadnycki, "Determining Your Born-Again Virginity," *Temple News*, November 1, 2005; and Haley Yarosh, "Parties and Visitors Yield Similar Results," *Emory Wheel*, November 16, 2004.

12. See Melissa Meinzer, "Suggestions for Boinking Beyond Boundaries of Bed," *Pitt News*, January 26, 2004; Sari Eitches, "Heading South," *Daily Californian*, October 5, 2004; Caley Meals, "The Age-Old Question: Spit or Swallow?" *Badger Herald*, April 9, 2003; Sari Eitches, "Morning-After Manners," *Daily Californian*, September 7, 2004; Laura Dlugatch, "Post-Hook-Up Etiquette: How to Save Face," *Review*, November 14, 2006; Archie Garcia, "Booty Calls," *California Aggie*, February 17, 2004; Emily Apatov, "Classroom Distraction," *Diamondback*, August 31, 2005; and Denise Brundson, "What You Should Know—Even if You Don't Want To—About the World's Nastiest Acronyms This Side of the U.S.S.R.," *McGill Daily*, January 6, 2005.

13. See Brook Taylor, "The Thin Line Between Admiration and Stalking," *Carolinian*,

November 8, 2005; Aly Murphy and Elena Gaudino, "Having a Gas," *Daily Campus*, November 30, 2005; Nadia Stadnycki, "Straight Up Sex," *Temple News*, October 26, 2004; and Jessica Ramsey Golden, "How to Get the Most Out of Your Fashion Bump," *Northern Light*, April 4, 2006.

14. John Bailey, "Obama and Your Sex Life," *Daily Campus*, November 5, 2008.

15. McLean Robbins, "Electronic Communication Ruins Our Sex Lives," *Old Gold & Black*, March 22, 2007.

16. Robin Cooper, "ED: Emotional Dysfunction," *New Paltz Oracle*, December 8, 2005.

17. See Dave Franzese, "Getting Wacky on Tabbacky," *Daily Nexus*, April 20, 2005; and Leonora LaPeter, "Sexual Curiosity Is College Columnist's Muse," *St. Petersburg Times*, April 19, 2004.

18. See Jessica Lee, "Are You Done Yet?" *Sophian*, September 13, 2007; Sari Eitches, "Pimp Your Ride," *Daily Californian*, February 22, 2005; Maria Medina, "Masturbation Is Healthy, Normal," *Ka Leo O Hawaii*, January 30, 2004; Roxy Sass, "Get More Out of Your Experience Here," *Stanford Daily*, October 13, 2006; Anthony Ciarrochi, "Early Ejaculation No Problem, Motorcycle Love Deadly," *Pitt News*, November 16, 2004; Jessica Lee, "Are You Done Yet?" *Sophian*, November 8, 2007; Glory Fink, "Sex Myths Mostly Untrue," *Student Printz*, November 16, 2006; and Lisa Hermann, "Introducing Your Local Friendly Health Columnist," *Cavalier Daily*, July 25, 2005.

19. See Liz Townsend, "Sexploration," *University News*, October 20, 2003; Valerie Arvidson, "What's Sexy, Dartmouth?" *Dartmouth Free Press*, November 12, 2004; Erin Granat, "Use Your Sincerity, Not Aphrodisia," *Nevada Sagebrush*, March 15, 2005; and Paul Shugar, "Is It a Flagpole or a Toothpick?" *Post*, April 24, 2003.

20. Madame Vixen, "Sexually Confused Women Want Questions Answered," *Acorn*, March 27, 2004.

21. See Samantha Levine, "Talking About Sex," *U.S. News and World Report*, April 9, 2005, 37; and Paul Shugar, "Smarter Than the Average Woman (At Least)," *Post*, April 3, 2003.

22. Jenna Bromberg, "Slut Pride," *Cornell Daily Sun*, August 23, 2007.

23. See Tom Ashbrook, "Hooking Up on Campus," *On Point*, National Pubic Radio, September 29, 2006: http://www.onpointradio.org/shows/2006/09/20060929_b_main.asp; and Elena Gaudino, "College Sex 101," *Daily Campus*, September 26, 2006.

24. See Elizabeth Stortroen, "Dating and Doing It: Anything Goes in Modern Dating Game," *Campus Press*, April 25, 2007 (*Campus Press* is now *CU Independent*); Elspeth Keller, "Dating at USC Is an Endangered Species," *Daily Trojan*, January 20, 2006; Erin Kaplan, "Where Has All the Dating Gone?" *Michigan Daily*, September 11, 2003; and Valerie Arvidson, "Sex and Sensibility: How Are You Spending Valentine's Day," *Dartmouth Free Press*, February 10, 2005.

25. See Scott Gentry, "Ask the Wise Guy: The Red Damn Line," *Broadside*, October 26, 2007; Eve, "The Do's and Don'ts of Getting Some This Year," *GW Hatchet*, February 12, 2007; Sumer Rose, "The Dating Game Is Dead in

Oxford," *Daily Mississippian*, January 15, 2003; and Miriam Datskovsky, "Defining and Defeating the 'Hook-Up,'" *Columbia Spectator*, October 18, 2004.

26. See Miriam Datskovsky, "Roller-Coaster Romance: Let's Get Rid of the Loops," *Columbia Spectator*, February 7, 2005; RJ Milligan, "Accepting Sexuality in College," *Heights*, March 16, 2004; Bonnie Sultan, "Virtually Dating," *GW Hatchet*, February 28, 2005; Laura Dlugatch, "Dating: Does It Exist?" *Review*, May 1, 2007; Kaplan, "Where Has All the Dating Gone?"; Brynn Burton, "Guys Should Have Agenda for Dates," *Post*, January 9, 2003; and Archie Garcia, "The Lost Art of Dating," *California Aggie*, October 28, 2003.

27. See Kate McDowell, "Wisdom of the Ages," *Cornell Daily Sun*, April 17, 2003; Julia Baugher, "Dating with a Lowercase 'D,'" *Hoya*, October 4, 2002; and Miriam Datskovsky, "No Dating: The Extremes Make More Sense Than You Think," *Columbia Spectator*, April 11, 2005.

28. See Heather Strack, "To Hook-Up, or Not to Hook-Up: The Horizontal Rule," *Dartmouth Free Press*, February 10, 2006; Nicole Wroten, "Getting Off the Hook," *Maroon*, November 16, 2006; and Mindy Friedman, "Hook Up for Communism," *Daily Californian*, November 15, 2005.

29. See Elizabeth Stortroen, "Below the Fold: 'Hooking Up' Shrouded in Confusion," *Campus Press*, March 7, 2007; and Denise Nilan, "What the Hell Does Hooking-Up Mean?" *Mustang Daily*, January 29, 2009.

30. See Liz Townsend, "Sexploration," *University News*, April 21, 2003; and Haley Yarosh, "If It Ain't Broke, Don't Fix It: Relationships Need No Update," *Emory Wheel*, April 5, 2005.

31. See Townsend, "Sexploration," April 21, 2003; and Anna Tauzin, "The Benefits from Friends," *University Star*, May 23, 2007.

32. RJ Milligan, "Rebound with the Ex-Factor," *Heights*, March 23, 2004.

33. See Paul Shugar, "It's Over . . . Except the Sex," *Post*, May 15, 2003; Jess Beaton, "Sex with Your Ex," *Johns Hopkins News-Letter*, February 27, 2004; and Jenny Kalaidis, "Time to Look at 'Ex Factor,'" *Badger Herald*, March 22, 2007.

34. See Julia Baugher, "To Booty Call or Not to Booty Call—Is There Really a Question?" *Hoya*, January 31, 2003; Dave Franzese, "Can I Stay Forever?" *Daily Nexus*, May 4, 2005; and Robin Cooper, "Girls Just Wanna Have Fun," *New Paltz Oracle*, November 17, 2005.

35. See Jessica Saunders, "Why We Should All 'Trick or Treat,'" *Cornell Daily Sun*, October 31, 2002; Jessica Saunders, "Single Me Out," *Cornell Daily Sun*, April 10, 2003; and Anna Ritner, "All the Kids Are Doing It," *California Aggie*, December 7, 2004.

36. See Miriam Datskovsky, "Otherwise Known as Walking," *Columbia Spectator*, October 24, 2005; Dlugatch, "Post-Hook-Up Etiquette"; RJ Milligan, "Victory Lap," *Heights*, January 20, 2004; Aly Murphy and Elena Gaudino, "The Morning After Blues," *Daily Campus*, October 12, 2005; James Whitaker, "Proudly Walking the Walk of Shame," *Mustang Daily*, January 29, 2004; and Elizabeth Stierwalt, "Sex Hair and the Strut of Infamy," *Crimson White*, October 13, 2005.

37. See Valerie Arvidson, "An Investigation into Sluts," *Dartmouth Free Press*, October 21, 2005; and Kate McDowell, "Mmmm Good," *Cornell Daily Sun*, October 10, 2002.
38. See Rachel Axelbank, "What Women Want: Sex, a Defense of the Female Libido," *Daily Princetonian*, April 29, 2004; Abi Medvin, "Promiscuous or Prude: A Question of Numbers," *Dartmouth*, February 2, 2007; and Tauzin, "Benefits from Friends."
39. See Beth Van Dyke, "Men Dangle Between Rock Hard and a Soft Place," *Daily Nexus*, May 28, 2003; and Marisa Picker, "Sexual Healing Makes Us Feel So Fine," *Diamondback*, April 4, 2006.
40. See Anna Schleelein, "The Secret Weapons," *Heights*, April 1, 2003; Amber Madison, "Why We Hook Up," *Tufts Daily*, April 7, 2004; Bromberg, "Slut Pride"; Anthony Ciarrochi, "Girls Gone Wild, Boys Not Wild Enough," *Pitt News*, October 18, 2004; and LaPeter, "Sexual Curiosity."
41. Datskovsky, "Otherwise Known as Walking."
42. See Kimberly Maier, "Ask Dr. Kim—Male Empowerment," *Clackamas Print*, May 22, 2007; and Arvidson, "Investigation into Sluts."
43. See Kate Carlisle, "Curiosity Killed the Kate," *Cavalier Daily*, September 5, 2005; and Lauren Morgan, "Concessions Essential When Dating," *Red and Black*, February 17, 2006.
44. See Jessica Pivik, "On Top," *Daily Reveille*, May 6, 2004; and McLean Robbins, "Sex Is Easy . . . Sometimes," *Old Gold & Black*, April 4, 2007.
45. See Randall Patterson, "Students of Virginity," *New York Times Magazine*, March 30, 2008, 38; and Jennie Yabroff, "Campus Sexperts: Erotic Magazines Run by Students at Elite Colleges Have Prospered: So Why Are They Having Less Sex?" *Newsweek*, February 25, 2008, 46–47.
46. See Yabroff, "Campus Sexperts," 46–47; and Dana Hull, "Sex Talk on Campus: Columnists Don't Shy Away from Explicit Advice," *San Jose Mercury News*, September 23, 2004.
47. Andrew Herrmann and Lori Rackl, "On College Campuses the Pressure Is Intense for One-Night Hookups, Without Emotion or Commitment," *Chicago Sun-Times*, March 18, 2005.
48. See ibid.; and Barrett Seaman, *Binge: What Your College Student Won't Tell You* (Hoboken, N.J.: Wiley, 2006).
49. Ben Shapiro, *Porn Generation: How Social Liberalism Is Corrupting Our Future* (Washington, D.C.: Regnery Publishing, 2005), 34, 38, 46.
50. Kolhatkar, "You Are Not Alone," 145.
51. Beth Van Dyke, "Face It, Nice Guys: Every Girl's Crazy 'Bout a Badass Man," *Daily Nexus*, February 26, 2003.
52. See Robbins, "Electronic Communication Ruins Our Sex Lives"; Lindsay Johnson, "Booty Calls: Read the Fine Print Before You Buy-In," *Rebel Yell*, May 4, 2006; Claire Fuller, "Something to Think About," *Lumberjack*, April 8, 2004; Brook Taylor, "My Love Role Models," *Carolinian*, November 15, 2005; and Natalie Krinsky, "What's Love Got to Do, Got to Do with It?" *Yale Daily News*, April 26, 2002.

Chapter 6. Clash of Cultures: Outside Criticism and Censorship of Student Sex Columns

1. See James Whitaker, "Nothing Fresher Than a Freshman," *Mustang Daily*, September 25, 2004; and Teresa Allen, "Sex Columns: They're Everywhere These Days, It Seems. Some Go Well, Some Don't: What Is an Adviser's Role?" *College Media Review* 42.2 (Spring 2004): 6–10.
2. It is important to note that student readers are certainly not a unified front. They express periodic concerns and anger in letters to the editor, e-mails, and personal asides with columnists and editors. Yet overall, they are admiring or indifferent toward the columns, with even the most vocal pockets of student opposition falling far short of the organized efforts by outside individuals and groups.
3. See Cristina Rouvalis, "Pitt News Columnist Dispenses Advice About Social Encounters in a Frankly Funny Manner," *Pittsburgh Post-Gazette*, April 8, 2004; Chris Bundgaard, "Racy Column Draws Mother's Ire Against College Paper," WKRN.com, September 20, 2005; and Allen, "Sex Columns," 6–10.
4. "The Rise and Fizzle of the College Sex Mag," *Playboy*, October 2007, 58.
5. Kate Prengaman, "Closing the Door One Last Time," *Flat Hat*, May 1, 2007.
6. See Tena Starr, "Sex Column Stirs Controversy at Lyndon State College," *Caledonian-Record*, November 1, 2007; and Keith Whitcomb Jr., "Letter from the Editor," *Critic*, October 19, 2007.
7. See Jordan Royer, "AIMing for a Better Sex Life?" *Critic*, September 28, 2007; Jordan Royer, "Don't Let Stress Get You Down," *Critic*, October 2007; and Jordan Royer, "Jackpot," *Critic*, October 2007.
8. See Elizabeth Norris, "Letters, to the Editor and Otherwise," *Critic*, October 19, 2007; and Starr, "Sex Column Stirs Controversy."
9. See Allison Maier, "Sex Column Causes Controversy; First Amendment Issues Raised," *Montana Kaimin*, March 11, 2009; and Chelsi Moy, "UM Student Newspaper's Sex Column Causes Stir on Campus," *Missoulian*, March 15, 2009.
10. See Lux, "Assignment 1: Get Acquainted," *Towerlight*, September 17, 2009: http://www.thetowerlight.com/blog-1.107/thebedpost?article155=19.10940 36&page155=BlogPosting; Robert L. Caret, "A Sense of Disappointment from Last Week's 'Bed Post,'" *Towerlight*, September 24, 2009; Childs Walker, "Sex Column Flap Forces Student Editor's Exit," *Baltimore Sun*, October 7, 2009; Loni Ingraham, "TU's Towerlight Editor Resigns in Wake of Column Controversy," *Towson Times*, October 7, 2009; senior editorial board, "Let's Talk About Sex," *Daily Californian*, October 13, 2009; and "Statement from The Towerlight," *Towerlight*, October 4, 2009: http://www.thetowerlight. com/statement-from-the-towerlight-1.1938159.
11. Editorial, "Freedom to Make Mistakes," *Baltimore Sun*, October 8, 2009.
12. Staff editorial, "Sex Column Aims to Educate: Staff Stands Behind Choice to Print," *News Record*, February 24, 2005.
13. "Orgasms: Do You Fake It?" *Wagnerian*, November 18, 2002. The sidebar accompanied the following column: Jackie Nguyen, "The Sex-Files: The Big Bang," *Wagnerian*, November 18, 2002.

14. See "College Pulls Papers Over Sex Column," *Quill*, April 1, 2003; Jackie Nguyen and Jill Higgins, "Wagnerian Pulled from Stand: Freedom of Speech Becomes a Campus-Wide Issue After Sex Column Is Published," *Wagnerian*, December 9, 2002; and "N.Y. College Readmits Adviser Following Sex Column Controversy: Confiscated Newspapers Remain in Administrators' Hands," Student Press Law Center, February 4, 2003: http://www.splc.org/newsflash. asp?id=548.

15. See Jerry Allegood, "Student Editor Fights Review; Column on Sex Spurs New Policy," *Raleigh News & Observer*, March 25, 2005; G.D. Gearino, "Out of the Briar Patch," *Raleigh News & Observer*, July 19, 2005; "Sex-Advice Column Prompts Debate—School President Wants Newspaper Reviewed Before Publication," *Charlotte Observer*, March 25, 2005; K. J. Williams, "Student-Run Newspaper at Center of CCC Meeting," *Chicago Sun-Times*, March 24, 2005; and Amanda Worley, "Fantasy Play Can Jolt Tired Sex Lives," *Campus Communicator*, March 2005.

16. See Jim Martyka, "N.C. School Considers Turning Paper Over to Corporate Publisher," *Trends in College Media*, May 2, 2005: http://www.studentpress. org/acp/trends/~craven.html; and "Curriculum Students Demographics: Enrollment by Age Groups," *Craven Community College Institutional Fact Book*, September 2003, 24.

17. See Martyka, "N.C. School Considers Turning Paper Over to Corporate Publisher"; Robert L. Shibley, "FIRE Letter to Craven Community College President Scott Ralls," Foundation for Individual Rights in Education, April 22, 2005: http://www.thefire.org/index.php/article/5815.html; and Gearino, "Out of the Briar Patch."

18. See Gearino, "Out of the Briar Patch"; Greg Lukianoff, "Victory for Press Freedom at Craven Community College," Foundation for Individual Rights in Education, June 22, 2005: http://www.thefire.org/index.php/article/5818. html; Rebecca McNulty, "N.C. College, Student Newspaper Reach Agreement to Grant Paper Independence," Student Press Law Center, June 13, 2005: http:// www.splc.org/newsflash.asp?id=1022; and Shibley, "FIRE Letter to Craven Community College President Scott Ralls."

19. See Paul A. Atkins, *The College Daily in the United States* (Parsons, W.Va.: McClain Printing, 1982), 5; and Bernice Ng, "Sex on Tuesday Steams Up Readers," *Daily Californian*, September 23, 1999.

20. See Alicia Ragonese, "Letters to the Editor: Parent Concern About Sex Column," *Muhlenberg Weekly*, February 17, 2005; and Maria Sudekum Fisher, "Dr. Ruth She Isn't, but KU Journalism Student Says Her Beat Is Sex," *Wichita Eagle*, March 4, 2002.

21. Romel Hernandez, "OSU Newspaper Cancels Graphic 'Ask the Sexpert' Advice Column," *Portland Oregonian*, February 17, 1999.

22. Bill Stauduhar, "Meanwhile, Back at UWF: Sex and the U. Complaint," *Voyager*, March, 19, 2009.

23. Ed Dalesdandro, "Sex Column Poorly Timed," *Penn*, October 27, 2006.

24. Kathleen Brasington, "Sex Column: Inappropriate for Readership," *Flat Hat*, October 29, 2004.

25. Timaree Schmit, "Get into Rhythm, Learn Technique," *Daily Nebraskan*, February 6, 2004.

26. Karen Knight, "Schmit Unrepresentative," *Daily Nebraskan*, October 22, 2003.

27. See Wes Hazard, "Sex Column Serves a Purpose," *Heights*, November 19, 2002; Anna Schleelein, "You've Got (Fan) Mail," *Heights*, April 29, 2003; and Anna Schleelein, "Protect and Serve, We Dare to Compare," *Heights*, November 5, 2002.

28. Schleelein, "You've Got (Fan) Mail."

29. See Ryan Maher, "As This Jesuit Sees It: So-Called Peer Wisdom Often Anything But," *Hoya*, November 21, 2003; and Rob Johansen, "Georgetown University: Committed to 'Inclusivity,' Not the Gospel," comment on Thrown Back, September 10, 2003: http://thrownback.blogspot.com/2003/09/georgetown-university-committed-to.html.

30. See Jodi San Lucas, "Wedding Night So Overrated," *Maroon*, January 25, 2007; and "Column Sparks Debate," *Maroon*, February 1, 2007.

31. See Sumer Rose, "Morning or Afternoon—Any Time's Good for a 'Nooner,'" *Daily Mississippian*, April 8, 2003; Wilson Boyd, "UM Sex Column Sparks Controversy," *Reflector*, April 25, 2003; Allen, "Sex Columns," 6–10; Karen Nelson and Tracy Dash, "Ocean Springs Student's Sex Column Sizzles," *Biloxi Sun Herald*, April 25, 2003; and Diane B. Quinn, "Sex Column Says a Lot," *Biloxi Sun Herald*, May 1, 2003.

32. See Max Seigle, "College Will Let 'Love Monkey' Continue Writing Sex Column," *Chicago Daily Herald*, October 24, 2002; Mary Beth Marklein, "Sex Is Casual at College Papers," *USA Today*, November 14, 2002; and Ian Stanford, "Not a Typical School Girl," *Daily Kansan*, September 14, 2006.

33. See Rebecca McNulty, "Ariz. Budget Prohibits: Measure Was Introduced in March, After Student Newspapers Published Controversial Content," Student Press Law Center, June 28, 2005: http://www.splc.org/newsflash.asp?id=1047; and Claire Fuller, "Something to Think About," *Lumberjack*, February 12, 2004.

34. See "Gimme Some Sex," *Daily Barometer*, March 1, 2004; Bob Purvis, "NAU Blow Job Column Ignites Controversy," *Arizona Daily Wildcat*, February 26, 2004; and Dennis Durband, "Humanist Education, Your Tax Dollars, and Instruction in Oral Sex," *Arizona Conservative*, n.d.: http://www.azconservative.org/durband7.htm.

35. See "Issue of the Week: Blow Job Backlash," *Arizona Daily Wildcat*, March 3, 2004; "University President Threatens to Cut Newspaper Funding Over Magazine Cover," Student Press Law Center, November 30, 2004: http://www.splc.org/newsflash_archives.asp?id=918&year=2004; "Arizona Lawmakers Threaten Funding for Campus Newspapers," Associated Press, March 11, 2005: http://www.firstamendmentcenter.org/news.aspx?id=14963; Sheelah Kolhatkar, "You Are Not Alone: College Newspapers Discover the Sex Column," *Atlantic Monthly*, November 2005, 144–147; and Kate Campbell, "Ariz. Lawmaker Proposes Eliminating State Funds for Student Publications," Student

Press Law Center, March 16, 2005: http://www.splc.org/newsflash_archives. asp?id=985&year=2005.

36. See "Arizona Lawmakers Threaten Funding for Campus Newspapers," Associated Press; Kate Campbell, "Ariz. Budget that Proposed Eliminating Funding for Student Publications Vetoed," Student Press Law Center, April 5, 2005: http://www.splc.org/newsflash_archives.asp?id=998&year=2005; and Campbell, "Ariz. Lawmaker Proposes Eliminating State Funds for Student Publications."

37. Kara Lindquist, "Blow Job Should Be Quick," *Collegian*, February 17, 2004.

38. See Toby Uecker, "Column in Collegian is Subject of Controversy," *Collegian*, February 24, 2004; Eric Novotny, "Letter to the Editor," *Collegian*, March 2, 2004; and Todd VanDerWerff, "Sex Column Important, Needs Closer Eye," *Collegian*, February 24, 2004.

39. Callie Elizabeth Butler, "Anonymous Women's Perspectives Give Ways to Spice Up Your Sex Life," *Sidelines*, September 13, 2005.

40. See Bundgaard, "Racy Column Draws Mother's Ire"; and Michaela Jackson, "Sex Column Offends Parent," *Sidelines*, September 19, 2005.

41. See Allison Moorhead, "Just a Spoon Full of Sugar Helps the Medicine Go Down," *Spectrum*, August 31, 2004; and Dana Hull, "Sex Talk on Campus: Columnists Don't Shy Away from Explicit Advice," *San Jose Mercury News*, September 23, 2004.

42. See "NDSU Board Against Student Columns," *Bismarck Tribune*, September 23, 2004; "NDSU Sex Columnist Switching Papers," *Bismarck Tribune*, September 5, 2004; and Matthew Perrine, "Editor's Note V: Break It Up," *Spectrum*, September 10, 2004.

43. See Janet Gillett, "Stirred Up About Sex," *Spartan*, October 31, 2007; Whitcomb, "Letter from the Editor"; and Terry Badman, "'Holy Sheet' Issue Got Out of Hand," *Spartan*, November 14, 2007.

44. See Robert Soave, "Free Speech Is Sexy," *Michigan Daily*, March 16, 2009; and "Individual Faculty Members Were Approached and Asked to Comment on the Situation," *Wagnerian*, December 9, 2002.

45. Christina Liciaga, "Twenty-nine Seconds: Reflections and Farewells," *Muhlenberg Weekly*, April 28, 2005.

46. See Dwight Bentel, "College Press Freedom Is Controversial Issue," *Editor and Publisher*, January 8, 1949, 18; Brandt Gassman, "College Papers Going Soft," *Washington Square News*, December 4, 2002; and Brynn Burton, "Women: Take Control of Your Sexuality," *Post*, November 7, 2002.

47. Erin Granat, "Sex Shouldn't Scare You So Damn Much," *Nevada Sagebrush*, May 3, 2005.

Chapter 7. *Playboy* for the College Set: The Rise and Influence of Campus Sex Magazines

1. "L'Universita' Del Porno," *Lucignolo*, Italia 1, April 4, 2005. *Lucignolo* is a news program on Italia 1, a commercial television station in Italy aimed at young people.

2. See Andrew Nusca, "Art Porn?: Harvard's H Bomb Is More of a Bottle Rocket," *Washington Square News*, March 21, 2007; Ashlea Halpern, "Art

School Confidential: Bryn Mawr's Virgin Mawtyr Gets Literary on Your Ass," *Philadelphia City Paper*, November 2, 2006; Andrew Rimas, "The Porn Princess of B.U.," *Boston Magazine*, January 2006, 98–102; Nicole Adamson, "Intellectual Masturbation: Nicole Adamson Probes How University of Chicago's New Magazine Takes Sex Ed to a Whole New Level," *Northwestern Chronicle*, January 23, 2005; Elizabeth Ehrenberg, "Sex and the Student Body," *In These Times*, August 15, 2003: http://www.inthesetimes.com/article/610/sex_and_the_student_body/; and Nina MacLaughlin, "Naked Ambition: BU's *Boink* Offers Porn for the People," *Boston Phoenix*, February 11–17, 2005.

3. See Sean Cole, "Is Boink the Next Playboy?" *Marketplace*, American Public Media, May 8, 2006: http://marketplace.publicradio.org/display/web/2006/05/08/is_boink_the_next_playboy/; Anita Davis, "In Bed with Boink Magazine," *Daily Free Press*, February 25, 2005; Alexandra Jacobs, "Campus Exposure," *New York Times Magazine*, March 4, 2007, 44; Kennan Knudson, "And Now, College Goes to Playboy: Sex Mags Emerge at BU, Harvard," *Boston Globe*, February 13, 2005; and Jodi Rudoren, "The Student Body," *New York Times*, April 23, 2006.

4. See Jeffrey P. Moran, *Teaching Sex* (Cambridge, Mass.: Harvard University Press, 2000), 156–157; Rodger Streitmatter, *Sex Sells!: The Media's Journey from Repression to Obsession* (New York: Westview Press, 2004), xi, 16–18; and Steven Watts, *Mr. Playboy: Hugh Hefner and the American Dream* (Hoboken, N.J.: Wiley, 2008).

5. See Streitmatter, *Sex Sells!*, 67, 74; Watts, *Mr. Playboy*, 300; and David Allyn, *Make Love, Not War: The Sexual Revolution: An Unfettered History* (New York: Routledge, 2001), 232.

6. See Adamson, "Intellectual Masturbation"; Aditi Eleswarapu, "Sex and Man at Yale: Sex Magazine to Be Distributed," *Daily Princetonian*, February 15, 2006; and Marcella Bombardieri and Jenna Russell, "Gray Is Out at Harvard; UMass Faculty Back In," *Boston Globe*, October 10, 2004.

7. Rimas, "Porn Princess of B.U."

8. See "Love in the Stacks (Part I): The Librarian," *Vita Excolatur*, Fall 2004, 4–8; and "Love in the Stacks (Part II): Extra Credit," *Vita Excolatur*, Fall 2004, 9–10.

9. Andrew Herrmann, "Magazine Peeks at the Sexy Side of the U. of C.," *Chicago Sun-Times*, January 13, 2005.

10. Michael Winerip, "In School," *New York Times*, November 17, 1993.

11. See ibid.; and Ben Gose, "Gay Students Debate Their Politics and Images," *Chronicle of Higher Education*, February 9, 1996.

12. Brandee J. Tecson, "'Yo, Is That My Lab Partner with No Pants On?' BU Undergrads Launch Porn Mag: Boink Plugged as 'Real College Porn for Real College Students,'" MTV News, March 15, 2005: http://www.mtv.com/news/articles/1498149/20050315/index.jhtml.

13. Jacobs, "Campus Exposure," 44.

14. See John Carroll, "Let's Talk About Text, Baby," *34th Street Magazine*, April 14, 2005: http://www.34st.com/node/2787; and Christopher Frizzelle,

"Nightstand," *Stranger*, April 5–11, 2004: http://www.thestranger.com/seattle/nightstand/Content?oid=17696.

15. See Suzanne Bell, "Sex Mag Editors Report Differences in Funding, No Censorship," *Student Press Law Center Report* 17.3 (Fall 2006): 38; Tara Lynch, "Hey, Isn't the Girl from Page 7 in Your Class?" *Fairfield Mirror*, April 14, 2005; Rimas, "Porn Princess of B.U."; Rudoren, "Student Body"; and Jenna Russell, "BU Students to Get Own Sex Magazine: School Officials Decry Senior's Plan," *Boston Globe*, October 6, 2004.

16. See Ehrenberg, "Sex and the Student Body"; Sarah Rutledge, "Literary Sex Magazine Debuts," *Rice Thresher*, April 11, 2008; Ryan Yacco, "Students Have Sex, but It's Not Something Campus Media Reports On," *Daily Targum*, April 20, 2006; and Cassidy Hartmann, "Let's Talk About Sex: Penn Students Launch the University's First Erotic Literary Magazine," *Philadelphia Weekly*, November 2, 2005.

17. See Bell, "Sex Mag Editors Report Differences in Funding"; Herrmann, "Magazine Peeks at the Sexy Side of the U. of C."; Patrice M. Jones, "Rated X on Campus: U. of C. Magazine Offers Erotica, Photos, and Advice for Sexually Liberated Students—but Don't Tell Their Parents," *Chicago Tribune*, July 13, 2006; M. L., "Let's Talk About Sex," UCHiBLOGo, February 7, 2005: http://uchiblogo.uchicago.edu/archives/2005/02/lets_talk_about.html; Rudoren, "Student Body"; and James Thornhill, "Porn in the USA," *National Student*, July 5, 2005.

18. "Other Campuses: Erotic Student Magazine Revived with Big Bang," *Daily Illini*, October 22, 2004.

19. See Alan Pappalardo, "Cloistered by Society's Eyes," *X-Magazine*, Spring 2005, 4–5; Rutledge, "Literary Sex Magazine Debuts"; Michelle Crentsil, "Dreaming in a New Body," *H Bomb*, Spring 2008, 68–69; "Meeting Sasha Grey: A Cultural Anthropological Inquiry," *H Bomb*, Spring 2008, 50–55; and Alex Meyers, "Gloria," *H Bomb*, Spring 2008, 7–8.

20. Colleen Davis, "Rag Doll," *X-Magazine*, Fall 2007, 14.

21. Frizzelle, "Nightstand."

22. See "Dirty Diction," *Boink*, May 2005, 22–23; and "Ask Syd Anything," *Vita Excolatur*, Spring 2005, 22.

23. "H Bomb at the New Hampshire Primaries," *H Bomb*: http://www.youtube.com/user/hbombmag.

24. See Charlotte Rutherfurd, "Discus," *Vita Excolatur*, Spring 2005, 12–17; "Kaz," *Boink*, May 2005, 42–49; "Douglas," *Boink*, May 2005, 62–69; and "Anna," *Boink*, May 2005, 88–95.

25. See Christopher Anderson and Alisa Lemberg, "Allison," *Boink*, February 2005, 74–79; Kasia, "Vaughn at 7B," *H Bomb*, Spring 2005, 36–37; Ming Vandenberg, untitled photographs, *H Bomb*, Spring 2005, 12–13; Rebecca Lieberman, "The Mermaid Parade, Coney Island," *H Bomb*, Spring 2008, 62–64; and Jan Lennard, "Stranger Than Life," *H Bomb*, Spring 2008, 73.

26. "Step-by-Step: A College Hook Up," *Sex Week at Yale: The Magazine*, February 2008, 23–26.

27. See Rodger Streitmatter, *Voices of Revolution: The Dissident Press in America* (New York: Columbia University Press, 2001), 75–78; Ben Shapiro, *Porn Generation: How Social Liberalism Is Corrupting Our Future* (Washington, D.C.: Regnery Publishing, 2005), 170; and Allyn, *Make Love, Not War,* 187.

28. See Allyn, *Make Love, Not War,* 185, 234–237; Ralph Blumenthal, "Pornochic: 'Hard-Core' Grows Fashionable—and Very Profitable," *New York Times Magazine,* January 21, 1973, 28; Bob Greene, "Beyond the Sexual Revolution," *Newsweek,* September 29, 1975, 13; Robert J. Glessing, *The Underground Press in America* (Bloomington: Indiana University Press, 1970); Esther Kitzes, "Before the Revolution Come the Words," *College Press Review* 8.3 (Spring 1968): 3–5; Abe Peck, *Uncovering the Sixties: The Life and Times of the Underground Press* (New York: Pantheon Books, 1985); "The Porno Plague," *Time,* April 5, 1976, 58–63; and Watts, *Mr. Playboy,* 303–304.

29. See Louis Chunovic, *One Foot on the Floor: The Curious Evolution of Sex on Television from I Love Lucy to South Park* (New York: TV Books, 2000), 88–89; Georges-Claude Guilbert, *Madonna as Postmodern Myth: How One Star's Self-Construction Rewrites Sex, Gender, Hollywood, and the American Dream* (Jefferson, N.C.: McFarland, 2002); John Leo, "The New Scarlet Letter," *Time,* August 2, 1982; Martha Smilgis, "The Big Chill: Fear of AIDS," *Time,* February 16, 1987, 50–59; Streitmatter, *Sex Sells!,* 104, 113–114, 126, 132, 134–135; and Watts, *Mr. Playboy,* 325–326.

30. See Rimas, "Porn Princess of B.U."; and "The Internet Is for Porn," from *Avenue Q:* http://www.allmusicals.com/lyrics/avenueq/theinternetisforporn.htm.

31. See Marc E. Babej and Tim Pollak, "Mad. Ave Goes (Soft) Porn," *Forbes,* October 5, 2006: http://www.forbes.com/home/columnists/2006/10/04/unsolicited-advice-advertising-oped_meb_1005porn.html; Streitmatter, *Sex Sells!,* 210–213; Martha Irvine, "Sex Peddled as Power in Pornified Girl Culture," Associated Press, June 3, 2007: http://www.msnbc.msn.com/id/18924743; Eric Gibson, "Go to College, Learn the Skin Trade," *Wall Street Journal,* February 13, 2004; Jeffrey Ressner, "Sex in the Syllabus," *Time,* March 26, 2006; and Rudoren, "Student Body."

32. See Ebonie D. Hazle, "Committee Approves Porn Magazine," *Harvard Crimson,* February 11, 2004; Jenna Russell, "Harvard Warns Sex Magazine Against Pornography," *Boston Globe,* February 14, 2004; Laura Sessions Stepp, "Fallout at Harvard over H Bomb Sex Magazine," *Washington Post,* February 14, 2004; and Rimas, "The Porn Princess of B.U.," 98–102.

33. See Hazle, "Committee Approves Porn Magazine"; Barbara Kantrowitz, "Dropping the H Bomb: After Months of Breathless Anticipation, That School 'in Boston' Finally Has Its Own Sex Mag: Does Anyone Care?" *Newsweek,* June 7, 2004, 45; Stepp, "Fallout at Harvard"; and Adam Schneider, "H Bomb Drops, but Not at Doors," *Harvard Crimson,* May 26, 2004. In a letter run in the *Harvard Crimson* the following day, Baldegg, Hrdy, and Hauser, the publication's faculty adviser, wrote, "Yesterday's article about the upcoming magazine, *H Bomb,* misrepresented the goals of our organization. *H Bomb* is not porn. . . . It is a literary arts magazine about sex and sexual issues at Harvard.

It will contain fiction, features, poetry, and art." See Katharina Cieplak-von Baldegg, Camilla Hrdy, and Marc Hauser, "Crimson Misrepresents H Bomb," *Harvard Crimson*, February 12, 2004.

34. See Marcella Bombardieri, "Harvard's Sexy H Bomb Magazine Drop: New Publication Draws Line Between Art, Pornography," *Boston Globe*, May 25, 2004; Davis, "In Bed with Boink Magazine"; Jim Martyka, "Magazine Startup: Too Hot for Harvard? Proposed Erotic Publication Meets Resistance from Committee," *Trends in College Media*, March 1, 2004: http://www.studentpress.org/acp/trends/~hbomb.html; and Rudoren, "Student Body."

35. See Bombardieri, "Harvard's Sexy H Bomb Magazine Drops"; and Katharine A. Kaplan, "Katharina P. Cieplak-von Baldegg '06 and Camilla Hrdy '04–'05: Women Behind H Bomb," *Harvard Crimson*, June 10, 2004.

36. See Nusca, "Art Porn?"; Bombardieri, "Harvard's Sexy H Bomb Magazine Drops"; Tristan Taormino, "Porn on Campus: Student Smut, Sometimes Unauthorized, Makes a Splash at Universities," *Village Voice*, June 11, 2004; Rudoren, "Student Body"; Neel Shah, "Columbia Delivers Pornless Porn Mag," Daily Intel, *New York*, October 23, 2006: http://nymag.com/daily/intel/2006/10/columbia_delivers_pornless_por.html; Adamson, "Intellectual Masturbation"; Chris Beam, "Whatever Happened to Good, Clean Ivy League Smut?" IvyGate, October 19, 2006: http://www.ivygateblog.com/2006/10/whatever-happened-to-good-clean-ivy-league-smut/; and Anthony Paletta, "College Sex Magazines," Phi Beta Cons, *National Review*, March 6, 2007: http://phibetacons.nationalreview.com/post/?q=MmE2ZGM0ZDYwNmVjZDZlNDhkZDFiYjNlNmZhOWZkNTA.

37. See Eliana Johnson, "College Students in the Nude," *New York Sun*, November 3, 2006, Fall Education Guide; Beam, "Whatever Happened to Good, Clean Ivy League Smut?"; Daniel Engber, "Surveying the Student Body," *Chronicle of Higher Education*, November 5, 2004; Halpern, "Art School Confidential"; and Jacobs, "Campus Exposure," 44.

38. Kimi Traube, "A Note from Editor Kimi Traube," *Outlet*, December 2006.

39. Jacobs, "Campus Exposure," 44.

40. See ibid.; Halpern, "Art School Confidential"; Rudoren, "Student Body"; Shah, "Columbia Delivers Pornless Porn Mag"; "The Rise and Fizzle of the College Sex Mag," *Playboy*, October 2007, 59; and Bobbi Epson, "Letter to the Editor," *Boink*, September 2005, 6–7.

41. See Jacobs, "Campus Exposure," 44; and Lynch, "Hey, Isn't the Girl from Page 7 in Your Class?"

42. See Watts, *Mr. Playboy*, 115–117; and Eric Wilson, "Smile and Say 'No Photoshop,'" *New York Times*, May 27, 2009.

43. Neil Swidey, "The Naked Truth: Is It Still the Same Old Pornography If the Model Is Your Classmate from Psych 101?" *Boston Globe*, March 6, 2005.

44. See Rudoren, "Student Body"; "Hot Girls Reading Books," *Vita Excolatur*, Spring 2005, 1; and Jacobs, "Campus Exposure," 44.

45. Matt Kinsey, "Student Sex Magazine Set for BU," *Daily Free Press*, October 5, 2004.

46. Arielle Brousse, "Flushed," *Quake*, Spring 2005, 4.

47. Untitled cover photograph, *X-Magazine*, Spring 2007.

48. Sarah Raymond, "Wo/Man's Room: Trans-activists Turn from Discrimination Polices to WCs, but It's Going to Take More Than Swapping a Sign to Achieve True Gender Neutrality on College Campuses," *Sex Week at Yale: The Magazine*, February 2008, 44.

49. See Rimas, "Porn Princess of B.U."; and untitled cover photograph, *H Bomb*, Spring 2005.

50. "Douglas," *Boink*.

51. Jacobs, "Campus Exposure," 44.

52. See Conor Graham, "Stop the Sexual Naiveté: Redlight Magazine's War on Prudes," *McGill Tribune*, March 27, 2007; and Jessica Haralson and Jessica York, "Letter from the Editors," *Quake*, Spring 2005, 2. According to Kyle, *Squirm*'s full title went through three early incarnations. At its founding, it was known as *Squirm: The Magazine of Sexual Praxis*. Some considered the name pretentious, leading to a new subtitle, *Squirm: The Magazine of Sex and Sensibility*. Kyle said the staff discovered a professional magazine with a similar tag line and subsequently switched to its current moniker, *Squirm: The Art of Campus Sex*. In Kyle's words, "That subtitle stuck."

53. "Rise and Fizzle of the College Sex Mag," 59.

Chapter 8. My College Paper Was Not Like That!:
The Journalistic Legacy of the Student Sex Column

1. Erin Kaplan, "Where Has All the Dating Gone?" *Michigan Daily*, September 11, 2003.

2. See Mary Beth Marklein, "Sex Is Casual at College Papers," *USA Today*, November 14, 2002; Eric Hoover, "The New Sex Scribes," *Chronicle of Higher Education*, June 14, 2002; and Lisa Hermann, "Introducing Your Local Friendly Health Columnist," *Cavalier Daily*, July 25, 2005. According to Fulbright, "I prefer sex expert, sex educator, or sexologist. I mean, I'll wear the sexpert hat because I know it goes with the territory once you're in the media eye and all that. I'm not offended by the term. I'm more offended when I get thrown in with a group that doesn't have the same background in sexology or training that I have."

3. See Dana Hull, "Sex Talk on Campus: Columnists Don't Shy Away from Explicit Advice," *San Jose Mercury News*, September 23, 2004; Kim Palmer, "Sex 101: College Scribes Add Sizzle to Student Newspapers," *Minneapolis Star Tribune*, March 22, 2003; John Burnett, "Letters to the Editor," *Nevada Sagebrush*, October 1, 2007; and Sheelah Kolhatkar, "You Are Not Alone: College Newspapers Discover the Sex Column," *Atlantic Monthly*, November 2005, 144–147.

4. See Miriam Datskovsky, "Toys 'R' Sluts?" *Columbia Spectator*, November 28, 2005; and Nadia Stadnycki, "Back by Popular Demand, I Give You the Orgasm," *Temple News*, February 21, 2006.

5. See David Gudelunas, *Confidential to America: Newspaper Advice Columns and Sexual Education* (Edison, N.J.: Transaction Publishers, 2007), 98, 157;

Dan Savage, *Savage Love: Straight Answers from America's Most Popular Sex Columnist* (New York: Plume, 1998), 9; and Carolyn Hax, *Tell Me About It: Lying, Sulking, Getting Fat . . . and 56 Other Things Not to Do While Looking for Love* (New York: Hyperion, 2001), 5–9.

6. Dana Delapi, "Not Just Sex: Born Again Virgins," *Central Florida Future*, January 15, 2004.
7. See Jenna Hall, "Size Doesn't Really Matter," *Tartan*, February 28, 2007; Jessica Ramsey Golden, "How to Get the Most Out of Your Fashion Bump," *Northern Light*, April 4, 2006; Amanda Baldwin, "Caught!" *Bottom Line*, November 15, 2006; Anna Schleelein, "Good Vibrations," *Heights*, February 4, 2003; and Nadia Stadnycki, "Straight Up Sex," *Temple News*, October 26, 2004.
8. See Gudelunas, *Confidential to America*, 2–3; Nahal Toosi, "UW-Madison Columnist and Her Colleagues Have Little Shame Exploring What Used to Be Pillow Talk," *Milwaukee Journal Sentinel*, November 17, 2002; and Leonora LaPeter, "Sexual Curiosity Is College Columnist's Muse," *St. Petersburg Times*, April 19, 2004.
9. Randall Patterson, "Students of Virginity," *New York Times Magazine*, March 30, 2008, 38.
10. Dave Franzese, "The Man Behind the Fly," *Daily Nexus*, September 29, 2004.
11. See Lena Chen, Sex and the Ivy: http://sexandtheivy.com/; Jonathan Zimmerman, "College Papers Aren't What They Used to Be," *Philadelphia Inquirer*, December 12, 2002; and Michael Strunck, "Crass and Tasteless Column," *Diamondback*, October 23, 2007.
12. See Brynn Burton, e-mail message to author, December 7, 2006; Andrew Peach, "Prof Dislikes Heights Sex Column," *Heights*, November 12, 2002; and Heather Walker, "Unnecessary Sexual Innuendos in Headline," *Oracle*, April 2, 2004.
13. See Brendan Cavalier, "My View from the Soapbox: Sex Columns Damage Integrity," *Daily Free Press*, February 11, 2003; and Leigh Shelton, "Senate Questions Sex Column, Thanks Campus Groups," *Daily Reveille*, November 12, 2004.
14. Gudelunas, *Confidential to America*, 205
15. Al Tompkins, "My College Paper Was Not Like That!" Al's Morning Meeting, October 11, 2002: http://www1.poynter.org/dg.lts/id.2/aid.7682/column.htm.
16. Kelly McBride, "Journalists Need More Sex," Poynter Ethics Journal, September 12, 2003: http://www.poynter.org/column.asp?id=53&aid=47732.
17. See staff editorial, "Sex Column Aims to Educate: Staff Stands Behind Choice to Print," *News Record*, February 24, 2005; and Ben Magid, "Sex—Everywhere with Good Reason," *Pitt News*, October 9, 2002.
18. Staff editorial, "Free Speech . . . and Sex," *Flat Hat*, February 24, 2006.
19. Jerry Hart, "Rights and Responsibilities—as Explained by a Student Editor," in *The Student Press, 1971: New Journalism During a Year of Controversy and Change*, ed. Bill G. Ward (New York: Richards Rosen Press, 1971), 55.
20. See Chloe Hurley, "Why Smart Sex Has Gone Stagnant," *The Buzz*, October 4, 2006: http://lamp.dailypennsylvanian.com/blogs/index.php?page=post&section=1&id=326; and Barbara Donlon, "College Sex Columnists Make Good Topic Dull," *Boston Herald*, October 20, 2002, 41.

SELECTED BIBLIOGRAPHY

Interviews

Afriyie, Rose. Interview with author, July 25, 2006.
Albert, Sasha. Interview with author, January 23, 2008.
Allday, Erin. Interview with author, December 7, 2005.
Anderson, Christopher. Interview with author, October 29, 2007.
Anderson Payne, Kaya. Interview with author, October 30, 2006.
Arenschield, Laura. Interview with author, September 2, 2006.
Arvidson, Valerie. Interview with author, August 9, 2006.
Bainum, Meghan. Interview with author, July 29, 2006.
Baldwin, Amanda. Interview with author, June 6, 2007.
Baugher, Julia. Interview with author, July 18, 2006.
———. E-mail to author, July 21, 2006.
Baugher, Robin. Interview with author, October 25, 2006.
Beaton, Jessica. Interview with author, July 16, 2006.
Belloni, Matthew. Interview with author, January 12, 2006.
Brown, August. Interview with author, October 27, 2006.
Brown, Sarah. Interview with author, November 30, 2006.
Brundson, Denise. Interview with author, July 27, 2006.
Burman, Alana. Interview with author, January 4, 2008.
Burton, Brynn. Interview with author, August 21, 2006.
———. E-mail to author, December 7, 2006.
Carlisle, Kate. Interview with author, July 25, 2006.
Chander, Kanika. Interview with author, February 3, 2006.
Cohen, Barnett. Interview with author, January 21, 2008.
Coleman, Michael. Interview with author, December 13, 2005.
Culleton, Serina. Interview with author, December 7, 2005.
Dana, Rebecca. Interview with author, January 13, 2006.
Datskovsky, Miriam. Interview with author, July 25, 2006.
Davé, Zoë. Interview with author, October 31, 2006.
Eitches, Sari. Interview with author, July 14, 2006.
Elliott, Phil. Interview with author, September 3, 2006.
Franzese, Dave. Interview with author, July 17, 2006.
———. E-mail to author, July 18, 2006.
Friedman, Corey. Interview with author, October 27, 2006.
———. E-mail to author, October 27, 2006.
Friedman, Mindy. Interview with author, July 20, 2006.

Fulbright, Yvonne. Interview with author, July 17, 2006.
Giblin, Katie. Interview with author, August 17, 2006.
Granat, Erin. Interview with author, October 11, 2006.
Grantham, Heather. Interview with author, July 19, 2006.
Grasska, Merry. E-mail to author, October 18, 2006.
Greaves, Kathy. Interview with author, September 27, 2006.
Griffin, Larry. Interview with author, August 30, 2006.
Hall, Caitlin. Interview with author, August 24, 2006.
Hrdy, Camilla. Interview with author, September 16, 2006.
Jay, Janet. Interview with author, June 12, 2007.
Johnson, Lindsay. Interview with author, September 1, 2006.
Kalaidis, Jenny. Interview with author, June 4, 2007.
Kaplan, Erin. Interview with author, July 26, 2006.
Katz, David. Interview with author, December 28, 2005.
Killian, Joe. Interview with author, September 3, 2006.
Kyle, Deva. Interview with author, January 21, 2008.
Lambert, Laura. Interview with author, December 6, 2005.
Liciaga, Christina. Interview with author, April 20, 2005.
Loewenstein, Lara. Interview with author, July 23, 2006.
Madison, Amber. Interview with author, August 24, 2006.
———. E-mail to author, October 26, 2006.
Maffeo, Gillian. Interview with author, June 12, 2007.
Maier, Kimberly. Interview with author, June 3, 2007.
McCabe, Alexis. Interview with author, August 7, 2006.
McDowell, Molly Kate. Interview with author, July 15, 2006.
Medvin, Abi. Interview with author, June 4, 2007.
Mielcarek, Stephanie. Interview with author, November 2, 2006.
Milligan, RJ. Interview with author, July 30, 2006.
Morgan, Lauren. Interview with author, August 28, 2006.
Muller, Wes. Interview with author, June 4, 2007.
Murphy, Aly. Interview with author, September 26, 2006.
Nigh, Kristi. Interview with author, January 15, 2008.
Perrine, Matthew. Interview with author, October 31, 2006.
Ponce, Mitzi. Interview with author, November 4, 2006.
Prengaman, Kate. Interview with author, July 20, 2006.
Riedel, Erin. Interview with author, July 25, 2006.
Ritner, Anna. Interview with author, July 14, 2006.
———. E-mail to author, July 15, 2006.
Robbins, McLean. Interview with author, June 12, 2007.
Rovzar, Christopher. Interview with author, January 12, 2006.
Royer, Jordan. Interview with author, November 5, 2007.
Saunders, Jessica. Interview with author, August 17, 2006.
Schleelein, Anna. Interview with author, July 23, 2006.
Schmit, Timaree. Interview with author, August 16, 2006.
Scott, Margo. Interview with author, June 3, 2007.

Shimura, Kaiko. Interview with author, April 19, 2005.
Shugar, Paul. Interview with author, August 24, 2006.
Stadnycki, Nadia. Interview with author, April 16, 2005.
———. E-mail to author, December 7, 2006.
Stortroen, Elizabeth. Interview with author, June 6, 2007.
Strack, Heather. Interview with author, October 4, 2006.
Sudhof, Soren. Interview with author, October 3, 2006.
Tauzin, Anna. Interview with author, June 11, 2007.
Taylor, Brook. Interview with author, July 26, 2006.
Taylor, Lane. Interview with author, April 18, 2005.
Thomas, Deb. E-mail to author, September 3, 2006.
Thomas, Erin. Interview with author, July 15, 2006.
Toler, William. Interview with author, January 15, 2007.
Trevick, Stephen. Interview with author, October 31, 2006.
Van Dyke, Beth. Interview with author, August 5, 2006.
Vandenberg, Ming Emily. Interview with author, September 14, 2006.
Wasserman, Martha Annabel "Martabel." Interview with author, January 23, 2008.
Wiesner, Lauren. Interview with author, April 20, 2005.
Wroten, Nicole. E-mail to author, December 8, 2009.
Yarosh, Haley. Interview with author, July 18, 2006.
Zumbrum, Josh. Interview with author, July 25, 2006.

Secondary Sources

Akass, Kim, and Janet McCabe, eds. *Reading Sex and the City*. London: I. B. Tauris, 2004.
Allen, Teresa. "Sex Columns: They're Everywhere These Days, It Seems." *College Media Review* 42.2 (Spring 2004): 6–10.
Allison, Julia. "Carrie Bradshaw 101: The Rise of the College Sex Columnist." *COED Magazine*, November 2006, 18–20.
Allyn, David. *Make Love, Not War: The Sexual Revolution: An Unfettered History*. New York: Routledge, 2001.
Ashbrook, Tom. "Hooking Up on Campus." *On Point*, National Pubic Radio, September 29, 2006: http://www.onpointradio.org/shows/2006/09/20060929_b_main.asp.
Avi, Rachel. "When Chloe Met Charlotte: MIICRNYCOAGNWMA? The Attack of the Female Sex Columnist!" *Village Voice*, April 12, 2005.
Bailey, Beth. *From Front Porch to Back Seat: Courtship in Twentieth-Century America*. Baltimore: Johns Hopkins University Press, 1989.
———. *Sex in the Heartland*. Cambridge, Mass.: Harvard University Press, 1999.
Cameron, Amy. "Campus Kama Sutra." *Maclean's*, April 4, 2005, 40–41.
Chunovic, Louis. *One Foot on the Floor: The Curious Evolution of Sex on Television from I Love Lucy to South Park*. New York: TV Books, 2000.
DiBranco, Alex. "The Student Sex Column Movement." *The Nation*, September 28, 2009: http://www.thenation.com/doc/20091012/dibranco.

Donlon, Barbara. "College Sex Columnists Make Good Topic Dull." *Boston Herald*, October 20, 2002.

Duscha, Julius, and Thomas Fischer. *The Campus Press: Freedom and Responsibility.* Washington, D.C.: American Association of State Colleges and Universities, 1973.

Eakin, Marah. "Sex and the Single College Grad." *WireTap*, May 4, 2005: http://www.alternet.org/story/21932.

Eble, Connie. *College Slang 101: A Definitive Guide to Words, Phrases, and Meanings They Don't Teach in English Class.* Mount Pleasant, S.C.: Spectacle Lane Press, 2003.

Ehrenberg, Elizabeth. "Sex and the Student Body." *In These Times*, September 15, 2003: http://www.inthesetimes.com/article/610/sex_and_the_student_body/.

Elliott, Leland, and Cynthia Brantley. *Sex on Campus: The Naked Truth About the Real Sex Lives of College Students.* New York: Random House, 1997.

Gibson, Eric. "Go to College, Learn the Skin Trade." *Wall Street Journal*, February 13, 2004.

Glessing, Robert J. *The Underground Press in America.* Bloomington: Indiana University Press, 1970.

Gudelunas, David. *Confidential to America: Newspaper Advice Columns and Sexual Education.* Edison, N.J.: Transaction Publishers, 2007.

Harris, Paul. "Columnists Lay Bare Sex and Single Student." *Observer*, October 16, 2005.

Hoover, Eric. "The New Sex Scribes." *Chronicle of Higher Education*, June 14, 2002.

Hull, Dana. "Sex Talk on Campus: Columnists Don't Shy Away from Explicit Advice." *San Jose Mercury News*, September 23, 2004.

Irvine, Martha. "Not Just Sex, but Advice, Too, Popular on Campus." *Miami Herald*, September 15, 2002.

Jacobs, Alexandra. "Campus Exposure." *New York Times Magazine*, March 4, 2007, 44.

Johnson, Tim. "Campus Newspapers Thrive." *Burlington Free Press*, October 21, 2008.

Kaufman, Leslie. "Channeling Carrie." *New York Times*, March 30, 2008.

Keller, Josh. "Student Newspapers Escape Most Financial Problems of Larger Dailies." *Chronicle of Higher Education*, September 11, 2008.

Knudson, Kennan. "And Now, College Goes to Playboy: Sex Mags Emerge at BU, Harvard." *Boston Globe*, February 13, 2005.

Kogan, Rick. *America's Mom: The Life, Lessons, and Legacy of Ann Landers.* New York: William Morrow, 2003.

Kolhatkar, Sheelah. "You Are Not Alone: College Newspapers Discover the Sex Column." *Atlantic Monthly*, November 2005, 144–147.

Krinsky, Natalie. *Chloe Does Yale.* New York: Hyperion, 2005.

Laverty, Rory. "College Sex Columnists Shift Gears." *Alameda Times Star*, October 29, 2002.

Mabley, Jack. "More and More College Newspapers Relying on Sure-Fire Sales Technique." *Chicago Daily Herald*, October, 9, 2002.

Madigan, Nick. "College Papers Deliver." *Baltimore Sun*, November 20, 2006.

Madison, Amber. *Hooking Up: A Girl's All-Out Guide to Sex and Sexuality.* Amherst, N.Y.: Prometheus Books, 2006.

Marklein, Mary Beth. "Sex Is Casual at College Papers." *USA Today*, November 14, 2002.

McBride, Kelly. "Journalists Need More Sex." Poynter Ethics Journal, September 12, 2003: http://www.poynter.org/column.asp?id=53&aid=47732.

Moore, Sonya. "Student Sex Columns Provide Service, Raise Eyebrows." *Editor and Publisher*, March 25, 2004: http://www.allbusiness.com/services/business-services-miscellaneous-business/4700750-1.html.

Moran, Jeffrey P. *Teaching Sex.* Cambridge, Mass.: Harvard University Press, 2000.

Munro, Pamela. *Slang U.: The Official Dictionary of College Slang.* New York: Three Rivers Press, 1991.

Murley, Bryan. "College Media Has Come a Long Way Online." *MediaShift*, Public Broadcasting Service, November 19, 2008: http://www.pbs.org/mediashift/2008/11/college-media-has-come-a-long-way-online324.html.

Murley Bryan, and Daniel Reimold. "ICM Discussion: Print and College Newspapers." Innovation in College Media, November 6, 2008: http://www.collegemediainnovation.org/blog/2008/11/06/icm-discussion-print-and-college-newspapers/.

Palmer, Kim. "Sex 101: College Scribes Add Sizzle to Student Newspapers." *Minneapolis Star Tribune*, March 22, 2003.

Peck, Abe. *Uncovering the Sixties: The Life and Times of the Underground Press.* New York: Pantheon Books, 1985.

Richter, Harvey, ed. *Best College Humor: The First Collection from the American College Humorous Magazines.* Reading, Pa.: Handy Book Corporation, 1920.

Rimer, Sara. "Sex and the College Newspaper: Student Columnists Explore a Familiar Campus Topic." *New York Times*, October 4, 2002.

"The Rise and Fizzle of the College Sex Mag." *Playboy*, October 2007, 58.

Schwartz, Rebecca. "Sex and the University." *Outloud*, March 2003: http://www.outloud.com/2003/March%202003/sex_university.htm.

Seaman, Barrett. *Binge: What Your College Student Won't Tell You.* Hoboken, N.J.: Wiley, 2006.

Semonche, John. *Censoring Sex: A Historical Journey Through American Media.* Lanham, Md.: Rowman and Littlefield, 2007.

Shapiro, Ben. *Porn Generation: How Social Liberalism Is Corrupting Our Future.* Washington, D.C.: Regnery Publishing, 2005.

Shulman, Max, ed. *Max Shulman's Guided Tour of Campus Humor.* Garden City, N.Y.: Doubleday, 1955.

Simigis, Antonia. "Co-ed Sex Advice: The Best New Trend in College Newspapers." *Playboy*, February 2003: 80–82, 136.

Steel, Emily. "Big Media on Campus: College Papers Around the U.S. Are Drawing Young Readers." *Wall Street Journal*, August 9, 2006.

Straus, Jillian. *Unhooked Generation: The Truth About Why We're Still Single*. New York: Hyperion Books, 2006.

Streitmatter, Rodger. *Sex Sells!: The Media's Journey from Repression to Obsession*. New York: Westview Press, 2004.

———. *Unspeakable: The Rise of the Gay and Lesbian Press in America*. London: Faber and Faber, 1995.

———. *Voices of Revolution: The Dissident Press in America*. New York: Columbia University Press, 2001.

Summers, Nick. "College Papers Grow Up: They Have the Ads, the Readers—and Budgets to Match." *Newsweek*, December 5, 2005, 48.

Swidey, Neil. "The Naked Truth: Is It Still the Same Old Pornography If the Model Is Your Classmate from Psych 101?" *Boston Globe*, March 6, 2005.

Takeuchi Cullen, Lisa. "Sex in the Syllabus." *Time*, March 26, 2006: http://www.time.com/time/magazine/article/0,9171,1176976,00.html.

Taormino, Tristan. "Porn on Campus: Student Smut, Sometimes Unauthorized, Makes a Splash at Universities." *Village Voice*, June 11, 2004.

Tompkins, Al. "My College Paper Was Not Like That!" Al's Morning Meeting, October 11, 2002: http://www1.poynter.org/dg.lts/id.2/aid.7682/column.htm.

Toosi, Nahal. "Sex 101: The Nitty Gritty." *Milwaukee Journal Sentinel*, November 17, 2002.

Tucker, Abigail. "Sex Writers Graduate to Real Jobs: Experience Adds Too Much Spice to Some Resumes." *Chicago Tribune*, May 1, 2005.

Watts, Steven. *Mr. Playboy: Hugh Hefner and the American Dream*. Hoboken, N.J.: Wiley, 2008.

Yabroff, Jennie. "Campus Sexperts: Erotic Magazines Run by Students at Elite Colleges Have Prospered." *Newsweek*, February 25, 2008, 46–47.

INDEX

Daily Bruin (University of California, Los Angeles), 121

Daily Californian (University of California, Berkeley), 11–13, 19–32, 54, 67, 70, 93, 117, 121, 163; editorial board, 11, 22–24; editorial independence, 21; financial slump, 19–20; newspaper theft, 11–12; newsroom, Eshleman Hall, 12; online edition, 31, 117; opinion columnists, 22–23; Proposition 209 editorial, 11–13. *See also* Sex on Tuesday column

Daily Campus (University of Connecticut), 87, 91, 171

Daily Cardinal (University of Louisville), 164

Daily Evergreen (Washington State University), 59, 73, 101

Daily Free Press (Boston University), 140

Daily Kansan (University of Kansas), 54, 78–80, 117, 124

Daily Mississippian (University of Mississippi), 92, 123–124

Daily Nebraskan (University of Nebraska, Lincoln), 103, 120–121

Daily Nexus (University of California, Santa Barbara), 59, 61, 64, 74, 98, 104, 167

Daily Northwestern (Northwestern University), 60

Daily Pennsylvanian (University of Pennsylvania), 141

Daily Princetonian (Princeton University), 97

Daily Reveille (Louisiana State University), 100, 168

Daily Telegraph (UK newspaper), 51

Daily Trojan (University of Southern California), 60

Dana, Rebecca, 40–41, 46, 50–51

Dartmouth (Dartmouth College), 61, 97, 165

Dartmouth College, 89, 97

Dartmouth Free Press (Dartmouth College), 64, 76, 89, 92–93

dating and sex terms, student, 47, 85–88, 92–95, 98, 104; "A Student Sexicon," 175–203

dating and sex trends, student, 9–10, 87–88, 90–96

Datskovsky, Miriam, 63, 65, 68–71, 76, 92–93, 98–99, 162

Davé, Zoë, 130–131

Dear Abby column (Phillips), 35–36

Details magazine, 21

Diamondback (University of Maryland), 98

Dlugatch, Laura, 92

Dorothy Dix column (Meriwether Gulliver), 34–35

Dr. HIPpocrates column (Schoenfeld), 36, 209n. 6

Drew University, 89

Driftwood (University of New Orleans), 173

Edington, Mark D. W., 149

Editor and Publisher, 131

Eitches, Sari, 67, 121

Elliott, Phil, 4, 61, 84, 109

Emory Wheel (Emory University), 74, 94, 163

Evans, Joni, 49

Exponent (University of Alabama in Huntsville), 18

Fargo Forum, 128

Female Chauvinist Pigs (Levy), 99

Fink, Glory, 1–3

Flat Hat (College of William & Mary), 52, 108, 120, 160, 171

Foundation for Individual Rights in Education (FIRE), 115–116

Fox News, 65, 75

Franzese, Dave, 59, 64–65, 70, 166–167

Freeburg, Alex, 71

Friedman, Corey, 115–116

Friedman, Mindy, 54–55, 70, 73, 93, 163

Frostburg State University, 70, 164

ABOUT THE AUTHOR

DANIEL REIMOLD, PH.D., is a journalism scholar who has published and presented research on college media throughout the United States and in Southeast Asia. He has taught journalism, mass communication, and new media courses at four universities in two countries. He currently serves as an assistant professor of journalism at the University of Tampa, where he also advises the *Minaret* student newspaper. He earned his doctorate in journalism/mass communication and an additional graduate-level certificate in contemporary history from Ohio University. He received his master's degree from Temple University and his bachelor's degree from Ursinus College. He worked for several newspapers in Greater Philadelphia, including the *Philadelphia Inquirer*, where he earned the paper's first Ralph Vigoda Memorial Award for passion in journalism. He maintains the popular daily blog College Media Matters (http://www.collegemedia matters.com/) and has been cited as the leading expert of the student press sexualization phenomenon.